"Flower delive

"Who is it from?"

"There's no name on the card."

"Which florist?"

"Emerald Hills."

Still apprehensive, she cracked open the wooden door just enough to see him. With a sudden, incongruous movement, the delivery man stuck his foot in the doorway and thrust the flowers at her with his left hand. As she reached to take them, he stuck a silver pistol in her face.

Marie started shrieking uncontrollably. She tried to run inside but the man grabbed her, one arm around her neck, grasping for her mouth with his hand. The flowerpot fell to the black-and-white marble parquet floor and shattered, pink petals scattering everywhere.

She stopped screaming when the hand formed a gag hard around her mouth. She realized the gun was at her temple. She couldn't stop looking at it.

"If you don't cooperate," the man said, "I'm gonna blow your brains out."

Other True Crime Cases by
Arthur Jay Harris
from Avon Books

UNTIL PROVEN INNOCENT

FLOWERS FOR MRS. LUSKIN

ARTHUR JAY HARRIS

AVON BOOKS ◆ NEW YORK

VISIT OUR WEBSITE AT
http://AvonBooks.com

FLOWERS FOR MRS. LUSKIN is a journalistic account of the actual investigation and conviction of Paul Luskin in 1988 for an attempted murder-for-hire of Marie Luskin in Hollywood, Florida. The events recounted in this book are true. Scenes and dialogue have been reconstructed based on tape-recorded formal interviews, local and federal law enforcement records, and published news stories. Quoted testimony and other court-related statements from before, during, and after trial have been taken verbatim from transcripts.

AVON BOOKS
A division of
The Hearst Corporation
1350 Avenue of the Americas
New York, New York 10019

Copyright © 1997 by Arthur Jay Harris
Published by arrangement with the author
Library of Congress Catalog Card Number: 96-96863
ISBN: 0-380-78182-4

First Avon Books Printing: February 1997

AVON TRADEMARK REG. U.S. PAT. OFF. AND IN OTHER COUNTRIES, MARCA REGISTRADA, HECHO EN U.S.A.

Printed in the U.S.A.

RA   10   9   8   7   6   5   4   3   2   1

CONTENTS

ONE

Flowers for Mrs. Luskin

Marie Luskin had just gotten her four-year-old Diana to sleep on the sofa in the family room, a little pillow underneath her head and a blanket covering her. She had been awake all night, throwing up, but Marie had given her children's CoTylenol and it had helped knock her out. She had an appointment later to take her to the doctor.

Diana's illness interrupted Marie's normal routine. Every weekday for the past six months, after the school bus picked up both Diana—who went to nursery school—and ten-year-old Shana at 8:10, Marie met her sister Joyce Elkin by nine to join a walking club at Hollywood Mall, a ten-minute ride away. It ended at ten when the stores opened, then most of the time the two women returned to Marie's house and ate breakfast together. But this morning, Marie called Joyce and said she couldn't make it. Marie told her not to come over, she didn't want Joyce's four-month-old to catch whatever Diana had.

While Diana slept, Marie sat across from her and opened the newspaper.

The doorbell rang. Marie got up to answer it.

Since her live-in housekeeper Silvia Mexicanos was off from Sunday morning to Monday afternoon, Marie was

1

home alone, and she knew not to open the door. Instead she went to the intercom.

"Who's there?"

It wasn't Joyce. It was a man with a rough voice.

"Flower delivery for Marie Luskin!"

That was a curious surprise. Her husband Paul used to send her flowers all the time, but those days had passed forever. A year and a half before, following Paul's affair with another woman, Marie kicked him out of the house his parents had helped them buy, then filed for divorce.

And what a spectacular divorce. If nastiness could be judged quantitatively, the civil war of the Luskins was the meanest, most aggressive divorce Broward County had ever seen. No other divorce file in the history of the county had produced as much legal paper. Its ceiling-high stack of boxes owned a corner of the clerk's office.

A few years before, none of Paul and Marie's friends would have predicted it. Most thought they had a model marriage. They were young, rich, socially up-and-coming, intelligent, and living in warm south Florida. That beat Baltimore, where Paul grew up and his family was prominent as TV and appliance retailers. When his dad came south, he began his own business and called it Luskin's, like the Baltimore store he had just left. In both places, Luskin's advertised heavily, so everyone knew their name.

Paul and Marie had married sixteen years earlier, after meeting at the University of Miami. Marie was a long blond-haired pretty girl from a middle-class family in Wilmington, Delaware. But as Paul took over management of his father's business, and his pay increased dramatically, she found a taste for expensive things, which Paul indulged. They had a $130,000 house in North Miami Beach, but when Marie called the neighborhood "the slum," they paid $600,000 for the biggest house in Emerald Hills, which was the most luxurious section of Hollywood—a town in between Miami and Fort Lauderdale.

Of course, there were no hills in Emerald Hills, or anywhere close. At its breathtakingly highest vantage point, south Florida is probably no more than ten feet above sea level.

Marie told her friends the house was "Georgia ante-bellum," which sounded like a reference to Tara in *Gone with the Wind*. Actually its exterior was a square, impos-ing, uninspired two-story brick box enhanced with white wooden columns and a front door framed in colonial motif. The backyard abutted the second tee of the Emerald Hills Golf Club. The community's winding streets were cutesy theme-named for famous names in golf; to reach Palmer Drive, you had to travel St. Andrews Road to Casper Court to Sanders.

"Who is it from?" she asked the deliveryman.

"There's no name on the card."

"What florist are you from?"

"Emerald Hills Florist."

She'd used them before to send flowers. "Oh, okay. I'll be right there."

But first she went to the front window, moved the white curtain aside, and peeked out. It was clear and sunny, just a perfect late-winter day. Standing on the porch was a thin man in his thirties, taller than her, handsome, she thought, with shaggy sandy brown hair, but he needed a shave. He was wearing a T-shirt and light-colored blue jeans, and he held a pot of pink azaleas, nicely wrapped in pink foil with a ribbon, obviously from a florist. His car was right in front of the door in the circular driveway, sky blue and new, one of those compacts that all looked basically the same, but with no commercial markings.

Still apprehensive, she cracked opened the wooden door just enough to see him. The temperature outside was warm, indistinguishable from room temperature.

With a sudden incongruous movement, the man stuck his foot in the doorway and thrust the flowers at her with his left hand, which obscured her vision of his head. As she reached to take them, he stuck a silver pistol in her face.

Marie started shrieking uncontrollably. She tried to run inside, but the man grabbed her, one arm around her neck, grasping for her mouth with his hand. The flower-pot fell to the black-and-white marble parquet floor and shattered, pink petals scattering near the foyer throw rug that read "Luskin" in the same design as the stores' logo. The wrap kept the clay shards in place.

"Shut up! Shut up!," he yelled, closing the door behind him. "I'm not going to hurt you. Shut the hell up, stop screaming!"

She finally stopped when his hand formed a gag hard around her mouth, and she realized the gun was at her temple. She couldn't stop looking at the gun, which framed his cruel eyes.

"Give me all your cash! Give me all your cash! Show me where you keep your cash! Just cooperate, and I won't hurt you. I just want all your money!"

"Okay, okay. Please put the gun down if you're not going to hurt me," Marie pleaded repeatedly. For a moment, the man did drop the gun to his waist.

"Now take me to your money!"

Marie thought, *Maybe he wants my jewelry.* She had a locked jewelry box upstairs, although it didn't have any really good stuff, like her seven-carat diamond ring, which was hidden elsewhere in the house. As she took him past the elevator, up the grand winding stairway with its dark-stained wood railings on both sides, a chandelier above, he followed in back of her, clenching her long blond hair close to the scalp, with the gun to the side of her head.

"Please put the gun down."

"I'm not going to hurt you, but if you don't cooperate, I'm gonna blow your fucking brains out!"

Together they went into the splendid master bedroom—seventeen hundred square feet large—and then to her ten-by-twelve-foot dressing alcove. There were three walls to the area, and all of them were mirrored to some extent; as they walked in, the wall directly in front was mirrored from floor to ceiling and slid open into closets. The wall on the right had entries to his and hers bathrooms, both doors mirrored.

The third wall had a built-in peach-colored Formica cabinet topped by an eight-foot-long, two-foot-deep red countertop. Over it was a full mirror framed by frosted bare bulbs, to resemble a backstage makeup room. In fact, it was a three-sided mirror, to cover the recessed areas perpendicular to the main mirror.

Marie stooped down and opened a cabinet door where she kept the box, pulled it out, and placed it on the thick pile cream-colored carpet. It was a large index card box—black metal, about eight by six inches, five inches high. Then she stood up and searched the counter, cluttered with her fragrance bottles. When she found a cup filled with Q-Tips, she chucked the Q-Tips on the floor, revealing a little key at the bottom of the cup.

Kneeling down on the carpet, she opened the box with the key.

"This better be loaded with cash," the man warned, standing in back of her.

But Marie knew there was no cash in it. "I don't know what I have in here, it's mostly my jewelry." She hoped he'd be satisfied.

Frantically, she started throwing things out of the box. She pulled out some U.S. Mint coin sets, a passport, two oriental brocaded purses, and a blue velvet Chivas Regal drawstring pouch. She also found a folded hundred-dollar bill her parents had given her for her last birthday, in November, that she had forgotten about.

She handed him the bill over her shoulder, but he let it flutter to the floor. She told him her diamond necklace and other good jewelry were in the Chivas Regal bag.

"Take it," she said, but again she had to let it drop when he wouldn't handle it. She told him she had $40 in her pocketbook, on the floor in the corner, but he didn't want that either.

Instead he got even angrier. "Where's all your cash? Give me all your cash!"

"It's in the bank!" she whined. "It's in the bank! This is it. This is all I have at home, I keep all my money in the bank!"

As the crescendo of voices in the Luskin house rose to a climax, exactly what happened next remains in dispute.

Marie fell to the floor, a terrible pain in the back of her head. She didn't see what had happened to her, the man was behind her the whole time. She didn't lose consciousness, but pretended to. She covered her face with her hands, trying to stop from hyperventilating. She literally saw stars.

Defenseless, she waited for him to shoot and kill her. But in the next moments she heard only profound silence, except the sound of her own self crying softly. A moment later the front door slammed. Meekly, she opened her eyes and didn't see him. That's when she noticed there was blood all over her. She thought she was going to die.

She made her way to the telephone. She called her sister first, so she could come over and get Diana. If she was going to die, she thought, she didn't want Diana to see her in that condition. But Joyce wasn't home, so then she called 911.

POLICE ARRIVE
10:25 A.M.

Barbara Alleva was the first Hollywood police officer on the scene. She was on road patrol nearby in Emerald Hills, and got to the house within minutes after dispatch put out a radio bulletin.

Marie opened the front door for her. She had a towel over the back of her head, and there was blood all over her shirt. She wasn't crying, but she was a little hysterical. She said when she thought she heard the intruder leave, she crawled to her bedroom door, pushed it closed, and locked it. Then 911 kept her on the phone until she heard the police siren arriving in her driveway.

The first thing Marie asked the officer to do was to check on Diana. Alleva went alone into the family room, and found she was still asleep. To make sure she was all right, Alleva woke her up. Then Marie and Alleva went upstairs, and Marie asked if she could change her shirt, it was all bloody and sticking to her skin.

Alleva asked for details of what had happened. She took a description of the assailant, then gave it to Officer Walter Schatzel, the second officer to arrive, who broadcast it on the police radio as a BOLO—be on the lookout.

About five minutes later, Hollywood Police ID Technician Marjorie Hanlon arrived to process the crime scene. She also talked briefly with Marie to get an idea where she might find latent fingerprints to lift. Marie told her she was pistol-whipped. When she showed Hanlon her wound, Hanlon thought it was the size of a key lime.

As Marie prepared to leave the scene in an ambulance, she asked Alleva to call her sister Joyce to take care of Diana; her mother Dorothy to pick up Shana from school later; and her divorce attorney Barry Franklin to meet her at the hospital. Alleva told Marie she would join her at the hospital later.

Leo Soccol, a detective in the robbery division, arrived at about 10:45, and Alleva told him Marie's wound was the size of a golf ball. Soccol talked to Marie for a moment, then the ambulance rushed her off.

Soccol roped off the area. Inside the house, Marjorie Hanlon went to work preserving the crime scene evidence. She photographed the entranceway, taking note of a card entitled "How to Care for Your Azalea *(Rhododendron hybrids)"* she found on the bare floor next to the errant flower petals. Then she took it into evidence, hoping that a latent fingerprint could be developed from it.

Upstairs, she photographed the dressing room, highlighting blood on the carpet and the metal jewelry box and its contents strewn about. Next she photographed some bloody spots leading to a telephone in an office area.

In her attempts to lift fingerprints, Hanlon dusted the jewelry box, the wooden railing leading up the steps, and the front door.

DETECTIVE LEO SOCCOL

While Hanlon worked inside the house, Leo Soccol worked outside, canvassing the neighborhood. He found three witnesses across the street at 2830 Palmer Drive: David Warner, a young man who lived there with his parents; and two gardeners, Daryl Brown and Ricky Jesel.

Warner told Soccol he was working on an automobile in his garage when he noticed a navy blue car—he thought a Honda Prelude—in the Luskins' driveway. He described the man who got out and stood at the Luskins' doorstep as wearing a blue short-sleeve shirt and possibly jeans, but Warner only caught a glimpse of his face.

Brown and Jesel saw what happened, too. They were planting cacti near the roadway and, therefore, were just a few yards from the Luskin house. Brown thought the car was a Toyota or a Honda. He saw the man carrying flowers and heard Marie's voice over the intercom talking to him.

Brown said he heard voices again a little later and a breaking sound from inside the Luskin house. It sounded like kids playing, so he dismissed the noise at the time. The man left in his car just after that, in a calm way, he said. It was as he was leaving that Brown got his best look at him, from about fifteen feet away. He was still carrying the flowers.

However, Jesel told Soccol that the man left in a real hurry. Warner had walked back into his house and missed it. Jesel told him he thought something might have happened, and Warner ran across the street to check.

Warner said the Luskins' door was closed, but unlocked. He walked in the house and noticed flower petals on the floor.

"Mrs. Luskin?" he called.

The rest of Warner's story contradicted Marie.

Warner said he walked into the kitchen and found Marie sitting on a chair in the corner, her hand on her badly bleeding head. She put down the telephone and told him she had just called the police.

"He hit me over the head with a gun," she told him. "He tried to kill me. Didn't you hear me scream?"

"I didn't hear anything," he answered.

Warner said he asked Marie where her kids were, and she told him one was gone, one was asleep. He helped her walk upstairs to her bedroom, and saw a hundred-dollar bill, a metal box, and some of its contents lying on the bloodstained carpet. Then the police arrived.

HOLLYWOOD MEMORIAL HOSPITAL EMERGENCY ROOM ABOUT 11:15 A.M.

Marie told nurses she was hit with a gun to the right side of her head. She was a little nauseous, had a terrible headache, and bone was exposed, but she was lucky; she didn't have an acute fracture. Although she felt dazed, she stayed alert and her speech was clear.

Barbara Alleva had stayed on the scene until Marjorie Hanlon finished her crime scene work, then Alleva left for the hospital.

By that time, Marie's head had been X-rayed, revealing foreign bodies embedded in the wound. Before the nurse shaved the palm-sized area of Marie's scalp surrounding the wound, Alleva called Hanlon back to photograph the action.

The photographs turned out grotesque. Skin exposed, Marie's injury looked like a liver-shaped gash with three deeper cuts through it. Below it, her blond hair was stringy—soaked in still-wet blood.

An emergency-room surgeon told Alleva he thought the foreign bodies were from the gun that hit her. He checked for black powder on the edges of the wound—which would have indicated a close-range gunshot—and found none. But when Marie told him she was wearing a hairpin at the time, he reasoned that was the origin of the metal fragment.

Doctors decided closing Marie's wound would best be done by a plastic surgeon, so they searched for one on Marie's health plan. They wrapped her head in gauze and sent her to the recovery room in a wheelchair. By this time, Barry Franklin had arrived.

Marie told Franklin and Alleva it was odd that the robber kept screaming, "Give me all your money!" but took nothing. Then, she informed Alleva, she was in the middle of a bitter divorce, and that her husband Paul or his family must have been responsible because he was being investigated for continuous failure to pay child support.

The intruder's demand for cash was curious, Marie thought, because Paul had kept a lot of money at home in the bedroom closet while he still lived there. The money was cash from the business, she said. But ever since he left and refused to pay support, she had had financial problems. The hundred-dollar bill and small change was the only cash in the house.

Sometime between 11:30 A.M. and Noon
2831 PALMER DRIVE
RUTH WAPNER

Marie's seventy-year-old aunt Ruth Wapner from Wilmington was visiting her youngest sister Dorothy—Marie's mother—in her Miami Beach home when police called to say Marie had been in an accident.

Dorothy was too upset to drive, so Ruth drove them to Marie's house, an hour's ride north through city traffic. By the time they arrived, all the police had left the scene, but Joyce was waiting.

Joyce assigned Aunt Ruth to stay at the house, look after Diana, and wait for Shana who would have to walk home. Then Joyce drove Dorothy to Hollywood Memorial, promising to call with details of Marie's condition as soon as they learned it.

Still short on details of what had happened, Aunt Ruth talked to one of the young men across the street before she went inside the house. She learned Marie had been attacked.

When Dorothy called, the news was that Marie was woozy, but okay. She also told Aunt Ruth not to touch anything in the house until after the police called her to say it was okay.

If it was up to Aunt Ruth, she would have cleaned up everything immediately. When she went upstairs—careful not to touch anything, she said later—she saw blood all over the dressing-room carpet. She thought, *This is a job for a professional carpet cleaner,* and she got on the phone to find one.

*   *   *

DETECTIVE LEO SOCCOL
EMERALD HILLS FLORIST
3343 SHERIDAN STREET

Since the assailant had mentioned he was delivering flowers from Emerald Hills Florist, Soccol decided to visit there. It was a store in a strip mall called the Park Sheridan Plaza, about two miles east of Marie's house, the first flower shop west of I-95 on Sheridan Street. Soccol found owner Denise Keltz, who remembered selling a potted azalea plant for cash at 9:45 that morning to someone close to the assailant's description.

He was the first customer of the day. They didn't make any particular conversation, but he did appear nervous. He browsed at the cooler in the front of the store, and when Keltz walked forward from the back of the store, he pointed at the plant he wanted to buy.

She remembered the exchange at the counter:

"Would you like a card to go with that?"

"No, I'm going to deliver it myself."

Keltz told Soccol she got a good facial view of the man. She described him as five-ten, slim build, late thirties, with sandy or brown hair parted on the side. He had fair skin, very smooth—like Don Johnson, the cop on *Miami Vice*. She thought she could identify him if he was caught.

From there, Soccol went to the hospital, hoping to speak to Marie. He began an interview, but because of her blood loss, she was too weak to continue.

A doctor showed Marie's wound to Soccol. "My God, that's a big hit," Soccol reacted.

"She must have really gotten walloped," the doctor said.

In the waiting area, Soccol spoke to Barry Franklin. Franklin repeated that her husband Paul might have been behind the attack because Paul, his family, or his associates had the potential of lining up something like this. He suggested Soccol look up the various reports of vandalism and disturbances that Marie had filed with Hollywood Police in the previous year and a half, since the divorce papers were served.

* * *

4:00 P.M.
OFFICE OF DR. ROSS CLARK
5012 HOLLYWOOD BOULEVARD

At 3:40, the hospital had released Marie to Dr. Clark's care.

When Clark did the surgery, a Hollywood police officer watched from behind glass. Clark cleaned the wound, removed the foreign body, and placed it in a clear plastic biopsy vial. Then he gave it to his nurse, Mary Anne Hartman, and then sutured the wound closed. The whole procedure took just thirty-four minutes, and required only local anesthesia.

When the surgery was done, Hartman put the vial containing the fragment in a tin box, then locked it in the doctor's safe, next to his computer diskettes.

In his medical report, Clark described the foreign body as either plastic or metal. His first impression, too, was that it was a fragment somehow related to a gun.

Sometime that afternoon
2831 PALMER DRIVE
RUTH WAPNER

While waiting for calls back later that afternoon, the phone rang. Ruth thought it was something like three o'clock or earlier.

"Hello, is Marie there?" asked a male voice she didn't recognize.

"No, who's this?"

"This is Paul. Who am I speaking to?"

"Oh, hi, Paul, this is Aunt Ruth. Marie isn't here. Can I have her call you back when she gets in?" she said, deciding not to tell him what had just happened.

"No, I'm leaving, I'm going out on a boat with some friends," she recalled him saying.

"I'll tell her you called," she said.

Later, Paul remembered the conversation much differently. He said he had called to talk to his children, and Aunt Ruth said they weren't home. They talked for another minute that Paul was coming to Florida at the end of the week for Shana's birthday. He didn't ask for Marie at all.

At the end of this very long day, Marie returned home.

TUESDAY, MARCH 10
HOLLYWOOD POLICE

That morning, Soccol found the slew of Hollywood Police reports that both Marie and Paul had filed against each other.

The first was November 29, 1985—the day Marie served Paul with the divorce papers. Soccol read:

> "Dispatched reference a possible vandalism, at the above location. Upon arrival, contact was made with the victim, who advised while she was out away from home, the suspect, being her husband, entered their residence and vandalized numerous articles inside said residence.
>
> "Further investigation revealed both subjects had been living apart for the past three weeks. The victim advised she believed this incident to be the result of divorce papers which were served to suspect this date."

Two weeks later, on December 11, it was Paul's turn to call police:

> "Upon arrival, contact was made with reportee Luskin who advised he is presently in the process of a divorce from Marie Luskin and requested to ascertain if his children were okay.
>
> "Investigation revealed that reportee Luskin and Marie Luskin are presently in the process of a divorce at which Marie Luskin is in custody of their home, being the above address. Reportee Luskin requested the police department to the scene to ascertain if his children were okay, due to the fact that Marie Luskin has a restraining order and would not allow reportee Luskin into the residence. Marie Luskin gave permis-

sion to Sgt. Korn to enter the residence to check on
the children, but she would not allow Mr. Luskin into
the residence.

"Reportee Luskin requested the undersigned (Ofc.
Paul Yancey) along with Ofc. Wagner and Sgt. Korn to
enter the residence to ascertain if a W/M subject
known to him as Gary Davis was inside the residence,
but Mrs. Luskin would not allow us into the residence
for that purpose."

On March 14, 1986, Marie called to report that Paul
might have taken letters from her mailbox two weeks
earlier. Missing, she said, were checks, a bank statement,
and correspondence from her attorney.

"The victim stated that she is undergoing divorce
proceedings at this time and suspects that her husband may have removed the mail but had no proof at
this time."

On August 30, 1986, Marie again told police something that had happened earlier, this time a week before:

"The reportee advised that she had a verbal alterca-
tion with her separated husband, Paul Luskin, on
8/23/86 in the early morning hours on that date. The
reportee advised that she felt somewhat threatened by
the actions of her husband and he had stated, 'You're
lucky to be alive.'

"The reportee could not advise any further reference her beliefs that she felt somewhat threatened by
his comments, but it should be noted that she stated
that he did make the comment with a closed fist and
that he did attempt to open her door and keep it open
with his foot in the door. However, this was unsuccessful by the husband."

The last two reports were "Malicious mischief," the
first filed September 17, 1986.

"This officer was contacted by the victim who advised
that her doorbell had been broken for the third time

at approximately 1800 hours on this date. She stated that her husband Paul Luskin responded to pick up the children and after he left, investigation revealed that the doorbell had been ripped out of the wall.

"She stated that she is in the process of getting a divorce from her husband and he had been causing nothing but grief to her during the period of time she has been seeing an attorney. She stated the doorbell cost approximately $35.00 to replace."

Then on October 5, 1986, police responded to the house to find two tires slashed on a car belonging to Marie's brother-in-law, Michael Elkin.

"Mr. Elkin stated that Paul Luskin, his future ex-brother-in-law, slashed his two tires on his 1980 Chevy Citation. It should be noted that Mr. Luskin has been slashing the tires of every member of his family's vehicles due to a divorce he is going through with Mr. Elkin's sister."

2831 PALMER DRIVE

In the late morning, Soccol returned to the Luskin house to continue his interview with Marie. They discussed whether Paul should be considered a suspect in the assault, but Marie answered that she didn't want to believe Paul would do something like that.

Soccol turned on a tape recorder. After describing what happened, she talked at length about her divorce.

"Do you normally keep large amounts of cash here?" Soccol asked.

"I never did," Marie answered. "My husband and I are going through a very, very nasty divorce. It's been going on for over a year and a half now. When my husband lived at home, it was before September 1985, my husband kept very large sums of cash in the house. He would bring it home from work, from the business, sometimes he would go back and forth to the bank, he always kept large sums of cash at home. But since the divorce proceedings, there hasn't been any cash at home.

There just isn't any cash. My husband had all the cash; I never had any."

"Was this kept in the metal box?"

"No, my husband usually kept it in a briefcase or a suitcase."

"In the bedroom?"

"Sometimes he kept some cash in the room next to the bedroom. Most of it was in what I call the locked computer room. It was his private room, and he kept a locked suitcase in there with money in it."

"Do you still talk with him on occasion?"

"Yes. We have two children and he's always in touch about the children and we're in court together all the time. Sometimes it has been very nasty. He refuses to pay child support or alimony, and he's had to be arrested twice in order to get child support from him. And it's become a very, very nasty case."

"Was he arrested here in Hollywood?" he asked.

"The first time he was arrested, we were in court and the judge had had a hearing with us and our attorneys at the Broward County Courthouse, and at the end of the four-hour hearing, the judge turned to the bailiff and said 'Take him upstairs to jail, he's in contempt of court.' So the first time he was arrested he was in the Broward County stockade.

"The second time he was arrested he was hiding at his parents' apartment in Turnberry Isle Country Club in Miami and the Metro-Dade Police came and had to batter down the door to get him out, and they took him to the Dade County stockade. That was about a month ago."

Soccol asked about the vandalism complaints she had filed with police.

"Yes," she said. "There were times he refused to leave the property. I was afraid. He's bigger than I am; he's always had guns. I am in possession of the home, and the judge gave me a restraining order to keep him off my property. The only time he comes on the grounds is to see the children, to pick them up."

"Has he ever assaulted you?"

"No, he's never assaulted me."

"Has he ever pointed a weapon at you, or threatened you in any way holding a weapon?"

"Never, no, he's never pointed a weapon at me."

"More or less, it's been vandalism?"

"Yes, the first time he did about $10,000 worth of damage to the home, when I filed divorce papers. He does things like ride over the flowers, ruin the flowers, back and forth over the flowers, riding back and forth to ruin all them and . . ."

"Tires?" Soccol asked.

"He's flattened our tires, my tires, he flattened my sister's tires, he flattened my parents' tires. I can't think of other things."

"Is he seeing another woman?"

"Yes, he had a girlfriend, which was the reason that I filed for divorce."

During the statement, the telephone rang. It was Paul, calling from Pittsburgh, where he had been living for the past few months. They talked for just a few minutes, and Marie didn't mention her assault the day before. Afterward, Marie explained she hadn't yet told Paul or his parents about it.

"He called to inform me that he's taking the children away next weekend, he's picking them up Friday and bringing them back Sunday. Which I said would be fine as long as I could have a phone number and an address where he's going to take them so my oldest daughter can call me. One time he took the children away and I didn't know where they were and wasn't able to reach them and I was frantic and I said I'd never let them go like that again."

"Did he indicate anything else regarding this incident?"

"No. He said that if he was going to take the children and not return them, he certainly wouldn't clear it with me by a phone call beforehand."

"Have you had any phone contact with Paul's parents?"

"No, they have not called me. They were here last week to see the children, but they haven't called this week. They normally see the children on Wednesday night—that was the normal visitation night that Paul

took them—and since he's been away, his parents come
and take the girls out."

"And the trial is set for June '87?" Soccol asked, in
regard to the divorce trial.

"Yes, June, and the trial against Luskin's Hi-Fi and
Mildred and Joe Luskin is set for August." That was a
separate trial, as Marie had sued Paul's parents for
conspiring to hide Paul's assets from her in the divorce.

"Have you had any real problems with your husband,
other than arguments over the telephone, in the past six
months?"

"Well, we've been in court many times. At this point,
it's mainly arguments on the phone, or my attorney
handles it through court, or the police handle it."

"Over . . . ?"

"Over visitation of the children."

"And . . . ?"

"And no support. He has not given us any child
support or any alimony since December. Paul has been
in contempt of court now about seven times, and the
judge arrested him once right in the courthouse, and the
second time Paul was hiding in his parents' apartment
and his parents lied to the Metro-Dade police officer,
saying he wasn't there, he wasn't there, but refused to
open the door for the police officers, even though the
police officers had an order to go into their apartment.
Finally they had to break into the parents' apartment
and they found Paul hiding there and they took him to
jail."

"Mrs. Luskin, how many stores does your husband
own?"

"There are eight Luskin's Hi-Fidelity stores that he
and his parents own."

Before Soccol left, he worked with Marie to draw a
picture of the assailant with the use of an "Identikit"—a
collection of facial parts that can compose a full render-
ing. When Marie ran out of steam, he ended the interview, but asked if she'd like to hire off-duty Hollywood
cops for security at $14 an hour. Marie said she didn't
have the money for it.

* * *

WEDNESDAY, MARCH 11

Soccol called Joe and Mildred Luskin at the Luskin's Hollywood store—where the executive offices were located—to tell them what had happened to Marie. He explained the flower delivery, the assault, the description of the assailant and the car, and Marie's injury.

Soccol wrote in his report that "upon speaking with them, they were unaware of the incident and seemed quite concerned over the matter." He also noted that Joe Luskin appeared to be quite surprised and alarmed when he learned that Paul's daughter was at home when it happened.

Soccol asked about Paul, and the Luskins said he was in Pittsburgh; therefore, he didn't know what had happened. For that matter, Joe said he had been out of town as well on the day of the assault, in Baltimore.

Soccol asked if he could set up a meeting with the family, and Joe offered to call Paul and have him phone Soccol back.

A bit later, Paul called Soccol. He sounded very surprised that something had happened, and asked how Marie was. When he realized he had talked with her the day before, he asked, "Why didn't she tell me?"

"Do you know your daughter was there?" Soccol questioned.

"What?" his voice rose.

Paul said he had been working as an attorney in Pittsburgh since January, but had planned to fly home Friday so he could take his children to Disney World for the weekend. He would meet with Soccol and his parents at the Hollywood Luskin's store, and assist any way he could.

Later that day, Soccol visited Dr. Clark's office to pick up the foreign body removed from Marie's head during surgery. Clark told Soccol that Marie was hit very hard, and in fact, she was very, very lucky to be alive.

Clark said he closed the wound with thirty stitches. He expected Marie would make a full recovery.

At the police station, Soccol placed the foreign body into evidence. He wrote on the property record:

> "One (1) clear plastic container, whitecap, marked Do Not Destroy + dates 3-9-87. Taken from the laceration of Marie Luskin, one (1) small metal fragment/foreign body."

The property clerk stamped the sheet "Received sealed."

FRIDAY MARCH 13
LUSKIN'S HI-FI
4150 N. 28th TERRACE, HOLLYWOOD

Soccol met the three Luskins for about a half hour in the morning. They reiterated they would assist the investigation any way they could, but Soccol noticed that the father was looking at the son kind of funny.

BROWARD COUNTY SHERIFF'S OFFICE
LAUDERHILL SUBSTATION

After the meeting at Luskin's, Soccol took Marie to see a police artist, John McMahon, who worked for the Broward County Sheriff. McMahon was a skilled free-hand artist who drew with pencil as he asked questions.

After an hour and a half the result was a black-and-white drawing of a rather handsome thin-faced young man. He had a straight nose, large eyes, and medium-length hair parted on the side and falling over his forehead. Marie thought the picture was a little off, but considered it 85 percent right.

Later, Soccol took the drawing to Denise Keltz at Emerald Hills Florist. She thought it was close, too, except the man's hair wasn't right. It looked too much like a wig, and the man wasn't wearing one. Also, the man as drawn looked too young.

After McMahon revised the drawing with Keltz's assistance on March 17, police released it to the press, hoping to generate some leads. In fact, the assault had not made news anywhere, not even the police blotter of the local *Hollywood Sun-Tattler*.

On March 19, the Fort Lauderdale *Sun-Sentinel* ran the story and drawing on page three of the local section, in the "Briefs" column. It was headlined "Police seek suspect."

> HOLLYWOOD—Police are looking for a man who posed as a florist's deliveryman and then struck a woman with a gun when she told him she didn't have any money, police said.
>
> The would-be robber, carrying a floral arrangement, rang the doorbell of a home in Emerald Hills on March 9, police said. The woman, whom police would not identify, allowed the man into her home, police said.
>
> Police said that once inside, the man pulled out a gun and threatened the woman's life if she didn't give him money.
>
> She told police she gave the man all she had, but the man didn't believe her and struck her on the back of the head.
>
> Police described the man as white, between 30 and 35 years old, 5 feet 11 inches tall and 180 pounds with sandy brown hair. He was wearing blue jeans and drove a late model, medium-blue, four-door Honda, police said. Anyone with information is asked to call 921-3361 or 921-3911.

Although the newspaper story referred to the case as a robbery, the *Weekly Information Bulletin* published by the Hollywood Police detective bureau on March 20 called the case a "Home Invasion/Attempted Murder."

The newspaper story brought a lead. Police in Oakland Park—another suburb in Broward County—had an informant who thought a possible suspect was a thirty-two-year-old man.

Oakland Park Detective Dusty Rhodes thought the man might be a match because he looked like the composite, drove a late-model blue Mustang, and his girlfriend was a florist. To get a picture of the man,

Soccol asked the state motor vehicle bureau to send a
duplicate of his driver's license photo.

The photo arrived eight days later, and Soccol showed
it to both Marie and Denise Keltz, but both were certain
it wasn't the right person.

The investigation stalled. On May 13, Soccol read
in *The Miami Herald* about an arrest that the robbery division of Metro-Dade Police had made in a
home invasion. He called Metro-Dade Sergeant Tony
Monheim, who said it was related to a home invasion
gang working out of Hollywood.

Soccol met Monheim in Miami, showed him his
composite drawing, and described the crime. Monheim
said it didn't match any of the gang members, nor sound
like the type of crime they engaged in. While talking, the
two detectives ruled out robbery as the motive for the
Luskin assault. Still, Monheim gave Soccol pictures of
his suspects.

Soccol placed the pictures in photo lineups and again
went to Marie and Denise Keltz. Again, neither made
identifications.

TWO

The Magnificent Luskins

BALTIMORE

A *Los Angeles Times* story about Baltimore's renaissance began by recalling the city's bad old days. Billie Holliday, who had lived there, said she always thought of Baltimore as a town that took pretty girls and turned them into prostitutes. Newspaperman H.L. Mencken, a curmudgeon on every subject except beer and his hometown, said he thought of Baltimore as a ruin of a once-great medieval city.

"Though it was America's second-largest city in the 1820s, Baltimore eventually came to be known as a place where anyone with all his teeth was a celebrity," the *Times* wrote.

For the first half of Baltimore's twentieth century, Mencken was its chronicler. In the 1980s a chronicler of Jewish Baltimore emerged, and in a new medium: film director Barry Levinson.

In a personal trilogy of films, Levinson went back three generations. *Diner* was about himself and his friends, who came of age in the fifties and hung out at the Hilltop Diner, near Pimlico Race Track; *Tin Men* was about a home improvement salesman in his father's generation, and *Avalon* began with homage to his immigrant grandfather, who landed at the Baltimore harbor at the turn of the century to begin a family.

After the end of World War II, Levinson's family got

into the retail appliance and television business. As Barry portrayed it in *Avalon,* they had a brilliant idea: sell at below full price. Their store was a smash.

When longtime Baltimoreans saw the film, they asked an obvious question: Was that Luskin's?

Levinson admitted to employing a certain amount of dramatic license. In real-life Baltimore, the first appliance discounters were in fact Jack and Joe Luskin.

The Luskin family had begun in business selling furniture and radios on the installment plan. In 1948, the two young sons Jack and Joe opened their own store, anticipating before anyone else yet another giant new trend: a suburban location.

Their first store was seven hundred square feet, on Park Heights Avenue next to the Pimlico Hotel—which wasn't a hotel, but the area's fanciest restaurant. The two brothers were a terrific match. Both handsome, Jack was the consummate salesman, and Joe was the backroom tinkerer. Back then TVs were sold in two pieces— picture tube and cabinet. Where other shops took custom orders and delivered weeks later, Joe was the only guy in Baltimore who could assemble a finished set in-house. Luskin's delivered in twenty-four hours, and besides that, discounted. They could sell a $600 piece for $450.

My dad, too, was in the same biz at the same time. He had a storefront in downtown Baltimore called "TV Club." He advertised a free five-day trial period; he'd come to your house and install a TV set, with no obligation to buy. If you didn't want it after five days, he'd take it back, no charge.

He never took back a single one.

The Luskins were better financed than my dad, and by the end of the fifties, when both businesses foresaw changes, the Luskins were in a better position to act. By the early sixties, my dad was out of the appliance business. Luskin's moved down the block to its present location, a huge store for its day. They bought broadcast time on local TV to sell TVs, and made themselves TV stars in the process. In an era when every business needed a slogan, theirs were "Jack and Joe Will Save You Dough," and "The Cheapest Guys in Town."

They did. And they were. And everyone knew it. In the appliance business, they owned the city.

There was enough success for both brothers, but instead they fought.

In the mid-1960s Jack correctly foresaw the next step in the evolution of Luskin's: a chain of stores around Baltimore. But Joe disagreed. They were making a good living, why risk it? One day in 1966 painters changed the slogan on the store's exterior wall. From then on it read "Jack, You Know, Will Save You Dough."

The brothers would never reconcile.

Whatever happened to Joe? Baltimore wondered. The answer was discovered by those who wintered in Miami. Jack had handed Joe $50,000 up front for his half of the business, the rest over ten years, and in 1969 Joe tried to go it alone by opening his own Luskin's. Jack wasn't happy about it, especially since the store used the same logo—a crown instead of a dot over the "i" in their name—and the same red and yellow colors, only reversed.

The Florida Luskin's was a little different. It, too, was in the middle of a bustling Jewish area—N.E. 163rd Street in North Miami Beach—but it only sold stereo equipment, cash and carry, no service department, no deliveries, no expensive fixtures.

Until Luskin's had opened, nobody in Miami discounted stereos at all. So, for years to come, they were the only place to shop for a bargain. Once again, in another time, another place, Luskin's was a huge success.

PAUL AND SUSAN

Paul Luskin was eleven in 1960 when he first went to work as a stock boy for Luskin's. He said he did it so he could see his dad, who worked from nine in the morning to ten at night. He was paid, and as a result, always had his own money in his pocket.

In 1966, during his senior year at newly opened Pikesville High, he offered to help a sophomore girl in library study hall with her geometry homework. She had brown hair and bangs, and her name was Susan Pruce.

In the next few minutes she fell in love with him. It
wasn't because he was a math whiz—he claimed to have
taken geometry, but it soon became obvious he didn't
know the first thing about it. Fudging a tortuous way
through a problem, he invented his own logic, then
caught her by complete surprise when he solved it. She
doubled over in laughter.

Right then Susan knew that Paul was intellectually her
match, and Paul realized she was whimsical enough to
follow him.

At halftime of a basketball game after school the next
day, Paul spotted her in the popcorn line, butted in,
bought her the popcorn, and asked to sit next to her for
the rest of the game.

Nothing could have elated her more. Although Susan
was in tenth grade, she was only fourteen since she had
skipped a grade. She looked like a junior-high kid, too.
The next week, on their first date, Paul violated Pikesville's "three-date rule"—the code of honor that kept
boys from attempting a kiss until the third date. And it
wasn't just a good-bye, Grandma kiss, it was the real
thing.

Susan didn't sleep much that night. *Did I lead him on?
Was he too fast? Is he taking advantage of me? He's three
years older than I am—what will people think?*

The sexual revolution was slow to hit Pikesville High.

They dated the rest of the school year although Paul
insisted Susan was too young for him. She saw him as a
rich kid who didn't require the trappings, and she liked
that. Her family was middle-class—her father Irv was a
pharmacist, her mother Gloria a Ed.D. schoolteacher,
and they lived in a tract house. Paul drove his mom's
car, a big blue Ford with a monster engine and bench
seats that only he thought was cool. When he and Susan
rode together, sometimes he would let her hold the
steering wheel. She never figured out he did it so their
bodies could touch.

They continued dating even after Paul began college,
at University of Maryland. By the time Susan graduated
from Pikesville, in 1968, she had blossomed. Her brown
hair was now blond, long and straight, and her little-girl
look was gone.

Her yearbook spoke to brimming sexual tension. One girlfriend inscribed "To the greatest man chaser of them all." But another girlfriend wrote the most poignant line, as seen from a distance of years: "I hope your kids and Paul's kids grow up to be the same people."

The couple had looked forward to 1968, when they could both live on campus at Maryland. But that was the year Joe Luskin moved south, and he had Paul transfer to University of Miami. That was too far away to keep a relationship going.

Paul didn't see Susan until the next summer, 1969, when he returned to Baltimore. He got a job at a day camp, Camp Milldale, as a counselor for nine-year-olds. He stayed with his older cousin Steve Miles, who lived blocks away from Susan's house.

That summer, Paul and Susan picked up where they had left off. They went on picnics, to Druid Hill Park, the Baltimore Zoo. Too young to do the bars, they did the delis. At night they took walks together.

Susan's parents weren't around much that summer, and it was easier to convince her grandmother that she was going to spend a weekend with a girlfriend when in fact she was going to spend two nights in a hotel room with Paul at Luray Caverns, in the Virginia mountains. Once they arrived, Paul held her hand and Susan imagined what life would be like being married to him. When Paul brought her back exhausted that Sunday night, Susan's grandmother asked her if she had had a nice time with her girlfriend.

The summer ended early. Paul had cut his foot on the job and was on crutches because it wouldn't heal. He wanted to go home.

The evening on earth that men first landed on the moon, July 20, 1969, was the last night Paul and Susan spent together. Susan didn't want him to go—at least alone.

Susan reluctantly lied to her grandmother again about where she'd be. That night was a milestone in the history of man, and Susan kept waiting for Paul to propose. But when the evening was over, only Armstrong and mankind had accomplished a giant leap. Paul wasn't ready; he was only twenty-one, and Susan just eighteen. It was too soon.

By morning he was gone.

PAUL AND MARIE

Just weeks after Paul arrived home, he got his draft notice; he was classified 1-A and preassigned as a second lieutenant in the U.S. Army infantry in Vietnam.

To Paul, that was the end of the world. University of Miami was full of Vietnam vets on the GI Bill, and it was impossible to ignore their horror stories of death, mutilation, and psychological terror. Paul's frat house roommate was a marine whose stomach had been shot out there, and he convinced Paul his chances of coming home in anything but a body bag were slim. He said second lieutenants especially were sitting ducks; the army couldn't resupply them fast enough because the Viet Cong was offering fifty-five-dollar rewards for each one killed.

The buzz on campus was how to beat the draft board.

Paul petitioned it for a student deferment and was granted one, but only month to month. He met with a Miami attorney who said for $2,000 he could influence the board into a favorable decision, but Paul nixed the idea when others on campus said he was a fraud. He tried joining the National Guard—it worked for Dan Quayle—but they said No because the army had already assigned him. Paul's dad Joe didn't want him to go either—Joe's brother, another Paul Luskin, had been killed in World War II. Joe suggested his son go to Canada and live with family friends.

It was in the midst of those uncertain times that Paul met Marie Reitzes.

Early that fall term at school, Paul returned from an overnight hunting trip in the Everglades and was informed that frat brothers were required to bring dates to varsity football games. A little later that morning, still dirty and dressed in camouflage, he gave four sorority sisters a lift across campus in his yellow Dodge Charger with a Jolly Roger flag on the antenna. The last one getting out had a pretty face, long blond hair, a great figure, and had been a cheerleader in high school. He asked if she had a boyfriend.

Marie did, but he was in the air force, stationed in Guam. Paul asked her to the game, and she accepted.

For the first year they knew each other, Paul and Marie stayed just friends. They dated only occasionally, but they did nice things together—day trips to Key West, and seaplane flights to Paradise Island in the Bahamas.

Meanwhile, Marie thought her air force boyfriend, who hadn't returned, was getting bizarre. To help Paul avoid the same fate, she suggested a way to beat the draft—eat himself over the weight limit.

She began baking. On Marie's sugar diet, he eventually put on fifty pounds—and Marie put on a few herself. Since Paul's deferment was month to month, the draft board had ordered him to take a physical each month. The night before one of them, he, Marie, and friends went to Coconut Grove for dessert. Scanning the menu, Paul ordered five-layer "Victory Cake," then followed that with "The Kitchen Sink." That night he waddled home, and next morning he flunked the physical.

Although Paul was grateful to Marie, he considered her a "fill-in" girlfriend, and never felt in love with her. Considering his tenuous draft status, it wasn't fair to marry someone. That's why he hadn't asked Susan. But after the summer of 1970 he learned that Susan was engaged to a Latin boy she had met when she was an exchange student in the Yucatán.

Paul was crushed. Susan hadn't lived with the reality of the draft, and didn't understand it. In the fall of '70, his relationship with Marie turned sexual. By the end of the year, with Paul now consistently beating the draft board physicals, they engaged and set a wedding date for June 1971.

The engagement was stormy, probably because it wasn't anchored by any deep love or passion. Twice Marie returned the ring; the second time she threw it at him.

In April 1971 Paul showed up unannounced at Susan's

house in Baltimore. He told her he was having second thoughts about marrying Marie, what should he do? He was trying to say he wanted Susan back.

Susan was still mad at him for not proposing two summers before, and didn't want to hear it. She snapped, "If you're so unsure that you have to ask, you shouldn't." What she didn't say was that she had broken off her own engagement three months earlier. If Paul had known that, all that followed would have been different.

SUSAN MEETS MARIE

Susan graduated from the University of Maryland in three years, at age nineteen. That put her two years ahead of herself. She wanted to teach high school, but she realized she wasn't much older than the kids. So instead, she entered a master's program in Spanish linguistics at Florida Atlantic University in Boca Raton, about fifty miles north of Miami.

When she arrived in September 1971, she called Paul, and he invited her to dinner at his apartment. He told Marie that Susan was one of the "kids" from Baltimore. Marie didn't suspect Susan was his old flame.

Susan had met a man at FAU named Gary Davis, from Chicago, and she asked if she could bring him along. Besides, he had a car and she didn't.

That night, Susan knocked on the apartment door she thought was right. A huge man opened it, and she was about to excuse herself for interrupting when the man grabbed and hugged her like a long-lost friend, scaring her. It was Paul.

In the six months since Susan had last seen him he had put on even more weight and had also let his hair grow long and wild. Susan, a string bean, was stunned. And his bride was almost as tubby. She thought, *Look at those fat polkies beneath her tight white cowboy outfit. Revolting.*

When Marie showed off her one-carat diamond engagement ring, she had no idea who it really was who was looking at it.

It was a horrible night. Susan knew immediately that

Paul had married someone he didn't have any special bond with. After Gary left her at home that night she had the biggest cry of her life. She resolved never to talk to Paul again.

As Marie had been Paul's fill-in girlfriend, Gary Davis became Susan's fill-in boyfriend. He was attractive, he liked cats, and seemed like someone she could have a regular life with. When the school year ended, he proposed and asked her to move with him to Columbus, Ohio, where he had taken a computer-programming job. Desiring to be married, she said yes. As she walked down the aisle she thought about Paul. She said to herself, *Well, it's too late now.*

MARRIAGE—FIRST YEARS

Paul and Marie's favorite topic the first year they were married was whether they should get divorced. When the University of Miami Law School placed him on academic probation, he transferred to the University of Baltimore. That meant going home.

It was almost the final straw. Marie didn't want to leave Miami, but at the last moment she agreed to go. They took a $150-a-month apartment in Randallstown, a few miles from Pikesville, Marie got a teaching job in Baltimore City that paid $6,000, and they bought a new Chevy Malibu.

During school Paul interned at the U.S. Attorney's Office, then the Maryland Public Defender's Office. On top of that, he created all the newspaper advertising for his father's store and mailed the art to him every week.

In 1975, Paul got his Juris Doctor degree and was ready to move back to Miami to work for his dad. But now, Marie liked Baltimore and didn't want to leave. Once again they almost separated.

Paul had always hoped he and Marie could build a love together, but after returning to Miami, he realized it would never happen. By 1977, Paul finally resolved they would both be better off divorced, but that's when Marie got pregnant. Now it was too late.

Before the baby was born, Susan came to Fort Lauderdale with Gary for a computer software convention. For six years Susan had kept her promise not to talk to Paul, but now she decided to call.

They had lunch. It made Susan think about what might have been. To expunge her anger, she asked why he had left her in 1969. "I've been thinking about it every day of my life since then. It changed my life, and I have to know the answer."

Paul was flabbergasted. She told him her life with Gary was as miserable as the life he described with Marie. That moment they both remembered that love, passion, and marriage were supposed to go together. They couldn't go back, but could they begin again? He suggested an affair.

She wanted to say yes but had to say no as a practical matter. With a new baby on the way he had no way out of his marriage. And if Gary found out, she would have no one.

Paul hoped the baby, Shana, would bring out the best in Marie, but it didn't. She had been teaching at a Jewish day school in Miami Beach, about to climb the ladder to assistant vice principal, and resented that now she'd have to pass up the promotion. Paul tried to appease her with a three-carat diamond ring and a full-time nanny, but neither solved anything. To escape, she locked herself in her room or ran to her mother, who would let her spend nights there, away from the child. She began seeing a therapist. Eventually she quit her teaching job, but still didn't spend more time with the baby.

AFFLUENCE

Instead of putting his energy into the marriage, Paul put it into his work. His dad gave him carte blanche; he could do anything he wanted with the business, as long as they made a profit. And it did; about a million dollars a year by 1980. Paul's salary rose to $200,000 plus bonuses and perks.

It was ironic that Joe Luskin and his brother had split over the issue of expanding the business, for by the 1980s, the Florida Luskin's was thirteen stores, from

South Miami to Orlando, and they were talking about covering the whole state and farther. Already it was the largest consumer electronics chain in the state, and arguably the most successful. They had sixty thousand square feet of retail space, and it now sold video as well as audio. In 1984 Paul's parents gave Paul a third of the business as a reward for running it.

After a while, the business began to run itself, and Paul looked for other diversions. He became friends with Gene Hawkins, national rep for Shure turntable cartridges, and husband of U.S. Senator from Florida Paula Hawkins. Paula suggested Paul run for Congress in 1982 as a Republican. Paul thought about it, then said no because he had watched his friend Alvin Entin get trounced when he tried in 1980.

In 1985, Paula tried to get Paul involved again. When she formally announced she would run for reelection, she made Paul her top fund-raiser—a complete surprise to him. In 1986, when Ronald Reagan came to Miami for a fund-raising gala, she made Paul a cochair, assigned to greet all the VIPs. He did the same for Vice President George Bush's dinner.

Paul had always liked to tinker in the back room, like his dad, and Gene Hawkins got him design work testing electronic tolerance levels for Shure cartridges. Following that, other audio-video companies asked Paul for technical, cosmetic, and packaging suggestions. Quasar used some of his ideas when they manufactured the first VHS camcorder.

Beyond that there was travel. As sales incentive bonuses, he went on paid trips to Japan, China, India, and Denmark. On a trip to France, he took both his parents and Marie's parents. But sometimes Marie turned him down, and he went alone. He'd go places on a whim; once a Panasonic rep told him about the shrimp Creole at a New Orleans restaurant. "Okay, let's go to lunch there," Paul said. They did. He called Marie first, but knew she'd say no.

A year after Shana's birth Paul and Marie moved from their modest $55,000 house in North Miami Beach to a $130,000 house not far away. New next-door neighbor

Diane Yariv thought they were the ideal couple. Marie was quiet and cordial, and neither ever raised their voice. "She was constantly getting gifts. I thought, what a lovely relationship, for a husband to want to do that."

But Diane also noticed Marie never laughed and didn't seem to share any of her husband's pleasures. She loved to talk about dieting. "We dieted together, she lost seventy pounds, and fit into size 10 Calvin Klein jeans," Diane said. But Marie didn't stay slim. "When Marie was upset, she'd eat. And Marie was a very unhappy person."

At a rare moment when Marie confided in Diane, she said she had been an only child until seven, then her mother had twin girls. After getting all the spotlight, her parents' attitude turned to "Get lost, we don't have time for you."

"Marie's not a loving person. She doesn't give it, and probably isn't able to receive it," said Diane. "Some people equate eating with childhood and mother giving you love for eating. But getting fat makes you feel worse, and then you punish yourself further by eating more."

When Diana was born in 1982, Paul bought Marie a seven-carat diamond for $18,000. Marie responded by having her tubes tied against Paul's wishes. Then she declared the new house too small. In 1983 they saw a nine-bedroom house in Emerald Hills. The sellers were separated and would take $600,000, but only if it was in cash and the sale could be completed within a week. Paul and Marie had $200,000, plus the value of their current house, and Paul's parents offered to write a check as a loan for the difference. Months later, when Paul and Marie sold the old house, they repaid $100,000 of it.

Marie took Diane Yariv on a tour of the new house. She was shocked when Marie pouted, "I wish I could be like you. You're so happy. You're so together."

"Marie, you're like a princess in a fairy tale. What's not to be happy? You have a wonderful house, children, a wonderful husband. And you don't have to work."

Years before, Diane and Marie had attended a womens' group meeting and the topic was "Do you know where your husband's assets are?" The speaker's advice was to continually better your surroundings, so should you divorce later, your husband will be forced to support you in the lifestyle to which you have become accustomed.

In the big house, Diane saw the first open rift between Paul and Marie. Sitting together on a sofa, Paul tried to take Marie's hand, but she abruptly moved it away. Diane couldn't believe it. She wondered if Marie had been following the speaker's advice all this time.

MARIE'S WITHDRAWAL

When Paul came home from work every night at eight, Marie locked herself in her room with her Harlequin Romances, leaving him to take care of the children and put them to bed.

Instead of complaining, Paul embraced the "Dad-daughter" time. He invented bedtime stories called "Daddy's Funky Fairy Tales," which included "The Pep Monkeys—Manny, Moe, and Jack Monkey," an inside joke that referred to The Pep Boys, an auto service chain with a cartoonish logo that had a store in Baltimore near the original Luskin's. When Paul would say Manny Monkey ate peanuts, the girls knew to shout "Monkeys don't eat peanuts! They eat bananas!"

Paul was a toy buyer—both for the kids and himself. Whenever he saw something for the kids he thought was neat—never dolls—he'd bring it home and they'd all get down on the floor together and play with it. Finger paints, Play-Doh, Paul had no prohibitions about making a mess.

Child discipline wasn't Paul's strongest suit.

Every Saturday he spent alone with Shana, every Sunday with Diana. They went to Grand Prix race-a-rama for go-carts and video games, picnics, every church fair, the Space Transit Planetarium, the Miami Sea-quarium. If there was nothing else to do, they'd drop in at Paul's sister Nance's shop, Le Chocolatier, and they'd dip fresh strawberries in warm chocolate.

Every November, Paul took his kids and Diane's kids to the Broward County Fair. Marie always stayed home.

Paul wouldn't miss a ride, except the ones adults couldn't fit onto. If the kids wanted to skip one, he'd go on it alone.

After a while, Paul would ask everyone if they were ready for some serious junk food. "Oh yeah," said Diane, "you got the right person. They ate corn dogs and cotton candy and DoveBars till they were sick. The kids loved it. It was a relief for them, because at home Marie always insisted they count calories." At the same time, Paul said, Marie would eat a bowl of ice cream.

Once Shana said she had never been to Washington, so they flew there and walked in on Paula Hawkins's news conference. Shana got on TV and was beaming.

"If you had all the money you needed, and had the time, why not do it?" he asked, blithely.

By 1985 Marie was impossible to live with, Paul said. In May they took a cruise around Greece but Marie wouldn't leave the boat when they got to the ports, and avoided his parents, who had also come. On their anniversary, June 6, he gave her roses, but she threw them in the trash and said this year she wanted carnations. She began taking evening tennis lessons at Emerald Hills Tennis Club, but returned without having broken a sweat. She wanted a $22,000 Piaget watch, but when Paul said no, she threw a screaming fit. Paul's mother Mildred gave Marie a pair of earrings for Shana, but Marie threw them back across the table. "These are inappropriate for a little girl. They're too big."

Mildred muttered, "Never again."

SUSAN RETURNS ONCE MORE

In April 1985 Gary Davis got a new job in south Florida, and flew there alone, leaving Susan behind in Columbus to care for the two kids, ages four and six, and to paint and spackle the walls before they listed the house for sale.

That sort of assignment was nothing new. When it snowed, Susan had to shovel half the driveway, and in the summer, mow half the lawn.

They had just had two big fights. When Gary suggested they move somewhere, Susan said Baltimore, but

he wouldn't consider it. Then when Susan's grandmother died, Gary didn't want to go to the funeral and
couldn't understand why Susan was angry about it.

Susan had never considered separating from Gary,
although she felt her relationship was crumbling. While
he was gone she was surprised she didn't miss him.

In June Susan flew to Florida to see the modest house
Gary had picked out. On the last day of her trip she
called Paul at work and offered to show him the place.
As they drove there, Paul couldn't believe it—it was in
Hollywood Hills, maybe a mile from his house in
Emerald Hills. The thought made Paul apprehensive.
While he and Susan had been far away, they had
controlled their feelings for each other.

As Paul had never told Marie the truth about Susan,
neither had Susan told Gary about dating Paul.

That summer, the Luskins put out the welcome mat
for the Davises. The Luskin girls and Davis boys were
about the same ages, and they played together around
the pools at both houses. On weekends, Paul took
everyone out on his boat, the *Jolly Roger,* followed by
barbecues afterward. At Paul's suggestion Marie took
Susan under her wing and she graciously introduced her
to Hollywood society.

But in the midst of the camaraderie, the inevitable
began. Paul observed that Gary didn't respect Susan and
told her she didn't have to put up with it. "I don't?" she
asked with an absence of sarcasm. It was then she
realized she hated Gary; nor would she be able to stay
just friends with Paul.

Almost everyone who saw Paul and Susan together
that summer noticed something between them. The
most notable exception was Marie, who tried to stay
aloof. The giveaway was Paul pushing Susan into the
swimming pool. Marie never let him do that to her; it
would have messed up her hair and her nails. All the kids
saw it and giggled. Richard Jehlen, Paul's sister Nance's
husband, sniffed something scandalous was up. "Who
the hell is she? And where did she come from?" he asked
discreetly. Gary, too, had suspicions.

By late summer tensions were ready to boil over.
Susan's six-year-old, Jeremy, asked Shana to come over

and play, and Marie said no. Then Jeremy appealed to his mother to ask Paul. Susan did, and predictably he said sure.

That got Marie's goat. She called Susan and screamed, "How dare you go around me? Don't you ever go around me again!" To Susan, it felt like Marie was talking to her as if she was the parent and Susan was the child. While Marie continued her tirade, Susan held the phone at arm's length, paying attention only to the din, waiting for Marie to pause for a breath. When she did, Susan said, "I'm hanging up now."

Marie said that by August, she and Paul were barely speaking.

That month, when a Miami TV station needed an expert to comment on camera about that day's U.S.-Japanese trade news, they asked Paul. That night, he and Marie watched the broadcast together, but she was completely disinterested in what he had to say. "You know, on TV you look ten pounds fatter," she told him. For Paul, that did it.

In September, the families were to attend Yom Kippur services together, and Susan told Paul she'd like everyone to break the day-long fast at her house. She didn't realize it was a *faux pas* to ask Paul, not Marie. Later, Marie called Susan to reproach her that "the social life in the family is my job, and goes through me. Business and moneymaking in the family is Paul's job."

The day was a disaster. Gary got bored and left services early to motorcycle to the beach. Susan, who is religious, got steaming mad at him.

Paul was just as angry at Marie. In the early afternoon, he had the honor of removing the Torah from the ark, which his kids wanted to see. Instead, Marie took them home because services were running late.

The two couples had sat in separate rows, but now that Paul and Susan were alone, they joined. They knew there was nothing in either marriage to save, and at that moment, they didn't even care. The week before, Susan had asked Paul if he still had his Pikesville High class ring, gold with a raised panther design and a purple glass stone. He had never given it to her when they went steady. That day in synagogue, nineteen years later, Paul took it off his finger and gave it to her. He admonished her, "If you run into trouble because of Gary, give it back to me, to let me know."

THE AFFAIR

In early October Paul was asked on short notice to go to New York on business.

He said he asked Marie to go with him, as always, but she wanted to go to Wilmington instead. "Are you going to see Leslie?" he asked, her old boyfriend who had since married.

"I'll probably see him," she said. "How big is Wilmington?"

Marie's version was that she did want to go to New York so she could shop. But for the first time, he absolutely forbade her to go, which raised her suspicions.

That weekend Susan was in Princeton, New Jersey, alone, for an annual computer convention called the Rainbow Fest, selling software Gary had created. She even bought him a "Rainbow Fest" T-shirt.

Paul finished his business in New York early, and showed up totally unannounced at Susan's booth. "I was in the neighborhood—in New Jersey," he said.

"Go away, I'm working, and you're distracting me," she told him. "I can't work with you here."

Paul was crestfallen. He stuck out his lip like a deflated puppy dog, so Susan asked him to come back at the end of the day, they'd have dinner. Paul left, but couldn't stay away. A short while later he returned with a tin of Famous Amos cookies for people who stopped at her booth. He put up a sign: Free cookies and a free smile.

That evening they strolled around the Princeton University campus. They ate dinner at a café and danced at the hotel disco. They asked each other why they didn't marry, the same thing they had asked at lunch in 1977.

He followed her back to her hotel room in the Hyatt Regency. "It didn't seem unusual for him to come to my room—it was just Paul," she said.

But once in the room she didn't want him to leave.

The lost years of emotion and passion filled the room. They were teenage lovers again, grown up. They knew it was wrong in 1969, and they knew it was wrong in 1985.

"I belong here. This is the way everything should have been," Susan cried the next morning. "I've always been drawn to you. It's always been hard to see you with Marie. Even when I sat next to my own husband."

"I feel so guilty," he answered. "Guilty for what I've done to you all these years, and guilty because we won't get away with this."

"I wasn't surprised you made an advance," she said.

"I was," he said. "I didn't go when I should have, and you didn't tell me to go when you should have."

Paul ordered breakfast from room service. It was a simple thing, but no one had ever done that before for Susan, and she thought it was the height of romance. But after it came, it struck her that these were fleeting moments.

"Oh shit. What are we going to do?"

"We have to pick up our regular lives," he said.

"I don't want to go home. The fairy tale will end. Real life's not so great."

THE TRANSCRIPTS

Paul and Susan never dreamed what would follow.

A few weeks later Susan was at home talking on the phone to Gary when she heard two clicks simultaneously: one from the earpiece and another in the room.

"What's that noise?" she asked. Following her ears, she found a recorder. "You've been tapping the telephone!" she freaked, then hung up on him. When she replayed the tape she heard the conversation they had just had—the noise was the sound of the recorder shutting off as the tape ended.

Susan's first thought was how much else he had captured. She had had some very discreet talks with Paul on the phone. She was more scared than angry.

When Gary got home they fought. Susan said she wanted to get out of the house with the kids, but Gary blocked the front of each door she tried. She called

Hollywood Police to escort her out. When she decided to return later that night—because she didn't want Gary to consider that she had abandoned him—she called the cops again. The cops suggested she stay away.

The next day Gary announced he was divorcing her because of her affair with Paul. His terms were, he would keep the house and kids, and she had three days to get out. Susan refused to leave.

That day, Paul said he 'fessed up to Marie. "I know. Gary told me. You shouldn't have done it," she answered. Then she walked away.

Gary transcribed conversations taped between October 29 and 31. Susan later found copies and entered them into evidence in an illegal wiretap suit she and Paul brought four years later. (The case was dismissed for lack of timeliness by a federal judge.)

The first was a conversation with Paul in which Susan described lunch with her single cousin from Baltimore earlier that day, October 29.

Susan: "She said if I really love you—and she said she can really tell it, you see the differences in what I look like when I talk about you and when I talk about anything else. She can really see it."

The cousin had asked how Susan managed still going to bed with Gary.

"I said, 'With great difficulty.' She said that's the one thing she can't do is two at a time. I mean, she's been damn near single since 1969. But she assures me that one at a time is her mind-set. And I said, that's my mind-set too, but you can blank it out. It's amazing what you can do and not be there; you can actually, mentally, and totally not be there. She asked me how you were."

Paul: "How I do it?"

Susan: "Yeah. I found myself get real red and start to smile. She said, 'That good? Huh?' It was a nice lunch, ha-ha. I told her about Yom Kippur. I told her about Princeton."

Paul: "What did she say?"

Susan: "She thought it was right. She said if we ever need to do anything like that again and can't find a day,

I've got an open invitation to spend as many days at her place, with the recorder on nonstop, no questions asked, anytime."

Paul: "You mean you can stay at her place?"

Susan: "I mean I can say I'm there, stupid. I wouldn't really be there."

Paul: "Well, when do you wanna go?"

Susan: "Anytime. She said the invitation is open. It can be for a weekday, a weekend, just let her know. And she will cover . . . I was there, we were together insepar-able, the whole time."

Paul: "Could you spend the night with her?"

Susan: "Absolutely."

Gary confronted Susan the next day by telephone with his new information.

Susan: "Sugar Software."

Gary: "Hello."

Susan: "Hi. How are you?"

Gary: "Good. Tell me about Princeton. (pause) Every-thing."

Susan: (long pause) "Why?"

Gary: (long pause) " 'Cause I wanna know."

Susan: (long pause) "I went to Princeton, I did the show. I came home."

Gary: "I'm setting up an arrangement with a marriage counselor, today if possible."

Susan: (long pause) "Are you crying?"

Gary: "No. But I should be. Obviously, things are worse than expected."

Susan: "What do you think happened?"

Gary: "I think you went with Paul."

Susan: "No, I didn't. What would make you think that?"

Gary: "I was talking with Marie this morning. She says Paul was gone the same days, to New Jersey, he didn't want her to come. Quite a coincidence. I don't think you are telling me the truth. Wanna try again?"

Susan: "He went to visit his sister Donna in New York. I know that."

Gary: (long pause) "I'm giving you a chance to come clean."

Susan: "I'm clean."

Gary: "I want the truth."

Susan: "You got it."

Gary: (long pause) "All right, bye."

Susan: "Bye."

Later that day, Marie left a message:

"Susan, hi, this is Marie Luskin. Please let the kids come for dinner around 4:30, 5:00. We'll feed them and carve pumpkins. Talk to you later."

Gary called back to tell Susan about an evening marriage counselor's appointment.

Gary: "Know I've been talking to all these people?"

Susan: "I knew, obviously, you talked to Marie."

Gary: "Paul called me."

Susan: "No. That I didn't know. [Gary's notes: Actually she was with him when he made that call.] I have not talked to him since this morning."

Gary: "I called what's her name, [Susan's cousin] this morning."

Susan: "What did you say to [my cousin]?"

Gary: "Just voiced my concerns."

Susan: "Yes, just like you were saying yesterday, or this morning, or whenever the hell it was, you don't think you're gonna change to be more of the things I was talking about, or provide me with the emotional support or whatever I need and you'd rather blame it on Paul and that's certainly your choice, but I do not have to participate in that."

Gary: "He agreed not to call you anymore. And he and Marie had a talk for a couple hours today . . . (Marie) called to say that she is pretty satisfied that there is nothing going on."

Susan: "She is satisfied?"

Gary: "Yeah. She feels that Paul loves her and doesn't want a divorce. I think he just gave her a snow job. But I didn't say anything."

Susan: "About loving her? Or about any of it?"

Gary: "I dunno. Well, if you don't go tonight, I assume you don't want to make good on our marriage."

Susan: "OK. And what does that threat mean?"

Gary: "That we are just gonna be unhappy forever. [Gary's notes: I don't want to tip my hand about divorce yet.] So, I'll be home early."

Susan: "Well, good."

After that, Susan dialed Paul at the store and told him that Gary had talked with Marie.

Paul: "Did she straighten Gary up to a degree?"

Susan: "Um, you love Marie, you always loved her, you never loved anyone else, you are never leaving, um, you are never calling me again."

Paul: "She told me that she loves me, that she always loved me, she doesn't want to lose me, and that even if you and I had an affair, she could accept it."

Susan: "I have a few ideas about how I'm going to handle it."

Paul: "But Marie at this point, in her mind-set, is trying so hard to believe that she will be a friend of yours, superficially."

Susan: "Well, I'll be a friend of hers, then. Like I told you, I'm a mensch. I can be a gracious guest."

Paul: "And if you went, you can stay, have a good time, have ice cream and tell Gary to schedule (the marriage counselor) for tomorrow. That you want to be with the kids."

Susan: "And tomorrow is Halloween. I don't want to do it then. I'll tell him that I'd like to talk to him a lot over the weekend, and if we don't feel like we are getting anywhere, I will consider talking about it one day next week. And not Monday, ha-ha."

Paul: "We're not going."

Susan: "Yeah, I didn't think so."

Paul: "We're not going."

Susan: "Are we still on for any of the other days?"

Paul: "We'll find . . . talk."

Susan: "Well, you were real sure this morning."

Paul: "Well, that was before I went home. Tonight will be the indication of whether he bought the story or not."

Susan: "OK."

Paul: "Marie says for me to show affection. Hold her hand. Put my arm around her. In front of the kids."

Susan: "And in front of me."

Paul: "That should give you an idea of what's going on."

Susan: "He said to me that she said, and I don't know if she said it or if he's making it up to make me feel that you are not part of my life, that you would never call me again, which you know I heard what you said to him, but . . ."

Paul: "Well, I told him that this morning."

Susan: "Yeah, I was there."

Paul: "OK, so that comes from me . . ."

Susan: "And that you loved her very much and that you were not having any more problems, and that you would never, ever, leave . . . That you went home to tell her that she shouldn't be upset and you weren't leaving and you know she was your life and all that."

Paul: "I went home STORMING." [emphasis Gary's]

Susan: "You were mad?"

Paul: "She called me on the phone to say hello. I said, there's something wrong. She said, 'You were in the swimming pool with Susan. The maid saw you.'"

Susan: "Whose swimming pool?"

Paul: "Yours. I said, 'Absolutely not.'"

Susan: "What maid?"

Paul: "The maid that was there that day? Remember that maid?"

Susan: "Yeah. Roz's cleaning lady?"

Paul: "I don't know. Marie says that people from ORT (her women's group) are calling her now. I'm telling you what Marie is saying. Marie said that one or two people from ORT have called and told her my car has been seen there once before and the maid saw me in the swimming pool with you."

Susan: "You weren't in the pool."

Paul: "Was I? No."

Susan: "No, you weren't."

Paul: "I was not."

Susan: "She saw you throw me in, I think."

Paul: "Probably. So that was part of it. What scared her, though, was that if you are thrown out of your house because of something she says, then I'm goin' too."

Susan: (pause) *"Going with me?"* [Gary's emphasis added]

Paul: "With you."

Susan: "No! I didn't say that you said that to her. (long pause) You can say no if it's true."

Paul: "Would I go with you now?"

Susan: "But . . ."

Paul: "But?"

Susan: "Yeah . . ."

Paul: "Yeah . . ."

Susan: "Of course but. What do you think I meant? The question is, if I'm kicked out, which I think is unlikely, and I'll tell you why . . ."

Paul: "Right now it is unlikely . . ."

Susan: "Yeah, 'cause I said to Gary that I'm not going to the marriage counselor and he said, 'We're just gonna be unhappy for a long time.' He didn't say, 'If you don't go—anything.'"

Paul: "I told Marie that you love Gary very much, and you're very upset 'cause he keeps walking out on you."

Susan: "Yeah, like in shul on Yom Kippur. She saw."

Paul: "When he talked to you this afternoon, how did he sound?"

Susan: "Burning up. Livid. 'You will be what I say.' It was almost like, 'Ha-ha, Paul isn't calling you anymore.' Like, ha."

Paul: "Let him have it."

Susan: "Oh, I am."

Paul: "No, no, no. Let him have the moment."

Susan: "Yes, I am, I understand you, and I agree with you. You told me this morning, 'Yes' him. And I will. I'm not going to the marriage counselor because I don't feel like it. I am absolutely too hostile right now to do it."

Paul: "I told Marie that I'm not goin' either. Forget it for next week, I've already been once. And that's my limit for the week."

Susan: "And I don't believe in counseling anyway. I think they are a crock of shit."

Paul: "So do I. Ha-ha. Now we know where you and I stand."

Susan: "Yeah. And you know I won't tell what's going on with you and me."

Paul: "Right."

Susan: "I know I won't. There is no question about it, you won't have to worry. I will not slip. Okay?"

The week after Paul was forced to admit the affair, Marie employed silent treatment on him, he said. When he walked into the house, Marie went into the bedroom and locked the door, which locked the kids out, too. She wouldn't even respond when three-year-old Diana cried, "Mommy, Mommy," pounding on the door.

Nor did Marie unlock it after the children were asleep. Seven-year-old Shana had a pullout guest bed in her room, and that's where Paul slept that week. When Diana found out, she wanted to be there, too. She cuddled with both her daddy and her big sister. In the morning the girls woke him: "Daddy, it's time to go to school!"

Ironically, Marie called Susan that same week and invited herself to Susan's for coffee. Susan said Marie forgave her for the affair and said everything would blow over. "Next year we'll all go out together as couples, and this will all be a bad memory," Marie said, "These things happen, it happened once and that's the end of it."

At the Halloween pumpkin-carving party, Susan said Marie offered her a wine cooler, then said, "You must be really upset. Why don't you take some Valium with it?"

Marie said Paul was very cold that same week, constantly tormenting her, nor did he come home every night to sleep. Paul denied it. On November 6, he moved out of the house and into a hotel room near his parents'. But he didn't want the kids to notice any difference, so after work every evening he went home to play with them and put them to sleep. Like before, he said, as soon as he walked in, Marie went to her bedroom and locked the door.

When Shana did discover that her dad wasn't sleeping at home, she told her mother she wanted to live with him, and little Diana echoed her.

The night before Paul left, he told Marie that his accountant had prepared a promissory note to his parents for $300,000, the remainder of the money they had put up for the house two years before. It was for tax purposes, he said. He asked her to sign it. She refused. A day or two afterward, she said he showed her the note and told her, "You better think about signing it." Again she refused.

In late September, Marie had begun seeing Shirley Cohen, the therapist she had first used when Shana was born. She asked Paul to see her, too, and he had gone October 7.

The first week of November was a busy one for Cohen; she saw them both together twice, and Marie alone once. On the day Marie was alone, Saturday, November 2, Cohen said Marie came to her house because she was afraid Paul was going to abandon her. Marie then "went into a very high-type anxiety reaction for fear of the loss of everything that she had held dear," Cohen said.

After a couple of hours, Cohen realized Marie was in no condition to drive home, and took her home herself. When they got there, she told Paul that Marie needed medication to calm her nerves.

Paul said Cohen told him Marie was suicidal, and that she had driven her home because she was too doped up. He said it didn't surprise him because Marie had said, "I think I'm going to kill myself" a few times before.

There was a second therapist, too; Paul said both advised him they should separate. The other said Marie was in Fantasyland and thought she was a real princess. Paul replied that Marie had ordered a duplicate of Princess Diana's wedding ring, had read a lot about the royal couple, and in fact their youngest, Diana, was named after Di.

DIVORCE SERVICE

On Saturday, November 23, Marie's thirty-sixth birthday, Paul sent her flowers and took her and the kids to dinner at Benihana, a Japanese steakhouse. At the restaurant Marie proposed, "Shall we get divorced or not?"

"Whatever you want, Marie," he answered. They

agreed to give the marriage another chance. Paul said he'd be in Tampa for George Bush's fund-raiser during the early part of the week, but he'd move back into the house the day after Thanksgiving.

Friday morning, November 29, began as a hopeful day. Paul checked out of the hotel, packed everything in his trunk, and drove to work. It was also the biggest shopping day of the year.

Every Thanksgiving weekend, Luskin's held their "Expo" sale at the Hollywood store. All the big-name manufacturers sent factory reps to show their merchandise in booths, as if it was a trade convention. Plus, the place was decorated like the circus had hit town—balloons, clowns, free popcorn, peanuts, prizes, and Luskin's baseball caps. Their two-page newspaper ad that morning included paste-up art of a turkey doffing its top hat, captioned "Luskin's Talks Turkey with Cheap Prices." Privately the Luskins called it their "million-dollar weekend," because that's what they typically grossed from it.

Paul pulled into the parking lot at nine, an hour before the store opened. It was full. Shoppers lined up outside the front door.

It was a gratifying day until 11:45. Then someone told Paul that two men wanted to see him. They were in the executive offices lobby, off to the side of the showroom.

"Here," said one, who handed Paul a thick stack of paper. He was a civil process server. "This is your wife's petition for divorce, and we have a warrant to search your office."

It didn't sink in at first.

"What are you looking for?" Paul asked.

"A half million dollars in cash," he answered. It was supposed to be in a safe in the blue room.

The second man was an attorney, court-appointed Special Master William Stern. He wrote later that Paul answered there was no safe on the premises, nor did he have authority to go into the blue office, which was his mother's.

Also present off to the side was Barry Franklin, whose

firm Marie had hired on Friday, November 22—the day
before her birthday—with a $10,000 retainer. He had
gotten a judge to sign the warrant on Wednesday.

His surprise attack was successful; Paul was entirely
flustered. He wouldn't even let Stern and the process
server in the door.

Stern walked back to tell Franklin. It was a hot day,
temperature already in the low eighties, the parking lot
was jammed, and drivers were blowing their horns
trying to claim spaces. Concerned that Paul had an
opportunity to remove any cash present and hide it
elsewhere, they decided to call the Hollywood Police to
help enforce the judge's order.

(Later, Paul said during that time he tried to reach his
mother and his attorney for advice because he didn't
know what to do.

Franklin said later Paul didn't seem terribly surprised
that his wife had filed for divorce, but he did act like
"someone with his hands caught in the cookie jar.")

Paul began reading the petition. Marie listed all the
marital assets she could think of: the house; their invest-
ment real estate, including the properties they rented to
the business; and their vacation town house in North
Carolina.

Then came the really good parts: she said he was using
a safe on the business premises to conceal assets from
her; his one-third ownership of the business was worth
$3 million; and he had wrongfully just transferred
$250,000 from their joint account to his parents, he said
to pay off the note they owed them on the house.

Further, since Marie alleged that Paul's parents and
Luskin's, Inc. had helped him shield marital assets,
Marie included them as parties to the dissolution of
marriage. At the same time, the judge froze the Luskins
from disposing of their assets.

Ten minutes later, three police cruisers arrived at the
store. Paul walked out and asked the two attorneys what
they were there for exactly. Paul changed his demeanor
and very politely led them into the building.

The offices were short of luxurious. The walls were
wood-paneled, and the Formica furniture looked sec-

ondhand. Paul's office had only a desk and a cabinet. Paul said Franklin was taken aback and asked, "Where's the rest of your office?"

Paul's parents' cubicles weren't any more deluxe. He unlocked his mother's office door, and showed them a tan filing cabinet, about four feet high and two feet wide. There were drawers on the left side and shelves on the right side, and below that, a small safe with a combination lock.

Paul said Franklin told him that was what they were looking for. "Your wife told us there is a briefcase with money in it in this particular metal cabinet—here," he pointed.

"You open it. It's not locked."

Stern disagreed with Paul's memory; he wrote that the safe was never open, Paul said he didn't know the combination, it had never been used, and that all the cash the store took in was picked up daily by a bank messenger.

However, Stern also said later that the filing cabinet was "flimsy" and the strongbox had a lock on it "that a child could have picked. It didn't look like the place where anyone would have entrusted anything of real value."

There was no briefcase in the filing cabinet, but the men did find a stash of sorts in three zippered bank deposit pouches. They counted out 170 one-dollar coins, 400 half-dollars, and the rest smaller change and Canadian currency. The grand total was about $600. Stern gave Paul a receipt and took it.

"Where's the rest of it?" Paul said Franklin asked. "Where's the suitcase?"

Paul said he opened his briefcase and let Franklin rifle through it. Inside were electronics trade magazines and two coloring books. He said Franklin then searched every room looking for another cabinet, then checked behind pictures, looking for a wall safe. He insisted that the $500,000 had been in the office that morning, but that Paul had hidden it after they had announced themselves.

Paul said Franklin taunted him on his way out.

"If you're going home tonight, it'll be the last time you

see it. You're going to lose your house, you're going to lose your kids, your business, everything."

(Franklin later said he wasn't inside the offices at all, and denied he and Paul had had any confrontations. When asked later, Stern said he couldn't remember either way.)

"They took the pennies?" Paul's mom Mildred said that afternoon. Since Luskin's had opened in 1969, she had kept that money as change. When the kids came to the store, Paul sometimes kept them busy letting them wrap and unwrap the coins.

That afternoon, Paul called the house twice but only reached Flori, Marie's live-in maid. She said Marie had left early in the morning, and had told her she was going to the park with the children. She didn't know when she would be back. Next, Paul called Hollywood Federal Savings and learned that Marie had cleaned out their joint account a week earlier. Then he drove to Barnett Bank to check their joint safe deposit boxes. They were empty. The log showed Marie had already been there that morning.

Around two o'clock he went to the house.

THE SLASHER

Paul knocked on Flori's door on the second floor. She was taking a shower. When she dressed, he told her that Marie had gone to a lawyer for a divorce, and he was afraid they weren't going to need Flori anymore. He said if he could get the children, he would rehire her.

Flori asked him if they could work things out, for the sake of the children. He said he was trying, but nothing had worked. He told her to pack, but wanted to make sure she had a place to go for the weekend. She did. He wanted her to leave right away and return Monday for her pay, because things were going to happen that would not be very nice for her to see.

While she packed, she saw him slash four oil paintings on the second floor. Marie had picked them out as her anniversary gift six months before, and Paul had paid $1,800 for them.

He used scissors from Marie's dressing table to destroy them. When he had bought them he thought they were awful.

In the bedroom he slashed two posters that were paintings of birds, shattering the glass.

He went again to Flori's door yelling her name, asking her to hurry up and go. She answered, "I'm leaving, I'm leaving." Before she left by the front door, she called out to say she was going, and heard him throwing and breaking glass and things.

Paul didn't know what Marie had told the children, so with a red magic marker he scrawled four messages on the foyer walls and the refrigerator:

"I love you Shana & Diana. I will never leave you. Love Dad." A second read "I will always be your Dad. With Love, Paul Luskin."

After fifteen minutes in the house he left. From there he went to see Brian Hersh, a divorce attorney he had already talked to.

Marie spent the day at her parents' house with the kids. She said Paul called her there, upset, asking why she had done this, and that he was sorry, sorry for what he had done.

"What did you do?"

"You'll see when you go home."

When Marie got home late that afternoon she called Hollywood Police, then a locksmith to rekey the doors. Barry Franklin said later, "It looked like Charlie Manson or his followers had been in the house."

At seven o'clock, police met with Paul at his office. He apologized, and admitted damaging the artwork and writing on the walls. But he said he didn't behead a porcelain Lladro of a mother strolling a baby carriage that Marie said he did.

Days later, Franklin got the court to issue a restraining order to keep Paul from Marie, and to require him to get a psychological evaluation. He wrote that Paul "intended to inflict bodily harm to his wife and/or the children when he damaged the house. Wife has good reason to fear for her safety and the well-being of the children . . . It appears he presents a clear and present danger not only to his family but possibly to himself as well."

That week, Paul took a $1,200-a-month unfurnished apartment at Turnberry Isle, near his parents. When he went to a waterbed store, the salesman asked if he wanted the waveless and motionless model.

"No," he said. "That was fourteen years of marriage."

December was a very unpleasant time. Paul said Marie told him on the telephone, during an attempt to settle the case, "I have decided that I will treat you as if you were dead. If you were dead, then I could inherit the whole thing instead of part of it."

To memorialize Paul's death, Marie sat shiva—the Jewish mourning ritual. He said she told him about it afterward. She explained that since Paul was now a dead spirit to her, she could justify doing anything she wanted to him, because you can't hurt a dead man. To his face she said, "As far as I'm concerned, you died."

Paul kept coming to the house most nights and put the kids to bed. But one evening, while playing with them, he felt a cold, icy stare on the back of his neck. Behind him on the stairs was Marie. She said in a low monotone, "I'm going to bury you."

Paul turned around. "If you're going to dig a grave for someone, Marie, dig two."

In late October, Diane Yariv had called Marie to borrow a garment bag for a trip to Seattle to watch a trial of some accused neo-Nazis. When she came over, she said Marie approached her with an idea:

"Diane, how about taking Paul with you? He's tired, he can use a week off."

"What? I'm not taking my husband, why should I take yours?"

Back then, Diane didn't know about Paul's affair, nor did she know that Marie had already consulted a divorce attorney.

In December, Diane scheduled a birthday party for one of her children. She told Paul to come if he had his kids that day.

Just as Diane was about to leave for the party, she said Marie called.

She was screaming. "What kind of friend are you? Why didn't you send an invitation to the house? How come I don't know about this birthday party?"

Diane, a registered nurse, thought Marie was psychotic, totally out of touch with reality, and it frightened her. She let Marie go on and on, but couldn't resist asking one question.

"What kind of friend would try to set me up after you've been to a divorce attorney?"

"There's no proof of that," Marie answered. Diane hung up and never talked to her again.

December 11 was another bad night. Paul took the kids to dinner, and Shana asked him to call the house later, after he went back to work. He called, and when Marie picked up, he heard a lot of noise in the background.

Paul drove to the house to make sure Shana was asleep, but Marie wouldn't let him in. She claimed to be alone, but Gary Davis's motorcycle was outside. Paul peeked in the kitchen window and said he saw papers and audiocassettes on the kitchen table, as well as Gary hiding under it.

Paul called the police. Marie let an officer in to see that the children were sleeping, but wouldn't let him look for Gary.

When Susan found Gary's wiretap transcripts, she also found a computer printout of his diary. Narrating the events of that night, he wrote:

December 11, 1985

Paul called and wanted to come over, he knew I was here. Paul called Hollywood Police, he wanted me out. I stayed until midnight. Paul had let air out of my motorcycle tires, Marie drove me home, Paul followed. At home, Susan came out in nightgown and drove away with Paul. Susan locked me out. Susan slept out that night.

Susan and Paul are paranoid about being followed,
about their cars being tampered with, phones bugged . . .
Without a doubt, these last 24 hours have been the most
exciting yet.

Susan said when Gary discovered his transcript and
diary pages missing, he told her it didn't matter because
he had given copies to Marie. Paul said Marie then told
him "You do not have them all," but Barry Franklin did.
Marie entered a private love poem into the divorce
file. It read:

> There once was a beautiful girl named Susan
>   who found life sometimes very confusing
> Given a choice of family or lover
>   not both, but one or the other
> It's serious and not very amusing.
>
> It's my fault that I tarried
>   in asking you to get married
> Or choosing one or another
> So take my love and not the pressure
>   not the grief, but the pleasure
> From your friend, your bondmate, your lover.

On succeeding days, Paul said Marie told him she
would "get even" with him; after she was through, he
would not be permitted to see the kids, she would end up
with everything, and he would be ruined.

HASSLING OVER ASSETS

On November 17, twelve days before Marie had the
divorce papers served, she filled out a questionnaire for
Barry Franklin. She wrote:

"I am in distress as I did not want this divorce. My
husband is involved with Susan Davis and they went to
New Jersey together for four days in October."

The sheet asked why the marriage had broken. "Paul
and I had a difference of opinion concerning our life-
styles."

What was she willing to settle for in a divorce? "A settlement which guarantees me the continuance of my and my children's lifestyle," she answered.

On November 4, just before Paul moved out, Marie inventoried their safe deposit box. She wrote that Paul's certificate for 16.65 shares of Luskin's stock was there. But between then and when Marie cleaned it out on November 29, Paul had removed it.

Paul responded he didn't own the stock anymore. He had given it back to his parents in January 1985 because his ownership was contingent on Luskin's making a profit while he had it, and in 1984, Luskin's lost money. He said he told Marie. Marie answered that was just a cheap ploy to keep it from being a marital asset he'd have to split with her in an anticipated divorce.

"I never, ever heard a word about that stock being transferred until this divorce case started," she said.

Besides, then why did Paul tell the credit agency Equifax in December 1985 that he was both an owner and president of Luskin's Hi-Fi?

Marie said the same thing about the $300,000 house note. It was a gift, not a loan. She recalled thanking Mildred for it: "I remember hugging and kissing my mother-in-law, saying how wonderful to be that nice."

Nice aside, it was a family loan, Paul insisted. Then it was pretty funny considering when Paul paid it back, she said, and just as funny that Paul demanded she sign a backdated note before he left the house.

There was a tale behind the cash valuation of the company as well. Marie said Paul's one-third share was worth $3 million, which made the whole company worth $9 million. She said Paul and his father had tried to sell the business for that much earlier that summer.

At some point the company might have been worth that, Paul responded, but not at the present. The whole electronics retailing industry was in a downturn, and Luskin's had declined with it, decreasing the current value.

From the beginning, Barry Franklin was very aggressive about discovery. He demanded a great deal of financial records from Paul, Joe and Mildred Luskin, and Luskin's, Inc.

From the beginning, Joe and Mildred—and therefore the business as well—balked. As sole owners they had never made their company finances public before, and weren't anxious to do so now, for reasons of taxes and business competition.

One of the first issues was temporary alimony and child support. Marie wanted $8,000 a month. To justify it, she claimed Paul's salary was $8,000 a week.

Paul produced his 1985 W-2 that showed $4,000 a week. His take-home pay was $2,600. Paying Marie $8,000 a month would leave him with almost nothing, he said.

Marie responded that his check was only half his income. The other half was cash he took home "in a little white envelope."

Luskin's did a lot of cash sales. For most of their marriage, they used cash to pay as many bills as possible, she said.

"I was told to pay in cash for as much as possible, and not to use credit cards, only very little."

Marie produced a legal-sized yellow page, in Paul's handwriting, that totaled his net worth. Under "Cash," it read:

Store	575
Home	75
CD	100
Law acct	33
M/P	80
(Marie and Paul's joint account)	
Misc	20
Total	$883

Those numbers indicated thousands. In addition, there was $875,000 value in property, minus $322,000 in mortgages, for a net of $553,000; $58,500 in 130 gold coins; and $150,000 in insurance. The grand total was $1,644,500 net worth.

Marie said Paul compiled the sheet around the time of his thirty-fourth birthday, which was in 1982—before they bought the big house on Palmer Drive. "Paul said he wanted to be a millionaire by thirty-five and on his thirty-fourth birthday he was overjoyed because he realized his net worth was over a million."

Marie testified she saw the cash in the store once, during the first night of the 1984 Expo sale. She was helping out that day—something she did rarely—selling her sister-in-law Nance's chocolate and counting money when her mother-in-law Mildred asked.

"It was there in the briefcase. Paul told me it was $500,000. Paul and I spoke about it often. I was always kind of upset that he left it at work because my feeling always was that he tried to keep it from me."

She said they called the money they kept at home their "cash in the briefcase." She last counted it in May 1985; it was about $75,000, in four bundles stacked across. But when Paul left the house in November, he took it, she said. All she had left after that was the $79,000 she had grabbed from the joint account; a few thousand cash she had given to her mother for safekeeping, plus another $2,000 cash, which she stuck away in her locked jewelry box.

Paul said his yellow pad accounting was not what he actually had, but merely one of a number of different projections of his net worth. He said he compiled them in case of emergency, because he hadn't been feeling well; about that time, his doctor had told him to lose weight immediately, or else obesity would shorten his life. He admitted he kept $5–10,000 cash in the house because he often traveled on short notice. But, he grumbled, how could he prove that the rest of it *didn't* exist?

Barry Franklin said later there was a period of time when Marie wanted to get back with Paul, but Paul "just did everything so terribly wrong. Any chance there was for a possible reconciliation went down the tubes." Paul refused to pay support until he was court-ordered, and took his name off Marie's credit cards and the utility services to the house—causing them to be cut off.

By February 6, 1986, nine weeks into the divorce, the time for reconciliation apparently had passed. Marie deposed that day: "I don't want the name Luskin anymore. I don't want to be part of that family, and I don't want to have anything to do with them."

In March 1986 Broward County Judge James Reasbeck ordered Paul to pay Marie $8,000 a month in temporary support, plus money retroactive to January, and $16,000 in attorney's fees to Franklin.

Two months later Reasbeck explained: "I entered a judgment against him for temporary support with the intention of making him understand he had better do what he is supposed to do to take care of his wife or he is really going to suffer some bad consequences. I have no intention of making a final judgment for him to pay support for her in the amount of $8,000 per month. The man cannot handle that. I know that. I am well aware of that."

Marie had trouble collecting from the get-go. In April, Franklin filed a contempt of court motion, then scheduled a hearing and got the judge to sign a writ of bodily attachment—an arrest warrant—if he didn't pay up immediately. Paul paid.

All summer Franklin filed contempt motions when Paul fell behind. Each time he paid at the last minute.

Paul convinced the appellate court that Judge Reasbeck was prejudiced against him, and he was thrown off the case. A new judge was appointed, Constance Nutaro, a never-married thirty-six-year-old who had been promoted from county court to circuit court by Governor Bob Graham earlier in the year. But from Paul's perspective, things did not improve.

In July, Franklin filed another motion for contempt, and on September 12, Judge Nutaro ruled for Marie. Paul paid up three days later.

Also in September, Susan and Gary's divorce became final.

On September 17, Marie amended her demands: now she wanted the house; lump sum as well as periodic alimony; child support; a new Mercedes 380 SEL; and attorney's fees.

But that was just to start. She also claimed that Joe and Mildred had fraudulently taken possession of Paul's one-third ownership of Luskin's, and she sued them for treble damages—three times three million dollars.

Half of Paul's third wasn't enough. Now Marie wanted all of Luskin's.

Late in September, Marie discovered that the Luskins had signed a letter of intent on September 4 to sell the business to Altex Industries, a Denver oil company with Baltimore connections, for $2.5 million plus incentives. The story even hit the Dow Jones business news wire.

Franklin immediately asked Judge Nutaro for an emergency hearing to stop the sale, claiming that the Luskins were violating a court order stopping them from disposing of their assets. The next day, the judge did stop the sale, and signed an order putting Paul, Joe, and Mildred in contempt of court for attempting to sell.

On September 10, Paul left Luskin's. He said his parents fired him because the business was slumping, and the divorce was occupying too much of his time and emotional energy. When Paul left, Joe Luskin came out of retirement to take over.

It wasn't the first time Paul had talked about leaving Luskin's because of the pressure. He said while he and Marie were still together in 1985, a law firm had offered him a $150,000 job. His idea was to sell the big house, buy a smaller house on the water in Fort Lauderdale which they'd pay for in full, then they'd have a million dollars in the bank.

But Marie was dead against his leaving Luskin's. In fact, he said, his warning that their days of high living would be soon ending triggered her desire for a divorce.

Marie denied it all. She said he had talked about retiring from work, period.

On short notice, Paul got a new job as a lawyer for an electronics firm that paid less than $3,000 net a month. When he added his investment income his monthly take was $5,160. He pleaded to the court for a reduction in his $8,000 monthly support payments, showing that he had already paid Marie $102,000 in support and fees for her attorney in the previous seven months. Of that, he had had to borrow $43,000 from his parents because the court had frozen all his liquid assets. Further, his parents refused to lend him any more.

"I do not have nor have I ever had the alleged cash my wife testified to seeing," he wrote in an affidavit. "My wife has advised me, in a taunting manner, that the purpose of her creating testimony concerning alleged cash in the house was so that she could attempt to convince the Court to give her all of our other assets and leave me solely with the fictional cash."

Franklin responded that Paul's firing was an obvious sham—the family staged it so he could ask for a reduction.

Judge Nutaro turned Paul down. Paul was now compelled to pay Marie almost twice his stated monthly income. On October 20, when Paul was late in paying, she placed him in contempt of court again.

CONTEMPT

Now Franklin pummeled Paul and his family with motions. On November 5 he called for a certified audit of Luskin's, Inc. Paul paid his October support bill on November 6, but on November 7, Franklin filed a motion for nonpayment of November support. November 12, at a hearing, Nutaro placed Paul in contempt a third time and ordered him to pay. Then on November 25, Franklin moved that Paul's pending pleadings be struck because he was in contempt—that is, until he paid up in full, he wouldn't be able to argue his case in court. Also on the same day, Nutaro ordered Paul to pay a second $8,000 that month for the children's private school tuition and summer camp.

On December 4, Mildred gave a deposition. "My husband has said that Marie is a very cold, indifferent person," she said. "When you walk into a person's house to visit grandchildren and the woman stays upstairs and never comes down to say hello, and when my husband turned to me and said, 'I don't think we're welcome here,' that's how we felt."

On December 12, Franklin got the judge to order both Paul and his parents to pay a total of $27,000 in attorney's fees.

Paul couldn't keep up. He paid the regular November support on December 5, but on December 10 his doctor diagnosed chest pains and put him in Cedars Medical Center in Miami. On top of it all, that month he had quit his new job and opened his own law office in Hollywood.

On December 15, with Paul still in the hospital, Franklin filed another motion for contempt to get Marie's December support plus the unpaid tuition and summer camp money due in November.

Judge Nutaro scheduled a hearing for December 19. When Paul's attorney Alvin Entin protested, she threatened to arrest Paul in his hospital bed if he didn't show up.

Paul appeared, though on medication. The hearing lasted ten minutes. Nutaro asked if he could pay December's $8,000. Paul offered $3,600 now, the rest at the end of the month.

Not good enough, she said, and ordered bailiffs to take him into custody for contempt of court.

Across the street at the Broward County Jail, Paul exchanged his suit for jail garb. That night he slept in the hospital section, although it was on a mattress on the floor because there were no open beds.

Next morning magistrate judge Jack Musselman accepted Paul's same offer of the day before. Paul said Musselman offered him advice: Get out of town.

That was the week of Christmas Eve, and the trial was set for January 5. Getting out of town until then sounded like a good idea—the trial would permanently settle the support issue. Paul's cousin Steve Miles had already asked him to spend the holiday with him in Baltimore, so the next day Paul packed up his apartment, then on December 24 he and Susan left by car after Susan finished work for the afternoon. The past year had been so chaotic, the couple hadn't spent much time together.

*   *   *

When Barry Franklin told Judge Nutaro on December 22 that another judge had released Paul without requiring him to pay the full amount, she angrily reissued the bodily attachment writ, placing Paul back in contempt. Marie reacted by taking the kids to Sanibel Island on Florida's west coast—but first she called police in Broward County and Sanibel to say Paul was looking for her and he was dangerous.

Also on December 22, Franklin took deposition testimony from Jack Luskin, in Baltimore.

Jack said Joe Luskin first approached him in May 1985 to buy him out as quickly as possible. He said he offered $2.5 million, and might have gone as high as $5 million. But Paul said it was worth $8 million—a "preposterous figure," Jack said.

"He indicated to me that they were able to get or had a deal brewing at eight million dollars, and that if I wanted to buy it, it would be ten million dollars. I was somewhat offended that I had to pay a two-million-dollar premium."

Jack replied that if Paul could get $8 million, he should "take it and run."

Franklin asked, "Did Joe run his business into the ground to avoid Marie getting a piece of it in the divorce?"

"Probably," answered Jack.

Paul and Susan spent New Year's Eve at dinner with her parents, then at the Hilton in Pikesville. On New Year's Day 1987 he dropped her off at Baltimore-Washington airport, then drove on to Pittsburgh, where a college friend, Bob Lipsitz, had invited him to stay.

But the week Paul was in Pittsburgh, Judge Nutaro delayed the trial until June at Marie's request. Meanwhile, Barry Franklin asked to depose Paul again.

By January, Paul was $16,000 behind again. Since Paul didn't want to go home and get tossed in jail for contempt a second time, Lipsitz suggested he stay indefinitely at his house in Pittsburgh and consult for his wholesale electronics business, at $500 a week.

That left attorney Alvin Entin to attend the next

contempt hearing alone. He argued that his absent client couldn't pay the money due all at once, and showed a letter from the children's private school waiving payment for six months.

Judge Nutaro didn't buy that either. Once again she placed Paul in contempt.

THE SLEDGEHAMMER

Paul returned to Miami Friday January 30 for Franklin's deposition, and stayed at his parents' twenty-fourth-floor penthouse condo at Turnberry Isle in North Miami Beach. That afternoon he said he answered the phone and heard a woman's falsetto voice say "Wrong number." His mom told him there had been calls like that all day.

Also that afternoon, Leonard Broom, a detective in the Metro-Dade Police warrants bureau, got a call from a woman who wouldn't leave her name but said that Paul Luskin was wanted by the Broward Sheriff's Office for contempt of court. She also told where they could find him.

Broom hung up and entered Paul's name in his computer. When it came up positive, he called the Broward County Sheriff's Office and found that the warrant was still active.

At 7:20 P.M., Broom and his partner, Detective Alicia Morrison—dressed in her raid jacket with the word "Police" clearly printed on the front and back—arrived at Turnberry. Enlisting the help of the building security officers, they rang the doorbell of the elder Luskins' apartment.

"We are police officers. We know that Paul is on the inside," Broom said.

No answer.

They kept knocking for about ten minutes, then decided maybe they weren't home. As they entered the elevator, the security guard with them got a radio message that someone in the apartment had called asking why police were knocking on his door, what their names and badge numbers were, and why security had let them up.

The cat-and-mouse game was on. Broom asked security downstairs to call back the Luskin apartment and have them open the door. From outside, the officers heard the phone ring, but no one answered. When they tried again, the answering machine picked up.

Detective Morrison got down on the floor and peeked into the apartment. She saw lights, shadows, movements.

Back at police headquarters, Sergeant Joseph Mussoline made another call to the Broward County Sheriff and found that the judge had issued a "break order" with the warrant. That meant that if all else failed, they had to break the door down.

"This judge wants him picked up real bad," Mussoline told another sergeant, Angel Nieves.

Broom asked if anyone had a passkey, and security suggested they contact building manager Carl Romano, who was out of town. While they waited two hours for him to arrive, they kept knocking and calling every two or three minutes—"Police. Police, open,"—with no response.

When Romano arrived, he discovered he didn't have a key. Meanwhile, someone on the police radio said the anonymous female had just called the warrants bureau again, asking if police had arrested Paul Luskin yet.

"No, we haven't," Broom radioed back.

Broom then requested uniformed officers to respond so the people inside could see them through the peephole. Also, Romano took Detective Morrison to the roof of the building—which was V-shaped—and showed her which apartment was the Luskins'. From there they saw movement and a heavyset man who matched Paul Luskin's physical description wearing a blue shirt.

After 10 P.M., Sergeant Nieves arrived, and they decided to announce—very loudly—that they were legally entitled to break down the door, and were about to.

Still, no one responded.

Nieves asked security if they had a sledgehammer, and they found one. Finally, at 11 P.M.—after four hours—Nieves took the sledgehammer and bashed in the wood door. It took about fifteen seconds.

They drew their guns and entered, and were met by Joe and Mildred. They were fuming and demanded to be shown a copy of the break order—which police didn't have—and insisted they had no right to force their way in without it or a warrant.

When police said they were looking for Paul Luskin, Joe Luskin answered, "I don't know who he is, he's not here, I don't have to cooperate with you.

"Who's going to pay for this damage? Who's going to pay for this damage?"

"You're making a big mistake," said Mildred. "He is not here."

There was a mirror on the back of the door, which was now shattered. Sergeant Nieves saw that Mildred was barefoot, and told her to watch out for broken shards.

Morrison and Broom then did a sweep of the apartment, with Joe and Mildred trailing them. They noticed two plates of partially eaten food on the kitchen table and another plate with steak on it in a bathroom.

Broom told Nieves the third plate meant a third person was around the apartment someplace, because there was only one entry and exit.

But Paul wasn't anywhere in the apartment. "He has to be around here someplace," Broom said.

As a last resort they opened the sliding glass doors that led to the balcony. No one was there, but they peeked around a five-and-a-half-foot concrete divider into the neighbor's balcony and saw a blanket. Morrison pulled it and underneath was Paul Luskin.

The detectives coaxed him back over the wall, then cuffed him. When they asked who he was, he answered, "Paul.

"I am not a criminal," he told them. "Why are you putting handcuffs on me?"

As police took Paul into the elevator, Joe Luskin began screaming to residents who were watching. "These people, they are taking my son, and I don't know who they are. Look what they've done to my apartment."

Police charged Paul as a fugitive from Broward County in reference to a contempt of court, then took him to the Dade County Jail.

Bond was $16,065.25, posted at 4 A.M. in cash by his sister and brother-in-law, Nance and Richard Jehlen. On Monday morning, police filed charges with the Dade County state attorney against Paul, Joe, and Mildred Luskin for resisting an officer without violence. Charges were later dropped.

Two months later, as Angel Nieves described for lawyers the moment he broke in the door, Barry Franklin commented, "I wish I was there."

"I bet you do," retorted Luskin's attorney Steve Glucksman.

"I would have given anything," Franklin said.

When Paul was released, he went to his parents' apartment for a few days, then returned to Pittsburgh, where he stayed most of February.

At a hearing on February 12, 1987, in front of Judge Irwin Berkowitz—substituting for Judge Nutaro, who was undergoing chemotherapy treatments for the cancer that eventually killed her in 1989—Barry Franklin complained that Paul had concealed his whereabouts all of January so police couldn't find him.

Glucksman responded that Paul had paid $178,000 in support and legal fees to Marie at that point, all the while Marie was living in a million-dollar house with only taxes and utilities to pay.

"Mr. Luskin, on the other hand, has not been quite so fortunate. He has had to go to the bank and borrow"— $70,000, Glucksman said.

"Paul Luskin's earnings are $50,000, and you can't support $8,000 a month on $50,000 a year. My client is tapped out, Judge. He is ready to go to jail until somebody realizes that everything he has filed is true."

Meanwhile, Paul missed his February, then his March support payments. On March 9, Marie was assaulted in her home.

Paul returned to Florida March 13, Shana's tenth birthday, and took her and Diana to Disney World with Diane Yariv and her kids. He said Marie showed him her wound when he came to pick them up, as well as described the incident. Paul stayed at Susan's house until March 23, then flew to Pittsburgh to work on his new project—opening a new TV and audio store in the Baltimore area. The plan was to use the name "Best Buys," but after a short break-in period, he said, he would change it to the one he really wanted to use, the one that would really upset his Uncle Jack—Luskin's.

Jack was negotiating to buy a chain of thirteen stores in the Tampa Bay area called Oldt-Waring. Paul believed that when the Luskin brothers split long ago they had set boundaries, and Joe had gotten Florida. So if Jack wanted to change the rules, then Paul could go into Baltimore.

ARRESTED AGAIN

On Thursday, March 26, Paul said he called Marie from Pittsburgh to arrange to see the kids. Judge Nutaro had ordered him to give another deposition on Monday, March 30, to be followed by another contempt hearing April 1, and he was going to fly in the next day.

Paul said they got into an argument and Marie told him, "I hope that you are killed in jail so that this is over with and I can get on without you. Anyway, I could at least get the $150,000 insurance while I can."

Saturday, Paul took his kids, Susan, and her kids to Disney World. Monday morning, Paul called Marie to ask whether he could pick up the children again and take them to dinner after he and Barry Franklin were through. Marie said six o'clock was okay, the kids would be in front of the house.

The depo was acrimonious. At one point, Paul complained about Franklin's tone and threatened to walk out.

"Do whatever you want at your own risk," Franklin retorted.

It ended at three-thirty. At six Paul's parents drove him to the house, but no one was there.

Out of view, however, were two Broward County Sheriff's officers. When Paul got out of the car, they cuffed him. After the depo, Franklin had asked Judge Nutaro to sign a *Ne exeat* order—prohibiting Paul from leaving the state. The cops were polite and suggested he get a lawyer.

"It was a trap," Paul said later.

Bond was $20,342, the amount he was in arrears to Marie, so Paul spent yet another night in jail. Two days later he was brought before Judge Nutaro for a contempt hearing. When Paul said he couldn't post the money in cash, she sent him back to jail.

While Alvin Entin appealed Nutaro's decisions and tried to get her thrown off the case as they had with Reasbeck, Paul spent eighteen nights in the stockade, missing Passover.

While Paul sat in jail, Luskin's, Inc. filed for Chapter 11 bankruptcy protection on April 13. They listed assets of $2.2 million, and liabilities of $3.4 million. Just before filing, they closed seven of their thirteen stores, but according to a *Miami Herald* story the next morning, the company planned to emerge from it, slimmer and trimmer.

Finally, on April 17, Florida's Fourth District Court of Appeals released Paul, but only temporarily, pending their full decision. For the meantime, he moved into Susan's house.

On May 5, Paul moved himself and his furniture to a new apartment in Pittsburgh. It was just in time, because on May 13, the appeals court ruled against him, and allowed Nutaro to stay on. That meant while he was in the state of Florida, he was again subject to arrest.

On May 27, Paul was supposed to show up for another of Barry Franklin's depositions. Having already danced that dance before, Paul stayed in Pittsburgh. Two days later, his attorney Steve Glucksman resigned the case.

In June, U.S. Bankruptcy Court-appointed trustee Robert Cullen wrote that Paul and Marie's divorce was keeping his parents from settling their Chapter 11 petition.

He said Luskin's had been a successful company selling stereo equipment until 1981, when they added video equipment to their line. They didn't know enough about marketing video to be successful, he wrote. It required high-volume sales, and that meant expansion, which "proved disastrous."

On the other hand, Cullen wrote that while Luskin's, Inc. lost $758,000 between 1982–1986, the Luskins paid themselves almost three million dollars in salaries.

Paul wouldn't return to south Florida until the beginning of August, and then just for a weekend. The next time after that wouldn't be until the end of September.

On August 1, Hollywood Police Detective Leo Soccol wrote his composite police report, tabling the case.

"Through the past several months, this detective has investigated and interviewed all parties possibly having any further information, or leads that would assist in this investigation, which as of this date, has proved negative.

"This detective also made a further check regarding latents lifted at the scene and upon checking, found that there were no latents of any value taken from the scene. The azalea card, which was left behind adjacent the front door, was also processed and found to have no latents. It should be noted that the victim did indicate at the time of the incident, suspect touched nothing as far as she could remember.

"All outside family members, employees, etc. appeared very cooperative and have agreed to assist in any way possible regarding this matter. Joseph, Mildred, and Paul Luskin were also given composites of the suspect and vehicle and agreed to distribute same within their respective Luskin stereo stores.

"Mrs. Luskin was contacted and explained the circumstances regarding this investigation and was satisfied with this detective's follow-up. However, Mrs. Luskin had indicated some peculiar/suspicious events which occurred:

"Suspicious incident #1) Suspect knew her name. #2) Florist shop, which she sometimes uses, was known to the suspect. #3) Suspect knew maid was off on Monday and that she would be home alone. Note that her daughter was home on that particular day, due to the fact that she was sick, but normally she would not be home and would be attending school. #4) Suspect was offered jewelry worth approximately $50,000 and money (U.S. currency—approximately $100) and took nothing, nor did he touch anything. Furthermore, nothing was taken from the entire residence. #5) Vase/pot was also taken by the suspect upon his departure.

"This is the reasoning of Mrs. Luskin's suspicions, to include the severity of her divorce proceedings and the monies involved in the settlement. To say the least, it is a very nasty divorce proceeding.

"As of this taping, there is no conclusive evidence linking any family members with this incident, nor the staff. At this time, detectives have no other information, leads or suspects in this incident. Therefore, this case will be placed in the pending and inactive file until new investigative leads are established."

Unknown to Soccol, the break in the case had just happened.

THREE

Silver Meteor

In 1987, Amtrak began getting wise that smuggled drugs from Florida were passing northward over their rails. Trains and buses had become the public transport mode of choice for smugglers; at airports, passengers and their bags were subject to metal detectors and x-ray searches.

Amtrak Police Officer Calvin Burns, based in Baltimore, was assigned to ferret out possible drug couriers by looking at reservation lists. On July 28 he spotted a likely pair: A person named M. Cohen had a reservation for two, round-trip from Baltimore to Fort Lauderdale on a sleeping car. They had left Baltimore the day before, were scheduled to stay one night in Florida, then be back in Baltimore July 30.

That alone fit the profile. Why else spend forty-six hours traveling, and only one night at the destination?

The tickets were paid for in cash, $449 apiece, at Baltimore's Penn Station ticket window. Burns called the contact number "M. Cohen" had left, and found it was a car phone that didn't answer.

Burns and his supervisor decided they should interview M. Cohen's party when he or she disembarked in Baltimore. On July 29, Burns alerted Baltimore City Police Detective Dorsey McVicker, assigned to narcotics, and he arranged to have drug-smelling dogs ready the next morning at the train station.

* * *

At 4:10 A.M., Thursday, July 30, Amtrak Police agent Robert Moss boarded the Silver Meteor in Richmond, Virginia, then it continued on its way hurtling northward through the pre-dawn. He found the two roomettes on car 8810 assigned to Cohen's reservation. When the train got to Union Station in Washington at 6:20, Moss first saw the two travelers, two men, then kept them under observation until the train arrived in Baltimore at 7:23.

Trackside, McVicker and Baltimore City Police Detective Christopher Rayburn looked for 8810 as it pulled in, then spotted their men. One, later identified as Milton "Sonny" Cohen, wore a light blue sport shirt, blue shorts, white tennis shoes, and was carrying a black nylon travel bag over his right shoulder. The other man, James Thomas Manley, wore a gray T-shirt with the word "Jaguar," black pants, and held a black guitar case in his right hand. Cohen was thin, and Manley had a belly. Both were white, clean-shaven, and had identical color steel gray hair although they were only in their early forties.

A few feet behind them came agent Moss, who pointed at the two men the Baltimore officers had already guessed were the targets.

The passengers walked quickly upstairs and toward the street exit. When they got a few feet from the doors, McVicker, Burns, and Moss approached them, and identified themselves as police.

"May I talk to you?" Burns asked.

"Okay," they answered.

The officers asked them to produce their tickets and identification. Manley said he had lost his wallet in Florida—later he said it was stolen—but gave an address on Luzerne Avenue, in Baltimore. Cohen showed his driver's license; his address was on Winner Avenue, also in Baltimore.

Both of the men were nervous. Manley was shaking so hard, McVicker saw the guitar case quivering.

The officers suspected they weren't musicians. Burns asked if they would allow a drug detection dog to sniff their luggage. He wrote in his report they answered, "Yes, go ahead."

The officers led the suspects to an office in the station. They put their luggage on the floor, had everyone step into the hallway where they could watch, then one at a time let dogs named Grizzley and Buck sniff for drugs.

Both dogs indicated positive.

McVicker then asked the men for a consent to search, adding that if they refused, he'd get a judge to sign a search and seizure warrant.

Manley said nothing. "Get a warrant," Cohen told McVicker.

McVicker typed an application, then left to find a Baltimore City judge to sign it. He returned at 10 A.M. with it signed by District Court of Maryland Judge Joseph Pines.

McVicker opened the guitar case, and Rayburn opened the duffel bag. The only kind of music the contents of the guitar case could make was a monotone staccato; it was a .223 caliber Colt AR-15 A2 semiautomatic rifle, equipped with laser beam light and scope, something McVicker thought Rambo would carry. It was loaded, and wrapped in an old white thermal blanket.

Inside the travel bag was a loaded .25 caliber black Beretta semiautomatic pistol and six-inch cylindrical black metal silencer without a serial number; a loaded .22 caliber Sturm-Ruger semiautomatic pistol; a single .38 caliber cartridge; a small kitchen knife; two sets of men's gloves; three rolls of tape; a pair of men's underwear and a T-shirt; shaving equipment; $3,861 in cash; and a gray plastic bag holding a paper bag filled with rice and thirteen plastic bags holding what they suspected was cocaine.

McVicker had made a hundred or so narcotics arrests at Penn Station before. But this was only his second time a narcotics arrest had involved the carrying of firearms.

At that point the men were placed under arrest. Rayburn read Cohen his Miranda rights, and Cohen said he wouldn't answer questions without a lawyer present, nor would he sign the Miranda sheet. Then when Rayburn advised Manley of his rights, Cohen turned to his friend Manley and said, "Don't say anything, all's they got was a couple of guns and some personal use."

Manley then also refused to answer questions, or sign the Miranda sheet.

At Baltimore City Jail, each provided a bit more information about themselves: Cohen was single and a bar manager at a place called Spectrum; Manley was married, and offered a different address—190 Westcott Road, Baltimore.

When police punched up Cohen and Manley's names on the state and federal crime computers, it came up cherries. Manley was a fugitive from neighboring Anne Arundel County, Maryland, for missing trial on May 26 on a burglary charge. The judge there had ordered him arrested and held without bail. Besides that, Manley had an FBI record back to 1959, which included arrests for things like assault, rape, stolen cars, receiving stolen property, and breaking into a post office.

Cohen was not a model citizen either. His FBI rap sheet had ten arrests dating to 1961 for bank robbery, assault, and robbery with a deadly weapon.

Later that day, both men were formally charged in state court with three drug counts, including possession with intent to distribute, and bringing cocaine into the state; plus four gun counts, including carrying a handgun by a convicted felon. Since the crimes were alleged to have occurred across state lines, it was decided to charge them in the federal court system as well.

Manley was denied bond. Cohen's bond was set at $500,000, but it was revoked before he could make it.

The next day, the Baltimore City Police crime lab determined the suspected cocaine to be 90 percent pure cocaine, weighing three and one-half ounces. Police estimated its street value at $48,000. They also found that all three of the guns were operable, and none were registered.

Since federal firearms violations were involved, the Bureau of Alcohol, Tobacco, and Firearms was responsible for the federal investigation. The lead was Special Agent Roy Cheeks, based in Baltimore.

Cheeks's first step was to trace the Colt AR-15 A2

rifle. He found it had been purchased by a woman named Patricia Widerman at a gun shop on June 25, 1987.

Cheeks and Baltimore City police interviewed Widerman and her husband Frank Liberto—who was legally blind but had limited sight—at their home on Monday August 3. She told them the gun wasn't for her. Frank's brother Jimmy had asked her to go to the shop, sign the purchase papers, and he would pay for it. She said she didn't know the first thing about guns.

Frank Liberto said his brother was a convicted felon.

Cheeks did a criminal check and found that James Liberto had convictions in 1975 for grand larceny and 1979 for false pretense. When Cheeks tried to find him, he was told he was away on a boat for a month and couldn't be reached.

Cheeks wrote a report calling for a full firearms license investigation on the gun shop and its owner, suspecting that he cooperated in a "straw purchase transaction" with Jim Liberto.

Also on August 3, in the Baltimore City Jail, Manley signed a sworn statement:

> "I, James Thomas Manley, under the penalty of perjury, do swear that on July 30th, 1987 I was traveling back to Baltimore with Milton B. Cohen. I had in my possession, in bags, 2 handguns, one rifle and cocaine. As I left the train I ask (sic) Mr. Cohen to carry one of my bags to the lobby so I could catch a cab home.
>
> "At no time did Mr. Cohen know that the bag he was carrying contained any drugs or guns.
>
> "When the police arrested us Mr. Cohen found out about that bag he carried contained guns and drugs. He was totally surprised."

Considering all of Cohen and Manley's firepower, Baltimore City Police checked outstanding murder investigations to determine if they could be linked. They found Cohen closely resembled an artist's sketch of someone wanted for the shooting of a federal witness in Anne Arundel County.

But on August 7, the Baltimore City Police crime lab made a solid hit: the .25 caliber Beretta pistol seized was the same gun used in an unsolved shooting of James Manley on June 10, 1987.

According to the Baltimore City Police report, at 10 P.M. that night, Manley was shot in the upper left leg inside the Belnord Inn in East Baltimore. Manley and the suspect, Billy Beard (aka Billy Bird), came in together, got drunk, and argued whether Manley owed Beard money. During the argument, Beard allegedly shot Manley and he fell to the floor.

When the officer tried to interview Manley, he said, "Fuck you, I'm not telling you a fucking thing because I'm going to kill that motherfucker."

On August 6, a federal grand jury began hearing testimony against Cohen and Manley.

Assistant U.S. Attorney Gregg L. Bernstein began with Patricia Widerman Liberto. She recalled a dinner at Palughi's Restaurant with her new husband Frank and her brother-in-law Jimmy:

"Well, Jimmy asked me if I had ever been in trouble, and I said no, and he said I want to know if you could buy a couple of guns for me, and I kind of hesitated and I looked at Frank and Frank says, 'Oh, don't worry, my brother wouldn't cause you any trouble,' and Jimmy says, 'I just want them for the house.'"

"Did Jimmy say why he wanted the guns for the house?" Bernstein asked.

"He just said he was having trouble and this person— I don't know who it was."

"What kind of trouble?"

"Well, the person came to his house and had a gun."

"So he wanted these guns for his protection, he said?"

"That's what he told me."

"That's what he told you. Did he tell you why he couldn't purchase the guns?"

"Well, he said that if he—if he purchased them he would get checked out. I guess he's been in trouble, you know. I don't know."

The next day she and Frank went to the gun store.

"I walked in and I said I'm supposed to come here and sign some papers for Jimmy Liberto for some guns and he said, 'Okay, I got the papers ready for you.'"

She signed the forms and walked out of the store without the guns. Nor did she even see the guns. "He never handed me no gun. I didn't even know what kind of gun Jimmy was getting."

She returned weeks later. "He had the papers there and he said, 'All you have to do is sign here.'" Again she left the store without the guns.

"Have you spoken to Jimmy Liberto about this matter since the agents came to see you?" Bernstein asked.

"No. His lawyer, his lawyer told Frank to tell me I had nothing to worry about, that he was going to be my lawyer."

Next up was Frank Liberto, who testified that Jimmy wanted the AR-15 because somebody had tried to kill him three weeks before the gun purchase.

"Someone tried to kill your brother?" Bernstein asked.

"Went to his house and the bullet was still in the floor."

"They shot at your brother?"

"Yes."

"How do you know this happened?"

"I seen the bullet hole."

"Did he tell you that someone had come in and shot at him?"

"Yeah."

"Continue."

"So he said he wanted to get some firearms and I says, well, okay. I'll ask my wife, you know, if she'll sign for them, and then I want to get her firearms because I knew I was going away for five years and she was molested, she was cut and she was almost killed."

"Mr. Liberto, what are you going away for five years for?"

"I got caught with dope."

"What kind of dope?"

"Coke."

"Cocaine?"

"Yes."

"How much?"

"Three—

"Kilograms?"

"Kilograms, three kilos."

"And you've been sentenced?"

"Yes. I'm going away tomorrow."

"Tomorrow you begin your sentence?"

"Yes."

"What's the period of your sentence?"

"Five years."

"Now because you were going away you wanted to get your wife a firearm?"

"A firearm, yeah, you know, for protection."

"But it was also your brother who wanted weapons as well?"

"Yes. He wanted weapons, but I didn't know what type. I have no idea of what type he got."

Bernstein asked if he knew whether his brother had a criminal record.

"Not that I knew of. Not that I know of now."

That contradicted an earlier statement, and Bernstein challenged him on it:

"Do you recall having a conversation with one of the Baltimore City Police detectives where you said your brother had, in fact, been convicted of a crime?"

"He told me that, but I didn't believe him because my brother, he'll tell you one thing today and another thing tomorrow."

"Mr. Liberto, do you know an individual named James Manley?"

"No."

"How about an individual named Milton Cohen?"

"No."

"Those names don't mean anything to you?"

"No, nothing at all."

Testimony resumed two weeks later, on August 20, with ATF Special Agent Roy Cheeks as a summary witness. After he reviewed the evidence, a grand juror asked if Cohen and Manley were acquainted with the Libertos.

"At this point in time we do not know that," Cheeks answered.

"Isn't it true that because of the good work of your office and the Baltimore City Police in arresting these two individuals, that it has come to light that the FBI has been investigating Mr. Liberto for some time?" Bernstein asked.

"Yes. The FBI is definitely investigating Mr. Liberto."

"Which one?" asked a grand juror.

"James Joseph."

"Can we ask why they are investigating him?"

"That has nothing to do with the subject of this indictment. At this point it is somewhat speculative, so I would rather wait until we have some concrete information."

"Agent Cheeks, isn't it true that there has been some evidence that indicates Mr. Cohen may know Mr. Liberto?" Bernstein asked.

"Supposedly some rumor has it that Mr. Cohen is an enforcer for Jim Liberto."

That day, August 20, the grand jury returned seven-count indictments against Cohen and Manley, charging them with handgun and drug violations. At arraignment August 28, Cohen pleaded Not Guilty. Manley's arraignment was postponed a week so he could obtain counsel.

On September 3, the FBI interviewed Denise Spring, Cohen's twenty-two-year-old blond girlfriend. The week before Cohen was arrested, she threw him out of her home because she suspected he was seeing other women. He'd leave town for varying lengths of time, and when she asked what he was doing, he would tell her, "It's none of your business."

On September 4, Manley had Assistant Federal Public Defender M. Brooke Murdock enter a plea of Not Guilty. But the same day, Murdock approached Bernstein with an off-the-record proffer:

Her client knew something about a contract murder on a woman in Florida named Luskin. In return for a break, he would be willing to testify for the government.

Murdock offered Bernstein a few tidbits: Mrs. Luskin needed to be killed because she was contesting a large amount of business assets in her divorce. Cohen had been hired by Jim Liberto. Jim Liberto's connection was his brother, Joe Liberto, who worked for the Luskins in Florida. Cohen had posed as a flower deliveryman in order to kill her, but had failed. After that, he hired Manley to help him try again. Together they tried twice more, without success. After the last try they were arrested on Amtrak.

Bernstein called FBI Special Agent Pat Connolly that day to check it out.

On Saturday the fifth, Connolly investigated Manley's lead that Jim Liberto had reserved a Dollar Rent-A-Car for Cohen to pick up in Fort Lauderdale on their end-of-July trip. Connolly confirmed it.

Monday was Labor Day. On Tuesday, September 8, Connolly attempted to find the woman Manley said was the intended victim. He teletyped FBI in Miami for assistance, and the next day, September 9, Miami FBI replied they had found her—Marie Luskin.

On September 10, Connolly flew to Florida to interview her. She told Connolly in fact she was embroiled in a nasty divorce, that she had been assaulted in her home by a man carrying flowers, in March, and that Joe Liberto was a very close friend of the Luskin family.

Connolly showed her pictures of Cohen and Manley, but she couldn't identify either one.

Marie told Connolly a number of other details, including Paul's affair with Susan Davis. On Friday September 11, the FBI put a tail on Susan.

The tail was immediately productive. That day, Susan drove to Fort Lauderdale airport and caught a flight to Baltimore. At the gate, Baltimore FBI agents watched Paul meet her, then they drove away to Washington together in his gray Mercedes with Florida tags.

Agents wondered if Paul had been in Baltimore to

meet with Jimmy Liberto—and speculated whether
Susan was involved in his plan.

On Sunday the thirteenth, agents watched as Paul
dropped Susan off at the airport for her return flight.
Then they tailed him again. He wove through traffic as if
he knew he was being followed, heading for a house in
Alexandria, Virginia, later determined to be a friend's.

The case looked solid. On Wednesday September 16,
Bernstein struck an agreement with Manley. He would
plead guilty to one gun count, which exposed him to ten
years in prison, and the feds would drop the other six
counts. But without help on Manley's various state
charges, the federal deal was worthless. Although Bernstein couldn't guarantee anything on the state level, he
promised to speak up for him wherever he needed it.
That vague promise apparently had some teeth in it,
because it was good enough for Manley. Also, if he
wanted, he could go into the federal Witness Security
Program—colloquially known as Witness Protection.

That day, the FBI met with Manley for the first time.
He identified pictures of Marie's house and a restaurant
where he had already said he and Cohen had stalked
Marie, using the AR-15 with laser and scope. The FBI
had taken the pictures after interviewing Marie Luskin.

When Manley didn't come back to Baltimore City
Jail, Cohen realized he had made a deal. On September
17, Cohen called the FBI and left a message that Pat
Connolly should come see him immediately.

Connolly, however, had already left for Florida again,
so two other agents, Charles Hedrick and Harold Moran,
went to the jail. Cohen was fishing for his own deal. They
told Cohen he should communicate with the U.S. attorney through his defense attorney, but Cohen replied he
couldn't trust his attorney to act in his best interests
since he had been hired by his partners in crime.

The FBI wrote:

"Cohen is a courier for a drug operation which is
responsible for trafficking 500–1,000 kilograms of cocaine per month to the Mid-Atlantic area. Cohen trans-
ports the drugs through a middleman, who traffics the

drugs locally. Cohen is supplied by a female from the South Florida area . . . Cohen desires to take over the middleman's territory and is willing to pay this individual $40,000 per month to 'retire.'"

Cohen told the agents to tell Connolly that he wasn't the murderer of the federal witness in Anne Arundel County although the sketch looked like him; nor did he have anything to do with an armored car robbery. However, his friends had told him he had a look-alike in South Baltimore named Bud Kelly.

On Friday September 18, FBI agents Connolly and Jeff Hill, and ATF Agent Cheeks, went to Luskin's Hollywood store to look around. While one of them asked for a demonstration of a Sony Walkman, Connolly got within ten feet of Joe Liberto, whom Marie had described for them.

The purpose was to solicit Joe Liberto's cooperation without anyone else knowing about it. They also wanted to see what Paul Luskin looked like, but after browsing forty-five minutes without seeing him, they gave up.

That night, agents called Joe Liberto's home number, posing as Hollywood Police officers. A teenage girl answered and said her parents were out to dinner.

The agents then drove to Liberto's home, a house on a cul-de-sac in Coral Springs, an affluent suburb of Fort Lauderdale. It turned out that night was the Libertos' anniversary, and they had been to a Chinese restaurant.

After they arrived home at 11:45, Connolly knocked on the door and introduced himself. He asked Liberto if he'd be comfortable talking at home, or elsewhere. Liberto suggested elsewhere; then he got in the backseat of the agents' rental car and they drove to a hotel and took a room.

Sitting at a table, the agents broke the news: they believed Liberto was involved in a plot to kill or seriously injure Marie Luskin and that his brother Jim was also involved. They told him he wasn't under arrest, he was free to go at anytime, and there were no plans to arrest him.

Soon after, Liberto appeared to be sick. He thought it

was something he had eaten, and he asked to take a walk. Cheeks took him down the hall to a soda machine.

Liberto was a garrulous sort. He said he had begun working for the Luskins in Baltimore in the early 1960s, at which time he became friendly with Paul Luskin. In the late 1970s, Joe and Paul Luskin asked him to leave Baltimore and come work for them in Florida.

But in 1984, the Luskins blamed him for a deceptive practices case lodged against them which had hurt business. Since then, the Luskin family had demoted him and treated him very badly, he thought. Although Paul Luskin had allowed him to stay rent-free at a town house he owned, they fought over who should pay the utilities. Paul was sued for nonpayment, and he made Liberto pay his thousand-dollar legal fee and forced him to move out.

Liberto said he quit Luskin's in December 1986 during a fight with Joe Luskin. But he asked for his job back in March 1987, and took reduced pay.

The agents showed him pictures. He identified Sonny Cohen and said he was an associate of his brother Jim's. He had met Cohen at Palughi's, he thought in December 1986.

Then they showed him Hollywood Police pictures of Marie Luskin's wounds. Liberto said he didn't realize how serious the injury was, and denied involvement in the crime.

Liberto said his brother Jim had been in south Florida five or six times that year, usually staying at the Marco Polo Hotel on the ocean in North Miami Beach. He said he had talked with Jimmy frequently, both on the phone and in person, but "I never really know what Jimmy is talking about." Nor, he said, did he want to know because he suspected Jimmy was involved in question-able things.

Liberto also said he was worried that some of his telephone calls might make him criminally liable. But he denied passing on any information about Marie Luskin's routine, or spying on her.

When the agents asked Liberto whether he had made

any phone calls to his brother on March 9, 1987, he said he wanted to think about it and talk to an attorney. That ended the interview, and the agents took him home. In the car, Connolly noticed him getting pale, sweating, and holding his stomach.

"I'm not feeling well," he said.

On September 23, Barry Franklin suddenly changed his mind and asked Judge Nutaro for a new trial date. Up to then, he had only asked for continuances. The judge gave him the week of December 27.

September 24, eight days after Manley signed his plea agreement, Gregg Bernstein paraded him in front of the same grand jury that had indicted him a month before.

Manley testified he had known Sonny Cohen for thirty years.

"Have you ever met (James) Liberto?" Bernstein asked.

"Not to shake hands, no. I've seen him quite a few times," said Manley.

"Does he know who you are?"

"I think he does now."

"Do you know the relationship—what relationship exists between Sonny Cohen and James Liberto?"

"Yes, I'm an eyewitness to this, that's how I know. I've seen Sonny, who would buy cocaine from Liberto and pay him x amount, thousands of dollars."

"Do you know how long they've had this narcotics relationship together?"

"Just about two years, I would imagine."

"And you know this from?"

"Sonny."

"He traveled for Mr. Liberto to purchase narcotics?"

"He's been to Florida quite a few times. I know other people that do travel for Liberto to bring the narcotics back."

"Now, do you know an individual named Joseph Liberto?"

"No, sir."

"Do you know who he is?"

"Yes, I know who he is. I've never met him."

"Who is he?"

"Jimmy's brother."

"Do you know where he lives?"

"Yes, sir, he lives in Florida."

"And do you know where he works?"

"Yeah, he works for a guy named Luskin."

"How do you know that?"

"Well, during the course of the last four or five months I've had an occasion to go to Florida and it's been pointed out the stores that Mr. Luskin owns."

"Who pointed those stores out to you?"

"Sonny."

"How about an individual named Paul Luskin? Do you know him?"

"No, I've never met him."

"Do you know who he is?"

"It was my understanding through Sonny that he owns the Luskin's stores up and down the East Coast."

"Do you know if he's married?"

"Yes, I know he's married."

"What is his wife's name?"

"Marie."

"And have you ever met her?"

"No. I saw her several times, but I've never met her."

"Now, at a certain time you were approached by Sonny Cohen to go down to Florida?"

"Yes, sir."

"When is it that he approached you?"

"Early May of this year."

"Would you tell the members of the grand jury what it is he approached you about?"

"He said he was getting $30,000 to kill Marie Luskin."

"Did he say where the money was coming from to kill her?"

"Yes, from Jimmy Liberto."

"Did he tell you how Jimmy Liberto came to offer him $30,000 to kill Marie Luskin?"

"He said Liberto's brother, Joe, lived in Florida and worked for Mr. Luskin and that there was a big divorce disagreement over diversement (sic) of property or whatever."

"The divorce is between Paul and Marie Luskin?"

"Yes, and she wouldn't agree to the terms of the divorce and it was worth $50,000 for her to be killed before the divorce was final."

"So, it was your understanding that Mr. Luskin had contacted who to have this—"

"Joe Liberto."

"That's what Mr. Cohen told you?"

"Yes, because he worked for him and they were all in Florida."

"And you mentioned—first you said it was $30,000 and then you said it was $50,000. Could you explain that?"

"Well, $30,000 for Cohen and $20,000 for Jimmy to set it up and make the arrangements because it had to be somebody from out of the Florida area."

"Why?"

"That's the only understanding I got because she's too well-known down there for a local guy to come up on her like that, especially in the area she lives."

"What was your involvement?"

"I was going to drive the car to Florida with Sonny and the weapons."

"And you were hired to do this by Sonny or Jimmy Liberto?"

"By Sonny."

"Did Jimmy Liberto know that you were now involved in this murder scheme?"

"Not at first."

"Sonny did not tell him?"

"No, sir."

"Did Mr. Cohen tell you about a prior incident in which he had gone down to Florida to attempt to murder her?"

"Yes, he said he had been down there several times, at least six times that I know of because, like I say, I've known Sonny a long time and I know when he goes out of town, where he goes. He explained to me that the trip to Florida was to stalk Mrs. Luskin with the intent to kill her."

"So he went down about six times before this conversation you had with him in May?"

"Well, first I told him I wanted no part of that, I'm not a killer, I work for a living and my wife works. He said, well, he couldn't do it himself because he already went down there and tried to kill her and shot her in the head and she lived. So it had to be a different face to get close enough to her to open the door where we could get in and shoot her."

"Did he describe to you the circumstances under which he had gone into the house to try and shoot her?"

"He said he got some kind of pot of flowers from the Emerald Village Estate in the shopping center right near where the lady lives. He knocked on her door—he had a rented car, and he knocked on the door and she seen the flowers and he said he was a deliveryman from the—I can't remember the name—it was the Emerald Shopping Center, I know that. It was a florist shop there inside the shopping center.

"He went into pretty good detail of how she wouldn't open the door at first and wanted to know who they came from and he said there is no card on it. He said he talked her into opening the door and then he attacked her."

"Did he say what he did when he attacked her?"

"He said he dropped the flowerpot on the floor and grabbed her around the head and said Where is your money and stuff, your diamonds and all of that. Then he put the .32 caliber gun to her head and shot her."

"That's what he told you?"

"That's what he told me."

"And he also told you that apparently she had not died?"

"He thought she was dead. He said he went back to the hotel, got his things together, and left in his own car."

"Now, did you later discover that she, in fact, had not been shot in the head?"

"On the same day that Sonny discovered it, I discovered it."

"How did you find that out?"

"Sonny went to Liberto to get his money and Liberto

started laughing and said I ought to shoot you because the woman is still alive. She wasn't even hurt."

"Did Liberto tell Sonny what really happened to him?"

"The way I understand it is Liberto said that the woman wasn't really shot, she was hit in the head."

Manley said he and Sonny drove to Florida in Sonny's black Mercury Cougar on the weekend after Memorial Day. When they arrived, they checked into the Marco Polo Hotel.

"And did you have a plan at that point as to how you were going to carry out the murder?"

"Well, Sonny had a plan, but I more or less talked him out of it because somebody else would have to be killed. Sonny's plan was to, any way I could, open that door so that he could go in. The original plan was to get a UPS driver, tie him up, and put him in the back of the truck and I would wear his clothes, knock on the door, and Sonny would come out of the truck and go and kill her."

"Did you drive through the neighborhood at all?"

"Yes, sir, constantly."

"Did you sit anywhere or do anything to watch where she was going?"

"Well, the most convenient place was at a 7-Eleven shopping center in the Emerald Isle Estates itself, on the corner."

"And were you able to observe her driving back and forth?"

"Yes, sir, that's the first time I ever saw her was in her car driving by."

"Did you have any information that she would be driving by?"

"Well, we had information that every Monday her housekeeper never worked and her children were in school. She has two younger daughters and I imagine they're like eight and ten or eleven and twelve. They're awful little."

"How about what kind of car she drove?"

"Well, we had information that she drove an off-white or light green Mercedes-Benz with a state tag, personalized tag."

"A vanity tag?"

"Yes."

"What was the vanity tag?"

"I remember the first and last initial. I can't remember the middle initial. It was an L or an R or something like that, but it was P and L. The first one was P and the last one was L for Paul Luskin."

"Did you have her phone number or photograph, or anything like that?"

"Well, Sonny had all of that, but he threw all of that away because he didn't want to be caught with material on him."

"Do you know how you obtained—how you had all that information?"

"Yes, sir, from Jimmy Liberto."

"And how do you know that?"

"Because Sonny told me that, the way things would come down. It would be Sonny in my car and I would have to go down to see Liberto to get some money or whatever and we would wait outside of (Liberto's) restaurant for Sonny and he would come back and tell me different things, you know."

"He would tell you what?"

"Different things like that's how I learned that the baby-sitter—not the baby-sitter, but the housekeeper never worked on a Monday. It was my information, so I believed that everything we learned was coming from Florida."

"Did Sonny ever tell you how Jimmy Liberto was obtaining this information?"

"He said his brother was on the end of everything that went on down there."

"Joe Liberto was calling up Jimmy and telling him things?"

"Well, he knew where she took the kids, to McDonald's or Burger King. We knew everything."

Bernstein asked what their ultimate plan was to kill Marie Luskin.

"Well, it was really my idea, but Sonny went whole heart with it. The security guard just happened to pull up in the 7-Eleven parking lot. He looks a lot like me, believe it or not, gray hair, older guy, black pants, black shirt, the whole nine yards. So that was our answer right there, we will knock on her door as a security guard up the street where she lives. They're very familiar; they're in and out all the time."

"Did you do anything to try to make yourself look like a security guard?"

"We went to J.C. Penney's and bought black shoes, black shirt with epaulets, and a black belt, like the type a policeman would have on."

"Did you buy anything else to make yourself look like a security guard?"

"I can't remember the name of the stores we went to, but they were in Miami–

"Was it a Kresge's?"

"Something like that, a McCoy's or something. It was a place where you buy anything you wanted, really, and I bought the badge, a kid's toy badge but it looks real— especially a silver badge with a black shirt on and a silver chain."

"Where was the chain supposed to go?"

"From the epaulet."

"Around the shoulder?"

"Yes, it curls around and goes down by your pocket."

"You bought a whistle also?"

"Yes, we bought a whistle, too."

Manley said he dressed up in the uniform that Monday night, which would have been June 1.

"Well, I had no intention of killing the woman even though I had put out quite a few thousand dollars of these people's money."

"Hold on a second," said Bernstein. "You had already been paid some money?"

"Yes, sir."

"From whom?"

"Sonny."

"This was part of the money that Jimmy Liberto had given you?"

"Yes, sir."

"How much had he given you at that point?"

"I think I had just about $4,000 then."

"And how about expenses?"

"Liberto paid for everything, the hotels, the plane fares, and anything like that."

"That was over and above the $30,000 you and Sonny were getting?"

"Yeah, it had nothing to do with the money."

"Now, I think you were describing what it was you did that night after you dressed up as a security guard."

"Well, Sonny stayed in the car and I got dressed and we waited until after dark because it gets dark late down there and it's always summertime. I had a long-sleeve shirt. I had everything that a policeman had on and I told Sonny to wait around in front of the shopping center, not by the 7-Eleven because they're getting tired of seeing us sitting outside. It was like I lived there for a while, and this is a very exclusive residence. Rich people live there, not people like us.

"As I was going by the 7-Eleven I got a six-pack and we went down in back of the lady's house, which we had already been through before. I knew exactly where it was at, through the golf course, which house it was, and the brick fence around the property—the whole thing."

"Was the golf course near her house?"

"Yes, the back of her house overlooks the golf course. There is nothing else there but her backyard and there was a little river, like a little creek that runs through there."

"What did you do?"

"I got up under a tree and drank a six-pack."

"What did you tell Sonny you were going to do?"

"I told Sonny that I was going to knock on the door and tell her some kids had knocked down the bricks off of her backyard and she would come out to investigate and I was going to shoot her."

"Did you have a gun with you to shoot her?"

"Yes, sir."

"Which gun?"

"The .38 special."

"You say you drank the whole six-pack?"

"Yeah, I stayed there about an hour and a half."

"What did you do after you drank the six-pack?"

"I went back and told Sonny that there was nobody at

home, nobody answered the door, and I didn't see nothing at all."

"What was his reaction?"

"He got a little mad. He said, 'Look, go down there and kick the door in,' and I said, 'Oh yeah, security guards will be everywhere and we have Maryland tags on the car. We're real top gangsters, plus all the hardware we got in the car.'"

"The four weapons you described?"

"Well, on the way over I didn't want to get caught with all of those weapons. One is bad enough. I told Sonny let's leave them in the hotel room. He said if anything does come down, they will check our hotel room and they've got the guns anyway. We compromised to throw the shotgun away. I got rid of the sawed-off shotgun."

"What did you do with it?"

"As you leave the Marco Polo Hotel you make a right-hand turn and you come across a real high arched bridge and I told Sonny to stop the car and throw the shotgun in the river."

"Now you were describing that you weren't able to kill Mrs. Luskin the first time," Bernstein prompted.

"I told him she must be out somewhere we didn't know about, maybe her kid is sick or something or maybe she might have just went out and got something to drink. I told him I would go back and I went back at eleven o'clock and went to the 7-Eleven and got more beer and went back under my tree and smoked a few cigarettes and drank the beer and then I went back and I told Sonny that I knocked on the door and an elderly lady answered the door. Then he calmed right down and said, 'Yeah, that's her mother, she's out somewhere. She may be baby-sitting the two little ones.'"

"Did you make any efforts to try to find her at that point?"

"Yeah, Sonny said her usual haunts were these restaurants. I don't think we've ever been able to—everywhere we ever go is a restaurant. I was wondering if she ever had any food in her house."

"How did Sonny know that she might have been at a restaurant?"

"Well, Sonny had a list from Jimmy Liberto of the

places she did go. She would go to a certain restaurant and eat there every Thursday night or whatever. I don't know."

Manley said they drove to each of the restaurants, looking for her car with the personalized license tags, without success. Then they gave up and drove back to Baltimore the next morning so Sonny could pick up his narcotics from Jim Liberto, as he did every Thursday.

On Saturday morning, July 25, Cohen found Manley drinking coffee at a bar in Highlandtown—Manley's neighborhood in Baltimore.

"I was playing the poker machine and Sonny came through the door with a big jar of coffee, a big 7-Eleven coffee and he said 'Come on outside, I want to talk to you.' He had his brand-new car with him then."

"What kind of car was it?"

"A brand-new Monte Carlo. We were standing in front of the car and he said, 'We've got to go to Florida, can you get away?' and I said, 'Yeah, what are you going to do this time, get drunk again? That's about all we've been doing.' He said, 'Well, here's a couple of hundred dollars to hold you over until Monday because I just left Liberto at Doughboy's and the woman will be in the restaurant in Florida exactly seven o'clock Tuesday night and there was time to get on the train Monday and get to Florida and relax and enjoy ourselves and then get her on the parking lot.'"

"Did he say what the name of the restaurant was?"

"He said it was Branigan's or something like that."

"Could it have been Bennigan's?"

"Yeah."

"He told you that Jimmy had given him that information?"

"Yes, sir, he said he got a phone call from Florida to verify that she would be there for dinner and she would be by herself."

"Did he tell you who made that phone call from Florida?"

"It was my understanding that Joe Liberto made that phone call. He's got two brothers, but I don't think the other one could have made the phone call. Joe had to make it."

"Who was his other brother?"

"His other brother was named Frank."

"He lives in Baltimore?"

"Yeah."

Manley speculated that Cohen wanted to take the train because he didn't want to risk spilling coffee on the seats of his new car. He said Liberto arranged for a rental car in Fort Lauderdale. When Manley next saw Cohen, on Sunday morning, Cohen opened his trunk and showed him a rifle with a laser and scope, which he said he got from Jimmy Liberto.

"I was going to have trouble getting away from my wife and he was already arguing with his girlfriend and moved his stuff back to his mother's house," Manley said.

"He had moved out from his girlfriend's house?"

"It's a temporary thing. They fight every week."

Cohen called Manley early Monday morning and said to meet him at Penn Station before the train left at 9:05. There, Cohen gave him $500 to buy his ticket, which cost $449.

Manley opened Cohen's travel bag to put his things inside. "I saw the .22 Ruger automatic pistol and there was a stack of money maybe three inches high. I asked Sonny if he thought he brought enough money and he said it's Liberto's money, hell with it, we'll spend it. He told me it was expense money for going down and back."

"Did Sonny have any conversations with Jimmy just before you left?" Bernstein asked.

"Yes, sir, and the train was delayed an hour and a half and we drank coffee and talked and he called Liberto while I was standing next to the phone. He called Liberto at his house and Darlene answered the phone. Darlene is Liberto's girlfriend. They lived together for quite a while. Sonny said, 'Hi, Dar, can I speak to Jimmy, this is Sonny.' Liberto was talking to Sonny and I couldn't hear what Liberto was saying, I could just hear what Sonny said."

"What were they talking about?"

"About the money to get to Florida. Sonny said, 'Yeah, I got plenty of money to get there and back,' and then Sonny said, 'That's good,' and he hung the phone up. Sonny said if we kill her Tuesday night there is a $25,000 bonus because time is running out. Sonny would have $25,000 to split."

"Do you know what he meant by 'time is running out'?"

"Yes, I think it's got to do with the divorce settlement. It's purely between Mr. Luskin and Mrs. Luskin, I know that."

Manley said they got to Fort Lauderdale Tuesday morning, and took a cab in from the train station to Dollar Rent-A-Car, near the airport. There, Cohen picked up a car reserved under Jimmy Liberto's corporate name. They drove around Marie's neighborhood, then got to the Marco Polo. The rest of the day they lounged at the hotel's beachside bar.

At six, Cohen announced it was time to go to work, and they loaded the car with their guns.

"We drove around the same area we had been driving both trips and never saw her car. We went to the parking lot at Bennigan's and we circled the parking lot several times. There are four or five exits on and off, and we didn't know which way she was coming in. She was supposed to be by herself, and Sonny was in the backseat. He was the one that actually was to pull the trigger, and we had three guns in the car within reach of either one of us."

"Which weapon was he going to use to kill her with?"

"Well, it was going to be up close and people were around and he was going to use the silencer, the .25. If we've got a clear shot going down the road somewhere we would use the .22. The bottom line was why we brought the rifle down. Well, if we had to have a long shot, especially from the golf course to her house, we had to use the automatic rifle."

Bennigan's was near a Burger King, and Manley went inside to get a Pepsi.

"We were looking for her regular car with the tag. It was a brand-new Mercedes that came up in back of us to my right and went around and it had the shaded windows where you couldn't see. It was past us before we could even see it."

"You mean tinted windows?"

"Yeah, real dark, and you couldn't see in the back of her car. It was just about a quarter to seven in the evening. She went right in front of the restaurant, up the main driveway, and parked right in front of the restaurant."

"What happened next?"

"Well, we still didn't know it was her, really. We were looking for the original car. This is not the car we were looking for. So, a lady got out of the car, kind of tall lady with blond hair and a shorter lady with reddish-looking hair, auburn maybe. Sonny said, 'There she is.' He was cussing now—I'm trying to be nice to you all. He said, 'There—she is there.' I said, 'What are you going to do, it's broad daylight?' He said, 'We'll wait until she comes out and then kill her.'

"Well, to start with, she was supposed to be by herself and—"

"Where did she go when she got out of the car?" Bernstein asked.

"She went directly into the restaurant. There was a great big guy, bigger than I am standing there, and she stopped and talked to him for a while. I went to get the sodas because I knew we had a wait coming. You don't eat dinner in five minutes in there, it's not McDonald's. I brought the sodas back and I told Sonny that we can't get her from here, we've got to go up in front of that parking lot.

"We pulled around the side and looked for a place. There was no way we could get a shot at her from the car. Sonny had the rifle in the backseat and he was sitting in the back. So, I pulled the car around and we had a direct line of vision to the front door of the place and everything.

"Meanwhile, I seen Mrs. Luskin a second time after she came back out of the restaurant, maybe five minutes after she went in the first time. She was still talking to that big guy, and she had her two younger children standing there talking to her. I don't know if they were her children or a neighbor's kids or whatever. I told Sonny 'It's off' right there, the children are with her. I didn't want to do it anyway, I just wanted some more money.

"So, Sonny said, 'No, when she comes out of there she'll be by herself because that's the information we got.' I said, 'Well, she didn't come in by herself and now she's got two kids with her, and I don't know if they were her kids or not.' All I knew for a fact is that she had two young daughters and I wouldn't touch them. I wouldn't even try. I probably would have shot at Sonny if he tried to shoot in front of those kids. He said, 'We'll wait and see what happens.'

"We were on the parking lot and I went down to Burger King and got two more sodas about an hour later."

"Did you do anything with the laser scope?," Bernstein asked.

"Well, it was in the backseat and there was a guy approximately my size that got out of a car after it got dark. We were sitting there for two hours before it got dark and the cars were coming in and out from Burger King. Sonny put the scope itself and the laser light, which is maybe as big as a quarter that far away. It was a couple of hundred yards away and (he) said, 'Now see how easy it is.'"

"The light was shining on the person?"

"Yeah, you could see the light that it was throwing and you could see it fluttering, and then he steadied it. He said all you have to do is put the laser light on the woman, look through that scope and pull the trigger, and it would hit the laser.

"Then the lady finally came out around ten o'clock."

"Was she with anyone when she came out?"

"She had quite a few people there. I didn't bother to count them. I said, 'Look, Sonny.'"

"You couldn't get a clean shot?"

"Sure you could get a clean shot. Sonny put the thing right on her. I said, 'Don't shoot her, Sonny, there are people coming across the parking lot and in front of us and there is no left-hand turn down in there. There is no way out of it.'"

"When she came out of the restaurant, was there any kind of disturbance?"

"Yeah, two cars had sped away from the Burger King without their lights on and a bunch of kids were running across the lot. When I say kids, I'm talking eighteen or nineteen years old. They were chasing the cars. Evidently they had done something to somebody and I said, 'There it goes, Sonny, it's not meant to be. Tell Liberto what you want to tell him, I'm not involved in this anymore.'"

"What did Sonny say?"

"He said, well, he said he will tell Liberto to jam his money, you know, and we politely left and got drunk."

"Did you see where Mrs. Luskin went after she came out of the restaurant?"

"Yes, sir, she stood in front of another car. I'm not sure, but I think it was a later-model Cadillac with the big guy and a couple of people. Evidently they knew each other, neighbors or whatever."

Manley said they followed Marie as she left in her car with her female friend.

"She turned left down to the main highway and that's where the 7-Eleven is at and the golf course is at. They're right next to each other. As she was approaching it, she slowed down and put her signal on to make the right-hand turn. Sonny said, 'Shoot her! Shoot her!' and there were cars everywhere. I didn't want to shoot the lady."

"I said, 'Are you crazy, what if she veers into us,' and there is another woman in there, and Sonny said, 'Shoot them both.' I said, 'Sonny, let's go home, I'm out of this. This is crazy anyway.'"

"What did you do the rest of the evening?"

"We went back to the Marco Polo Hotel, walked up the street to the Waikiki, and did some drugs."

After Manley finished, grand jurors asked him questions.

"Which Liberto paid for the expenses when you were down in Florida?" asked one.

"James," said Manley.

"And where did he get the money to pay the expenses?"

"It was my understanding—this is not something I can say, but it's my understanding that he was given x amount of dollars in front for the actual setting up and killing, and hiring the contract killer."

"Who did Jimmy get the money from?"

"I'm pretty sure it was his brother. I can't swear to that. This is just conjecture."

"Mr. Manley," asked Gary Jordan, another assistant U.S. attorney, "are you saying that your source of that information is Mr. Cohen, you don't have firsthand knowledge?"

"Right," Manley said.

"Do you know where Mr. Liberto got the money?" asked Bernstein.

"Mr. Liberto is wealthy anyway, but I'm pretty sure that Liberto had to get it from Luskin."

"You didn't have any information to indicate that Joe Liberto—" Bernstein started.

"I didn't know Paul Luskin's name," Manley said.

"Well, what was your understanding—who was the person that requested this be done, Joe Liberto or Paul Luskin?"

"The killing was for Paul Luskin over the divorce settlement. He said—here's the story Sonny told me. Mr. Luskin offered Mrs. Luskin $200,000 cash money and everything she owed, he would sign over the car and the house and whatever, plus a few of the stores in Florida, and she refused and said she was going to take it all in the divorce because she was raising the two children and Mr. Luskin decided to kill her before the divorce became final and he lost everything he had."

"It was your understanding that Mr. Luskin contacted Jimmy Liberto, or Joe Liberto?" Bernstein asked.

"Joe Liberto. He contacted Joe because he worked there. From what I understand—"

"This is what Sonny told you?"

"Yeah, Joe had worked for Mr. Luskin for, like, twenty years."

*   *   *

Marie testified the same day. She told the grand jury about her divorce, her assault, and a few more details.

"I'm not real sure of the date, but I think it was about a month after this incident, after the home invasion. My husband brought the children back on a Sunday night from visitation. My big daughter Shana came in the house and my little one Diana just jumped into my arms. I was, like, standing back from the door so when she came in the house, she jumped in my arms.

"While I was holding her, Paul said I need to talk to you just for a few minutes, come outside. I said I'm not going outside with you. So, he said, tell Diana to go in the other room. She wouldn't leave me. She was clinging to me, and my father or mother came in and took Diana away from me and I stood at the front door, but I couldn't close it all the way because I was afraid of him.

"He said, 'You better settle this case already and quit horsing around down there.' I looked at him and said, 'Don't threaten me, I'm not afraid of you.' Meanwhile, I was scared to death, but I was pretending not to be scared of him. I said, 'We'll settle the case in court legally and properly like it's supposed to be settled.'

"He said, 'Remember, Marie, there are always other florists.'

"I looked at him and I said, 'I don't believe this,' and I ran in the house and closed the door and ran over to the telephone." She called Detective Soccol and left a message for him.

Assistant U.S. Attorney Gary Jordan solicited testimony about a "Single Parent Support Group" Marie had organized at the Hollywood Jewish Community Center.

Marie said both Susan and Paul were members. Paul went to one picnic, but after the Broward County Court issued an arrest warrant for him, for nonsupport, he didn't attend any other meetings.

She said the group sent out a newsletter in the beginning of July for a dinner meeting July 28, at Bennigan's restaurant in Hollywood. But Susan, who had regularly attended past meetings, didn't sign up for this one.

"To your personal knowledge at that time, there were no remarkable events that night?" Jordan asked.

"Nothing that I remember. I do remember being so relieved that finally Susan Davis didn't show up and I didn't have to watch her staring at me all the time."

"And that had been a problem at other meetings?"

"Yes, she sits there and stares at me."

Jordan asked Marie if she knew Joe Liberto.

"Joe was Paul's right-hand man. He helped Paul run different stores. He was a trouble-shooter. If he needed help—let's say if a manager was sick that day, Joe would go to a store and take over."

"You personally spoke with Joe Liberto over the years?"

"Yes, he's like a friend of the family."

Marie testified that Paul had never been violent with her. A grand juror asked if Joe Liberto had a violent temper.

"No, Joe Liberto was always warm and friendly and nice. I never saw any violent temper at all."

Jordan asked if Marie had vanity license tags on her gray four-door Mercedes.

"Yes, the license plate on the back of the car was PBL. It was Paul's initials."

Then Marie had a question. "Did they find the man who held the gun to me?"

"Yes," answered a grand juror.

"Do you know of anyone being arrested?" Bernstein asked her.

"Only from my testimony here that I know that someone—there must be somebody arrested for this."

On September 25, the FBI and ATF got a warrant to search the home of a friend of Sonny Cohen's. Manley said Cohen was afraid that his girlfriend Denise Spring might have told the FBI about his rented garage, where he kept a silencer, rifle, and two handguns, including a .38. Manley said he had seen the weapons himself.

Manley said Cohen had his mother bring the garage

key to the jail so she could give it to Denise. Denise then gave it to Cohen's friend, who took the weapons out of the garage and put them in his apartment. Then Denise told Cohen it had been done.

But when the feds arrived, they found two girls in the apartment who said Cohen's friend had left a week before, and had given them no forwarding address. Agents searched but didn't find the guns they were looking for, although they did find a nine-shot revolver one of the girls claimed was hers.

On September 29, the FBI served Denise Spring with a subpoena to testify to the grand jury. At that time, she gave agents Pat Connolly and Charles Hedrick a statement:

She did get the key to Cohen's garage from his mother, and passed it on to his friend. But she believed his friend was simply going to remove some tools and clean the place up.

But she also volunteered that she had gone to Florida with Cohen and stayed at the Marco Polo Hotel sometime at the end of February or beginning of March (she later corrected herself it was January). At first she said she stayed at the Dunes Hotel—which was down the street from the Marco Polo—but then she said Cohen told her to lie to the FBI about staying at the Dunes, when in fact they had stayed at the Marco Polo.

She knew James Manley through Cohen. Cohen had told her that Manley was in protective custody because he was giving information to the feds. Cohen told her he hadn't done anything, but Manley had. He didn't elaborate.

She also said she believed Cohen was involved in narcotics trafficking, considering all the trips he had taken to Florida. She also mentioned an escape attempt, but she wouldn't say anything more about it.

On October 15, the grand jury convened again.

In part it was Girlfriend Day; Denise Spring told them she thought Sonny was dealing cocaine, but in any event he had supplied her with the drug. She also knew Jimmy Liberto, whom she saw at the Marco Polo; after Sonny was arrested in July, Liberto told her not to worry because he was going to bail Sonny out.

She also added to the garage incident; although Sonny didn't tell her, she figured it contained guns and drugs. She later asked Cohen's friend if he found any tools in it, and he said no.

Jimmy Liberto's girlfriend Darlene Armstrong testified she had gone to the Marco Polo with Liberto two or three times in the previous year and a half. She knew Cohen from seeing him at their restaurant, Palughi's, as well as at the Marco Polo. She had also seen Joe Liberto meet Jimmy at the Marco Polo.

However, Darlene said she didn't know Jimmy was a drug trafficker, nor that he had tried to bond Cohen out of jail.

Susan Davis appeared that day as well. She faced a conundrum; she didn't want to testify against Paul, but her subpoena compelled her to appear. She also had a potential problem of self-incrimination should the government have believed she was involved in the scheme as well—although she wasn't a target of the grand jury.

To solve the problems, Susan hired an attorney to work out a "use immunity" deal that the government offered her. That meant she would have to answer everything the government asked, but they couldn't use her testimony, or anything derived from it, against her later. In practical terms it meant the government had concluded that Susan had played a part, but most likely inadvertently. Rather than prosecute her, they preferred to use her testimony, and this was the way to get it.

But the deal had limits; it only covered what she would testify to. If it turned out she was more involved and hadn't said so, she could still face charges. Plus, if she perjured herself, the government could indict her for that.

She said she had been with Paul in Baltimore four times in the previous twelve months; Christmastime, Father's Day in June, mid-August, and mid-September. She also confirmed she was a member of the Hollywood

JCC's Single Parent Support Group. But since both her
ex-husband Gary and Marie were among the leaders, she
attended meetings only sporadically.

Jordan asked if she had ever discussed the group with
Paul.

"Yes, I have," she said.

Then he showed her the flyer promoting the group's
July 28 dinner meeting at Bennigan's, with Marie's
home phone number as RSVP.

"Do you remember receiving this?"

"Yes."

"Did you choose to attend this?"

"No, I didn't."

"Why not?"

"Because I mainly just liked to go to the meetings
where there is a topic. I really don't want to eat with my
ex-husband."

"I believe you mentioned this meeting or dinner in
passing to Paul Luskin; is that correct?"

"Yes."

"Did he express any interest in attending it?"

"No, he was living in Pittsburgh."

The government called FBI Special Agent Charles
Hedrick as a summary witness. He had reviewed police
reports, court records, telephone records, travel records,
and done a number of interviews.

He offered the grand jurors a chronology: in November 1985 Paul separated from Marie, and later that
month, a Hollywood Police report showed Paul had
done about $35,000 damage to Marie's home. In De-
cember the police were called again to settle a verbal
argument between him and Marie.

In 1986, he said, Paul was found in contempt of court
several times for nonpayment of child support and
alimony. In October 1986, Paul's brother-in-law complained to police that his tires had been slashed.

In January, 1987, Jim Liberto and Darlene Armstrong
flew to Fort Lauderdale, stayed at the Marco Polo Hotel,
and were billed for two rooms. Phone records showed
calls from one of the rooms to Joe Liberto's home
number. The other room had phone calls consistent with

numbers Sonny Cohen called, including Denise Spring's.

Also in January, Paul Luskin was arrested on a fugitive writ for contempt of court. Police saw him inside an apartment but couldn't get anyone to open the door. Finally they forced their way in and found him hiding under a blanket on a balcony.

On March 4, Jim Liberto registered at the Marco Polo, and his room was billed for calls consistent with his calling pattern. On March 8–9, calls from the room were consistent with Cohen's calling pattern. Plus, Cohen had used his car phone nearly every day in Baltimore, but not at all on those two days. His first two calls on March 10 were to Palughi's Restaurant and then to Jim Liberto's home.

On March 9 Marie was assaulted. "The intruder gained entrance by posing as a florist deliveryman. He had a bunch of flowers, and when she opened the door, the assailant had a gun behind the flowers. The intruder demanded money. She is assaulted in this, assaulted very seriously in this incident. She's struck on the head with the gun," Hedrick said.

"I interviewed Marie Luskin and she told me she offered the intruder a hundred-dollar bill and a bag of jewelry which she valued between $25,000 to $35,000 and the intruder took nothing, assaulted her, and left."

Jordan then showed grand jurors the police photos of Marie's head wound.

"The incident happened at 10:20 in the morning. The Marco Polo Hotel is about twenty minutes or so driving distance from the victim's house. Shortly, within minutes of the time it would take for a person to make that drive to the Marco Polo from the victim's house, we have a series of toll calls from the Marco Polo reversing the charges, charging these calls to Palughi's Restaurant. The first call goes from the Marco Polo to Palughi's, and then there are other calls that go from Palughi's to Joe Liberto—that's Jimmy's brother who works at Luskin's—and then a call to Luskin's in Hollywood, Florida, and these calls occur just after the assault on Marie Luskin."

Hedrick summarized James Manley's testimony, placing the July 28 Single Parent Support Group meeting in the time frame. He reminded that Manley testified Cohen told him he had "inside information" about Marie's schedule, to include a dinner at Bennigan's that same night. Manley also reported there was a $25,000 bonus if they were successful in killing her.

Then Hedrick added something Manley had not said to the grand jury. On the train going home, Cohen told Manley they needed to return in two weeks to try again, because "the divorce hearing is coming up shortly.

"Manley tells me that the contract is still open on Marie Luskin and he says that Cohen has made this a matter of pride. Cohen says that as soon as he's released he's going to go back to Florida to do the contract himself because it has apparently bothered him that he wasn't successful."

Hedrick said an electronic "trap and trace" on Marie's Luskin's phone showed "that as recently as the weekend of October 2 to October 4 Paul Luskin called Marie trying to find out what her up-and-coming schedule would be."

There was still more compiling work to do, he said. Only that morning they had received phone records of Luskin's, Inc. Still to come, under subpoena, were records of Susan's calls and Paul's calls from Pittsburgh.

At the end of the day, the grand jury returned indictments against Paul Luskin, James Liberto, Joseph Liberto, and Milton "Sonny" Cohen, for conspiracy and interstate travel in the commission of murder for hire, and weapons offenses.

Realizing in advance that the grand jury would probably vote to indict, Paul Luskin flew to Baltimore with his attorney Alvin Entin and presented himself to the U.S. marshal at the federal courthouse. Since he got there early, they asked him to take a seat. When the grand jury took its action, marshals took him into custody.

At 6 P.M., FBI and ATF agents surrounded Palughi's Restaurant and arrested Jim Liberto. After he was advised of Miranda, Liberto told ATF Agent Cheeks he had bought a rifle and loaned it to Sonny a day later. He also said he had a .357 Magnum pistol, and would have his attorney turn it over to authorities.

Joe Liberto, however, was allowed to surrender the next day at FBI headquarters in Baltimore. Four weeks earlier, the FBI had told him they had no plans to arrest him.

At a bond hearing, Gregg Bernstein called Paul Luskin a "cold and calculating man" who was likely to flee if granted bond and was still a danger to his wife. Despite that, U.S. Magistrate Paul Rosenberg set Luskin's bond at $2 million, which his parents posted in properties. U.S. District Court Judge J. Frederick Motz ordered that he sleep at a halfway house until the trial's conclusion.

The U.S. Attorney's Office in Baltimore anticipated "major publicity" because of Luskin's name, and prepared a press release. Friday evening, October 16, the story bannered an edition of *The Miami News:*

> Luskin indicted in attempt to kill wife
> Charges against Miami businessman
> come amid bitter divorce battle

The Miami News printed a quote from Entin: "My client categorically denies all of the charges, and he fully expects to be vindicated by a jury of his peers."

The next day, the story made the Baltimore *Sun, The Washington Post,* and *The Miami Herald.* The *Sun* story printed a comment from Jack Luskin: he said he had had only limited business contacts with his Florida relatives in the past fifteen years, and his company had no connection with them.

Paul had been invited to a dinner at the White House on October 25 as a reward for his Republican Party fund-raising efforts. He didn't attend.

FOUR

"Money's My Friend"

Two weeks after the grand jury indicted, yet another snitch witness came forward.

He was James Raidy, arrested in August for possession with intent to distribute an ounce of the drug PCP, but whose bigger problem was a parole violation. He had been convicted for second degree murder in Baltimore City in 1976, sentenced to seventeen years, and released early. Raidy first called Gregg Bernstein, who sent FBI Agent Pat Connolly to see him in the Baltimore City Jail on October 29.

Raidy said he had known Sonny Cohen and James Manley for a year. He knew Cohen was a cocaine trafficker, and had seen Manley use cocaine.

Raidy said three days earlier Cohen told him that he had gone to Florida to kill a woman, and that he "went up alongside her head with a gun." Cohen didn't believe the woman would be able to identify him because she had said her assailant was six feet tall and had brown hair.

After that, Cohen made two more trips to Florida to murder her, these times with Manley. Additionally, he and Jim Liberto made another trip there for purposes relating to the hit.

Cohen also told him he had offered Manley $20,000 to clear him of the gun charges. At some point, Cohen got suspicious of Manley and tested him. He said he kept some guns in a garage, but there were no guns there, Raidy said.

Raidy got information from Manley, too. He said Manley told him that Sonny got his cocaine from Florida.

Raidy's message was urgent because Cohen told him he was going to escape by using bedsheets to swing over the wall. He also had a hacksaw blade. Since the plan would take two persons, Raidy wondered if Cohen wanted him to come along. But Raidy also told Connolly that Cohen might be testing him as well by telling him this.

As a partial reward for his information, Bernstein arranged that Raidy be released on his own recognizance at his arraignment in state court November 18.

The next day, from the street, Raidy called again. Cohen was going to escape November 22, between five-thirty and nine in the evening, with two guys facing life terms. Cohen wanted Raidy to cut a hole in the jail fence and leave a car for him.

Cohen told him he knew the feds had put Manley at Anne Arundel County Jail to separate them. Once out, he planned to stalk the jail with a second AR-15 rifle with laser scope he had. He'd kill Manley when he walked past a jail window. If he couldn't kill him, he would kill one of Manley's children or grandchildren to to keep him from testifying, or to avenge his cooperation.

In the next few days, Raidy was a stream of information. Cohen told him Manley could "sink" him because he had told him that Marie Luskin was supposed to be at a particular shopping center. Only a few people, including Marie's husband, knew that. Cohen was also worried that Joe Liberto might be cooperating with the FBI.

Cohen wanted Raidy to know it wasn't true he wanted to cooperate with the government and give information about a five hundred-to-one thousand-kilo-a-month drug operation. However, he did say he was making two drug runs a month for $2,000 a trip. He had planned to buy the Florida connection for $40,000 a month, then use Manley as the courier.

On November 21, acting on Raidy's information, jailers searched Cohen's cell. They didn't find anything there, but in the next cell, Tommy Taylor had a saw blade in his shoe heel. Taylor said it was Cohen's. In addition, another inmate had a homemade rope made from bed-sheets, and he also said it was Cohen's. Cohen and Taylor were placed on lockdown and charged with attempted escape.

The FBI interviewed Marco Polo employees who might recognize Cohen's picture. They found one—bartender John Gioe—then on November 25, they found Keith Hellebrand, a lighting technician for a Las Vegas-style stage show called *Legends in Concert,* which had a three-month run at the Marco Polo during early 1987.

One day in March, Hellebrand had met Sonny at the bar. They talked baseball, and Hellebrand mentioned that the Baltimore Orioles were playing the Los Angeles Dodgers in an exhibition game early that afternoon at Miami Stadium. With one more person, they went to the game and arrived after two o'clock.

Hellebrand had kept his scorecard. The Orioles—just beginning a years-long decline—started Scott McGregor but fell behind 5–0 in the fourth inning, and lost 6–3.

The date of the game was March 9.

On December 9, the FBI interviewed twenty-three-year-old nursing student Patricia Parks, who had worked together with Cohen at a bar. Parks had entered the Miss Maryland pageant a year before; she was runner-up.

In late June, Cohen had asked her to ride with him to Florida in his car. They stayed at the Marco Polo for three days. There she saw Cohen talking to a couple he appeared to know. When the FBI showed her a photo lineup, she identified Jim Liberto's picture as the man.

On the way back to Baltimore, they listened to a radio discussion on capital punishment. She said Cohen asked her opinion. Parks answered killers should be electro-cuted.

Cohen then gave her some hypotheticals: what if all the evidence incriminated someone, yet there was still some doubt? What if a boyfriend kept beating up a girl, even after he got out of jail for it? Would it be appropriate for someone to hunt down the boyfriend and kill him? What if someone was paid to kill someone whom the killer didn't know?

After Cohen was arrested, he told Parks he was in jail on gun charges and was under investigation for a murder in Baltimore City. Later, he said authorities were trying to implicate him in another murder. A lady was supposed to see him in a lineup, but she wouldn't be able to identify him.

In federal criminal trials, the government is obligated to provide the defense with both *Brady* and *Jencks* discovery materials. *Brady* is evidence and some law enforcement investigation materials—which Gregg Bernstein turned over as he received them. *Jencks* materials have to do with witness credibility and prior witness statements, including their grand jury testimonies. Technically, the prosecution can wait to deliver this until absolutely the last moment—just before the defense begins cross-examination of the witness. Disgruntled federal criminal defense attorneys call that "trial by ambush." In this instance, Bernstein turned over Jencks two weeks before trial began.

As local counsel in Baltimore, Alvin Entin hired Steven A. Allen, a former assistant U.S. attorney in Maryland. At the insistence of Paul's cousin Steve Miles, a third lawyer was hired, Russell White, a bit of an elder statesman among Baltimore criminal attorneys.

Allen became lead counsel. On November 16 he filed a pile of motions complaining that the government hadn't provided any evidence against Luskin.

"Virtually none of the discovery even mentions Paul Luskin," he wrote. Existing discovery consisted of travel and hotel records proving that James Liberto and Milton Cohen had been in Florida several times in 1987; the codefendants' telephone records; records of Pat Widerman's gun purchases; information of Cohen and Manley's arrest; and police records of Marie's assault "which includes a composite drawing of the attacker which bears no similarity to the appearance of any of the defendants in this case," Allen said.

"The only information concerning Luskin's alleged criminal conduct which the Government has provided to defendant Luskin from which he can prepare his defense is the reference to him in two paragraphs of the conspiracy count in the indictment and the proffer made by the Government during bail hearings in this case that an individual named James Manley will testify he was allegedly told by defendant Milton Cohen, who allegedly was told by defendant James Liberto, who allegedly was told by defendant Joseph Liberto that Paul Luskin had arranged for the murder of Marie Luskin."

Allen called that "treble hearsay."

Allen moved for a severance. "If Luskin were to be tried with his co-defendants, all of the evidence of criminal activities of the three co-defendants, including drug trafficking and use of firearms, would be available for the jury to draw the inference that Luskin too, from his association with the co-defendants in the same indictment and at a joint trial, must also be involved in serious criminal conduct."

In another motion, Allen foreshadowed Luskin's defense. He would introduce evidence hostile to his codefendants:

"The sole purpose of James Liberto's and Milton Sonny Cohen's trips to Florida during 1987 was to participate in drug trafficking activities and not to murder Marie Luskin pursuant to a conspiracy involving Paul Luskin."

James Liberto was "significantly involved" in drug trafficking in Baltimore, and his drug source was in Miami. Joe Liberto knew about Paul and Marie's divorce, and during his trip to Baltimore in December 1986 after Luskin's had fired him, Joe told his brother Jimmy.

Cohen was one of Jimmy Liberto's drug couriers, as evidenced by his possession of three ounces of 90 percent pure cocaine when arrested. Both Cohen and Jimmy Liberto were in south Florida on March 9, 1987. Prior to that, Cohen learned from Jimmy Liberto that Marie "had obtained large quantities of money from her husband during the divorce.

"On March 9, 1987, Milton Sonny Cohen for the purpose of committing a burglary at 2831 Palmer Drive and robbing Marie Luskin at that location traveled from the Marco Polo Hotel, where he was staying, and attempted to rob and assault Marie Luskin. Milton Sonny Cohen assaulted Marie Luskin by striking her in the back of the head with a hand gun. Cohen's assault on Marie Luskin was unrelated to any plot involving Paul Luskin or the other defendants in this case."

When Cohen stalked Marie twice afterward, he did want to kill her, Allen wrote, but that was because he believed she would be able to identify him as her assailant on March 9.

Allen played the role of prosecutor—not an unfamiliar role—by investigating the telephone pattern of both Jim and Joe Liberto. He found repeated calls to three phone numbers of Hispanic women in northwest Miami whose homes, it turned out, were guarded by fences and iron bars.

Meanwhile, the FBI found sixty-eight Western Union money transfers from a pharmacy near Palughi's Restaurant in Baltimore, all to south Florida. There was a total of $188,300 sent between December 1986 and December 1987. Joe Liberto picked up two-thirds of the money; almost all the wires were sent by Jim Liberto or a company called Acme Tile—owned by Jim Liberto.

Allen, however, found even more. He subpoenaed Western Union himself and found a total of two hundred similar wire transfers beginning in March 1986, totaling $375,950. All the wires were less than $10,000, which avoided the IRS cash reporting requirement.

That was the drug ring, Allen thought. Money goes south, narcotics from Florida go north.

Luskin's defense asked the government to produce all its information of drug trafficking by the defendants and other coconspirators. In a reply, Bernstein said the government was in the process of collecting it, but he didn't believe he had to turn it over because it wasn't relevant to the charges.

The fight was on. Allen responded that the government's claim ignored the fact that Cohen had three ounces of cocaine when he was arrested on the train from Florida.

Proving the drug ring was important, but the key to winning the trial was to destroy James Manley's story, or at least, his credibility. And it turned out that would not be hard to do.

Manley personified the term "career criminal." He was forty-five, and his FBI rap sheet was five pages long; he had twenty-eight arrests, beginning in 1959, when he was sixteen years old. Most of the early stuff was small, like burglary, or breaking and entering.

But by 1970 he had turned more dangerous, with arrests for assault by pointing a pistol, robbery with a deadly weapon, and a jail escape.

He was moving up in the world by 1978, when he was arrested and convicted for breaking into a post office, stealing a money order machine, and imprinting the checks and selling them. He was also involved in a scheme forging other checks.

All in all, it appeared there were at least four adult felony convictions on his record: a 1966 burglary and larceny in Cincinnati; robbery with a deadly weapon in Baltimore in 1971; a stolen car in Baltimore in 1977; and the post office burglary in Baltimore in 1978.

That was significant because Maryland had recently passed a new career criminal act; now, merely a third felony conviction in state court brought a mandatory twenty-five year sentence without parole. The fourth carried mandatory life without parole.

Since Manley seemed to have four already, his possession of drugs and guns made him eligible; his back was to the wall. That was strong motivation, Allen knew, to invent a good story—or at least, embellish one perchance—to get a deal with the government. It wouldn't be inconsistent with the criminal class.

Plus, as it turned out, there were still more pending cases against him:

- Manley was indicted in 1986 by a grand jury in Anne Arundel County, Maryland—Annapolis—for a 1985 burglary. The case was set for trial on May 26, 1987, but Manley had failed to appear. The county judge then issued a bench warrant for Manley's arrest, with a no bond hold.

- He had also been arrested in Baltimore County on May 13, 1987, for carrying a fully loaded .357 Magnum revolver concealed under the driver's seat of his car. In addition, he was charged with driving while intoxicated, and driving with a suspended license.

Besides those cases, there were three crimes of violence involving Manley:

- On May 20, 1987, there was an assault with intent to murder Jimmy Liberto at his home in Middle River, in Baltimore County. A middle-aged man in a plaid shirt and maroon silk jacket rang the doorbell, asked Darlene Armstrong for the man of the house, then raised his hand with a gun. Liberto was fast enough to push the man's hand down, so the shot was fired into the floor. Liberto kicked him and threw a lamp at him, and he fled.

  Manley admitted to the FBI that he was Liberto's assailant. Cohen had hired him to kill Liberto so Cohen wouldn't have to pay for the drugs Liberto had given him on consignment.

- Manley also told the FBI that Jim Liberto had commissioned Cohen to murder a man named Ralph Watson and someone else named Jimmy, both of whom Liberto suspected had stolen $60,000 from the trunk of his car. In mid-June, Cohen asked Manley to help him, and together, they surveilled Watson in an attempt to shoot him. They never did.

  Since Watson was Cohen's friend, Manley said he asked why he would kill him for money. Cohen answered, "Money's my friend."

- There was also the incident on June 10, 1987, when Manley had been shot. He was taken to Johns Hopkins Hospital that night. Knowing police would arrest him when they realized he was a fugitive from Anne Arundel County, Manley left his room on crutches the next morning and disappeared.

James Manley had had a busy couple of months.

Steve Allen hired private detectives to investigate Manley.

First they found Doris Manley, his wife. She described her husband as a "loving father and grandfather who was attempting to get his life straightened out." She said he was a high-school graduate, extremely intelligent, who wrote poetry and had once studied for the ministry. He was an excellent cook and baker, and had recently worked as a security guard and an ice-cream truck driver.

No one else said anything remotely nice about him.

Next they found Joe Reeside, Manley's codefendant in a 1976 robbery case. Manley turned state's evidence against Reeside; Reeside got ten years, Manley walked.

"If I were walking down the street and saw Manley on the other side, and I had a gun, I'd kill him with no regrets. Manley is a snake," he said.

Michael Forame had been arrested at the same time with Manley and Reeside. He described Manley as a "bad dude" and "number one bad boy." Manley didn't have a job; "he just robs stores"—at least thirty that Forame knew of.

Reeside's girlfriend wrote him in prison that Manley had killed a state trooper. Forame said he knew Manley had killed a motel clerk in 1975 during a robbery. When the clerk reached for a cigar box, Manley thought he was going for a gun. Manley dragged him over the counter and stabbed him. He got away.

Manley was a heavy cocaine user, Forame said. Once, after robbing $5,000 from a grocery store, the money was gone within two days.

Forame said Manley always carried a pistol. He never turned his back on him because Manley would "kill you in a heartbeat." During a robbery, when a female clerk slammed her cash register closed instead of handing over her money, Manley "pistol-whipped the shit out of her."

Next, investigators found Tallman "Tommy" Johnson, who met Manley when they worked together at an A&P grocery in the early sixties. Johnson said Manley was a womanizer who had at least two husbands looking for him. He didn't know Manley was violent, but did call him a habitual liar and a bullshitter.

Herman Fried met Manley in 1986 in New Jersey. He said Manley was always high on cocaine, heroin, or booze. Manley didn't give a damn about his life, he said. If he liked you, he was generous, but if he didn't, he was capable of extreme violence. Many times he saw Manley "snap" and begin fistfights.

Burt Walls, who lived in Salem, New Jersey, was Manley's cousin. Manley stayed with him and his sister until the day he got drunk and slapped her around. Walls described Manley as a "singer"—when he got into trouble with the police, he would do anything necessary to get out of it.

Robert Cuffley said the same thing; whenever Manley got arrested, he had no qualms about telling police what they wanted to know about his associates, so he could get out of jail.

Cuffley remembered some stories: in 1972, Manley asked his stepfather to drive him to pick up his paycheck. His stepfather dropped him off, and while he waited, Manley robbed a business. His stepfather never knew what happened.

Another time, when Manley stayed at Cuffley's house, a passerby asked Manley for a match. The man lit his cigarette, then continued walking. Manley went into the house, found a baseball bat, and attacked him. Cuffley had no idea what had happened; Manley said afterward that the man hadn't returned his matchbook. Cuffley told him that was because there was only one match left in it.

Finally, detectives found Manley's girlfriend, Ruth Walters. She had known Manley ten years; she even posted $2,000 bond for him on his Anne Arundel County charges. But when she overheard Manley discuss sneaking out of Maryland with a girlfriend, she demanded her bond money back from the court.

Walters said Manley was intelligent, but he had a "criminal brain." He made money cashing bad checks and beating slot machines in bars by attaching nylon fishing line to the quarters he played with. When Manley slapped Ruth around, she bit off the tip of one of his fingers.

Manley was definitely a snitch, she said. Manley showed her son how to rob bars; but when Manley got in trouble for drunk driving, he turned in her son, who got convicted and sentenced to fifteen years.

Manley would do anything to stay out of jail because "he can't do any more time," she said.

Walters referred investigators to James Bates, who knew Manley from Maryland prison in 1972. Bates remembered that Manley had snitched on an escape attempt. He also said Manley had told him he was involved in the contract murder of someone named Owens.

Manley was a liar, a snitch, and an opportunist who would do anything to stay out of prison or shorten his sentence, Bates said.

At a motions hearing December 11 in front of Judge J. Frederick Motz, who would preside at trial, Cohen's attorney Paul Weiss tried to show that the train station search was illegal. If the arrest could be thrown out, the rest of the case would be, well, derailed.

He questioned Amtrak Police Officer Fred Wallace about some informal statements he had made earlier.

"Did you ever tell Mr. (Milton) Allen [Cohen's original attorney] during a conversation that, off the record, and I believe that was the line you used, that this was a bad search of Mr. Cohen and Mr. Manley?"

"I don't recall that," Wallace answered.

"And did you ever tell Mr. Allen that, in fact, prior to

the time that the warrant was issued and brought back and executed that one of the other officers had opened an end on the guitar case?"

"I don't recall saying that either."

"Now you and I had a brief conversation out in the hall prior to this hearing, isn't that correct?"

"Yes."

"And do you recall during the course of that conversation telling me that 'you were not going to lose your job over this'?"

"Did I make that statement?" Wallace asked back.

"Yes?" Weiss asked.

"I made that statement," Wallace admitted.

"What did you mean by that?"

"I was not going to lose my job over it. I did not mean anything about it."

A week later, James Manley testified about the search. He said he and Cohen did *not* give their consent to let the dogs search their luggage; and in addition, an Amtrak officer peeked into the luggage before the signed search warrant arrived.

"Officer Moss went over to the guitar case and bent it up and looked in it," Manley said.

"Did he say anything after he did that?" Weiss asked.

"Yeah. 'Jesus Christ, look at this'—pretty heavy exclamation. I thought he was talking to the people down the block somewhere. He screamed it."

"How did the other officers react to that?"

"Well, a couple of them started to look. Somebody, I don't know who it was, said, 'Don't look in there, don't dare look in that guitar case.'"

"Now, when you went to the back office, and the dog sniff occurred, how many minutes elapsed between the time that you went to that back office, and that dog sniff, approximately?"

"It wasn't very long, two minutes, three minutes. It wasn't long at all. Long enough for me and Sonny to tell them again they couldn't search our bags."

Either way Judge Motz ruled on the motion to suppress the arrest, the defense was going to win. If he

believed Manley was telling the truth and he tossed out
the arrests, the case was in big trouble. If he thought
Manley was lying, then the trial would be tainted by the
judge's failure to believe the sworn testimony of the
government's most important witness.

Motz turned down the motion to suppress. Manley
was lying.

Trial was set to begin January 19, 1988. At the end of
January 4, all the defense attorneys got the *Jencks*
material—about five hundred pages of grand jury testimony of witnesses who would appear for the government at trial, plus FBI "302" reports, outlining their
investigation. And more would come in the next few
days.

One of the 302s concerned James Raidy, whom
Luskin's defense had never heard of before. After reading it, Allen wrote another motion for severance, arguing
that Raidy's testimony about Cohen's escape attempt
would inflame the jury at a joint trial, unfairly to all of
Cohen's codefendants.

"It is the Government's choice. The statements made
by Cohen to Raidy are admissible against Cohen, but
introduction of those statements in a joint trial would
deny Paul Luskin and his codefendants a fair trial."

The government had to agree. They preferred to keep
all the codefendants in the same trial, so as a result, the
jury would not hear James Raidy.

Also on January 4, Bernstein wrote to all the lawyers
in the case that the FBI lab had begun comparing the
metal fragments removed from Marie Luskin's head to
the bullets seized from Cohen and Manley when they
were arrested. He would forward the results upon com-
pletion.

That was strange. Marie had told Hollywood Police,
as well as the FBI and the grand jury, that she had been
hit in the head. Bernstein earlier had also referred to her
assault in the same way. But Manley had testified Cohen
told him he shot her. Now the government was trying to
corroborate that.

The first step was viewing the fragments under
a microscope. FBI firearms examiner Charles Spaht

looked for spiral-shaped rifling marks, which guns cut onto bullets when they are fired. But the two fragments were much too small to see any—the largest was less than a tenth of a gram.

Next, the lab attempted to analyze the elements present. First they tried a test called x-ray fluorescence, in which x rays bombard a specimen so it will emit x rays itself. Because each element present will then give off x rays in a different proportion, it can be determined which elements are there.

The result was: both fragments were "essentially lead." Bullets are mostly lead, so that meant the fragments might have come from a bullet; then again, it didn't mean it for sure.

On the Sunday before trial was to begin, the FBI tried two additional methods that were more precise but worked on the same principles as the x-ray test: scanning electron microscopy, and neutron activation analysis.

Bullets vary greatly in their composition, not only by manufacturer but even from batch to batch. Still, the FBI hoped that by comparing the now-determined-lead fragments from Marie's scalp to the bullets seized from Cohen and Manley, they would get an elemental match. That would prove Marie was shot.

There were no matches.

On Wednesday January 20—the day of opening statements in trial, the government had another idea—if the lab couldn't determine that the fragments were from a bullet, perhaps a forensic pathologist could.

They called Dr. Charles Kokes, a state of Maryland medical examiner. The FBI gave him Marie's medical reports and x-rays of her head, and briefed him that lead fragments had been removed from her scalp.

Kokes looked it all over and said yes, her injury was most probably a gunshot wound.

He told the FBI the entrance wound was atypical, but the x-rays showed metal fragments consistent with fragments of a shattered bullet. The wound could have come from a hit on the head, but that was much less likely.

To Kokes, the topper was that the metal was lead. Blunt force trauma rarely left fragments behind.

The bullet had fragmented, he said, owing to one or

more of the following: either the bullet was faulty; a silencer had been used; the bullet was fired through another object, which slowed it down; or the bullet hit her at an angle.

Now at last, the prosecution had a theory that answered the defense—Cohen, the hired hit man, shot Marie Luskin. If it was only a robbery, why did he shoot her? And if it was a murder-for-hire, why go to all the trouble of getting in the house, then just hit her on the head?

FIVE

You're Going To Name the Business "Reitzes"?

The divorce trial opened December 28. For Paul to attend, two courts had to relax conditions: Federal Judge Motz allowed him out of Baltimore, but only in the custody of Alvin Entin, at whose home he slept; and Broward County Judge Nutaro temporarily waived her contempt order to have him arrested when he set foot in the state of Florida.

This would not be a jury trial. But even after all Paul's complaints that Nutaro was biased, he was still deflated when he saw that she had set up a metal detector outside the courtroom—something almost never seen in civil court. The first morning, only Paul and his side had to go through it. Entin complained, then Nutaro ordered everyone entering the courtroom to pass through.

Paul was the first witness, but with Gregg Bernstein present to observe, he didn't want to say much. He invoked his Fifth Amendment rights whenever a cross-examination question got too close to the criminal trial issues.

On January 3, Joe Luskin testified that after his experience in Baltimore having a family member as a partner, he resolved never again to share ownership of a business. He didn't even give his wife stock.

But Mildred badgered him for years to give Paul a one-third share, and he finally did it in 1984. However, the deal was "anytime I wanted the stock back, I could get it back."

Joe said Paul got power-hungry as soon as he took the stock. They fought continually. Paul had taken more and more responsibility in recent years, but now he tried to cut Joe out entirely of the business's day-to-day operation.

For instance, when Joe stuck his head into meetings with vendors, "I would get a look like 'What do you want?'

"He would tell me something and I would disagree. He would say now, 'Read my lips.' I resent very much that being used by anyone towards me."

Joe said he asked Paul to return his stock a number of times in 1984, and finally Paul told him, " 'Take your damn stock back,' if I may quote him."

Entin asked Joe if he would rehire Paul if the stores got out of bankruptcy.

"I would not even want Paul to be my employee," he said.

"Why?" asked Entin.

"Because I don't think he could ever take orders from his father."

"And would that be necessary?"

"It would be absolutely necessary for anybody working for me. I am not a hard employer, but I do insist on having the final authority on everything. At forty, I think he does not want to work for his father anymore."

In cross-examination January 4, Marie testified she was afraid of Paul, and that he had shoved her once.

"I think we were discussing him leaving the home and I was crying and asking him not to and I went to put my arms around him and he shoved me to the floor."

Entin reviewed her financial statements. While Paul was missing support payments, she canceled the kids' Disney Channel for lack of money, she said.

"During the same period of time you also kept two maids, did you not?" Entin asked.

"Yes," Marie said.

"And you could have afforded the $10 a month for the Disney Channel if you hadn't had a second maid?"

"It's a possibility," she said.

* * *

Entin further tried to show that Marie was less than the perfect mother she had made herself out to be. Some of his questions came from personal observations; Entin and his family had lived two doors from the Luskins in "the slum."

After Shana was born in 1977, "You were uncomfortable about having to make a choice between your career as a teacher and your responsibility as a mother?"

"No," said Marie.

"Isn't it a fact, Marie, that the reason you went to (therapist) Shirley Cohen was because you wanted a divorce at that time?"

"No, that isn't true at all."

"Isn't it a fact, Marie, that you wanted to give Shana to Paul and be a teacher on a full-time basis?"

"That's not true at all. I'll explain if you want me to, but if you don't want me to—"

"Please explain."

"I went to Shirley because I was teaching. I'm like a perfectionist, I want to do everything well. Here I was, I wanted to be a super teacher, I wanted to be a super new mom, I wanted to be a super wife, and I couldn't handle all the pressure and all that, and I couldn't get all my papers graded and change the diapers and use the special soap for the baby. And I just wanted to do everything right and it just made me nervous."

"Mrs. Luskin, so the Court doesn't get a misapprehension of the terrible and tremendous pressure that you were under at that point in time, wouldn't it be fair to tell the Court that during this period of time you hired a day maid, who stayed with Shana from nine in the morning until five at night?"

"We had a housekeeper come in four days a week while I was teaching. On Fridays my mom and my grandfather came to the house and took care of Shana."

Marie said she learned early on in her marriage to be compliant. "If you didn't listen to what Paul said, there was going to be a problem."

"That's true, too," Entin agreed. "If we were to characterize Paul Luskin, would pigheaded be a good word?"

"Paul liked to get his own way."

"Obstinate?"

"You're using your own terminology. When I lived with Paul he was stiff-toed. I learned to shut up. I learned to make peace and to do it his way, it was just easier than fighting about it."

"Was Paul a liar?"

"I didn't know Paul to be a liar when we were married."

"Was he a braggart?"

"No, I didn't think he was a braggart."

"You didn't think that Paul exaggerated things?"

"No."

"Marie, you were hurt, obviously, as a result of the affair; were you not?"

"Yes, I was."

"And isn't it a fact that your determination from the time you filed your initial divorce or dissolution complaint was to punish Paul?"

"No. I didn't mean to punish Paul."

"Isn't it a fact that from the very first time that you filed in this case you have asked for one hundred percent of the marital assets?"

Franklin objected.

"Didn't you ask today, or tell this Court that you want it all except for the Luskin name?" Entin asked.

"Yes, I don't want the Luskin name," she said.

"You're going to name the business Reitzes," he cracked, a reference to her maiden name.

Entin went over Marie's demands, starting with all the real estate, including the marital home.

"In addition to that, you want $8,000 a month in support, do you not?"

"That would be nice."

"You want three million dollars worth of something from Joe and Mildred Luskin; do you not?"

"Yes."

"You want one hundred percent of everything, do you not, Mrs. Luskin? Yes or no?"

"Yes," she said.

"And isn't the reason you want one hundred percent

of everything is because you're trying to punish him for the affair?"

"No, no, I need it for my security, me and for my girls. I mean, he hasn't paid any support. My husband's not going to make any child support or alimony no matter what any court tells him to do, he's not going to listen to anybody."

On January 6, Diane Yariv testified about a night in July 1985—three months before the divorce began—when she was a guest at the Luskins' home.

"In the middle of the conversation, Marie said, 'So-and-so down the street just got a divorce or a settlement of $8,000 a month.' A couple minutes later, she repeated it.

"Paul looked at Marie and said, 'I just walked in and in the last five minutes you mentioned divorce twice. Have I missed something?'"

"What did Marie say after that?" asked Entin.

"She said, 'Well, if we got a divorce, I could get $8,000 a month, too.'"

The trial lasted eight days and ended January 8. Paul's attorneys had just eleven days in between to prepare for the first day of the criminal trial.

Barry Franklin submitted his written closing argument on January 15.

"Paul's continuing crusade of aberrational and repugnant conduct must be compared against Marie Luskin's years of dedication to husband and family raising two beautiful, well adjusted children despite these terrible circumstances. Marie worked as a school teacher while Paul was in law school, worked occasionally for Luskin's, Inc., went on business trips with Paul and she gave back to her community through volunteer service and significant charitable work.

"The instant fact pattern cries out for a result of nothing less than the remaining, identifiable assets being awarded to the wife.

"There is ample case law justification and authority for this . . . Given the various types of misconduct and fraud perpetrated by Paul resulting in the dissipation of marital assets and increased financial need of his wife, an award of 100% of the marital assets to Marie, implemented by way of equitable distribution or under the guise of lump sum alimony, would clearly be endorsed by the Florida Supreme Court.

"In conclusion, Marie respectfully requests that all of the remaining assets to be awarded to her by way of either or both equitable distribution and lump sum alimony; that Paul Luskin be obligated to pay $4,000 per month child support ($2,000 for each child until each child reaches the age of majority); that Marie Luskin be awarded $4,000 per month non-taxable, rehabilitative alimony for a period of five years, even if she should remarry before the expiration of the five year period; and after the five years, for Marie to receive $2,000 per month, non-taxable; and a final judgment against Paul for all temporary support arrearages totalling approximately $120,000 plus interest."

On February 3, while the criminal case was in progress, Judge Nutaro ruled.

She gave Marie sole parental responsibility of the children. "The wife has been an excellent, nurturing parent for both children, at all times, particularly during the more than two years that this marriage has been in turmoil and Paul Luskin has been away from the home. Both the current and the former guardian ad litem agree that the children are generally well adjusted, doing well in school and their affections have not been alienated against their father or grandparents, despite the horrible surrounding circumstances. This is the best tribute to Marie Luskin's child-rearing ability and devotion to her children. At present, and for most of the time this action has been before this Court, Paul Luskin has not demonstrated the appropriate fitness and conduct necessary to be afforded any form of parental responsibility."

Nutaro also suspended Paul's visitation rights, pending a "comprehensive mental examination/evaluation" by a psychiatrist.

The judge agreed with Marie that Paul's income from Luskin's included large amounts of unreported cash, and that Paul's parents staged his firing from the business. She didn't believe his poor-mouthing: "The greater weight of the evidence demonstrates that if Paul Luskin's financial ability has changed during the last two years, it has been as a result of voluntary, temporary, and conspiratorial acts."

Nutaro wrote that Paul's actions affected how she distributed the marital assets: "The misconduct and wrongdoing perpetrated by Paul Luskin was willful, continuing, malicious, and conspiratorial, in part based upon the solicitation and assistance of his parents." She said both Paul's transfer of the $230,000 to pay off the house note and his divestment of Luskin's stock were fraudulent.

She also said that Paul hid "large sums of cash and gold coins" just before the litigation began, and had the opportunity to remove them from the business safe in the few minutes after he was served with divorce papers.

This is what Judge Nutaro considered "equitable distribution." Marie got:

The house and personal property in it; one hundred percent of Paul's one-third interest in Luskin's, which she said was worth $2.5 million at the time the divorce was filed. (She admitted the current value had dissipated but only due to a "calculated and conspiratorial effort on the part of the Luskin family.") The full amount in cash was payable by Paul; proceeds from the sales of their investment and vacation real estate, worth $700,000; her Mercedes; the value of their $150,000 life insurance policy; alimony of $2,000 a month for three years; child support of $4,000; past support arrearages of $134,400; and attorney's fees.

Paul got: the $230,000 he transferred to his parents, which the judge ordered his parents to return to him—although Nutaro implied that once they did, it would be seized to pay his support arrearages; all the cash Nutaro said he concealed, but was never proven to exist; his jewelry; and $2,000 of miscellaneous stock.

That was a shutout if there ever was one.

Nutaro couldn't resist a parting shot. She issued a permanent injunction for Paul to keep away from Marie, but in doing so, she seemed to make her own judgment on the criminal case's merits: "The greater weight of the evidence demonstrates the well-founded fear of Marie Luskin being afraid of Paul Luskin. The likelihood of irreparable injury is more than imminent."

During a recess in the federal courtroom, a reporter for the *Baltimore Evening Sun* asked Paul for his reaction.

"I'm thrilled. I'm a free man, whatever that means."

"He wants his maiden name back," Entin joked.

On February 12, still in the midst of the criminal trial, Entin petitioned Nutaro to reconsider.

"In light of these findings of fact, the Court achieved an almost logical impossibility. The Court apparently believed almost every fact and witness presented by the wife and willfully refused to believe every fact and witness presented by the husband. The Court in effect conducted *ex parte* hearings, listening to only one side of every issue and always the same side at that. Husband and his witnesses could have achieved the same result or better by not appearing at all.

"The Court has aimed its wrath at the husband and scored a direct hit on the children . . . But where the Court really errs is in the distribution of property between the parties. The Court ignores each and every exhibit inconsistent with the wife's theories, the testimonies of each and every witness for the husband, and each and every direct contradiction of the unsupported testimony of the wife in order to arrive at the conclusion that the husband is lying or incorrect on every point. This is a logical absurdity.

"The Court concludes that huge amounts of money were skimmed (from Luskin's). The Court totally fails to mention the Cullen report commissioned by the U.S.

Bankruptcy Court which totally rejected this possibility." As for her finding that the family intentionally dissipated the company's value, "It assumes Luskin's went into bankruptcy for the sole purpose of cheating Marie Luskin." That was contrary to the best interests of all the family members and employees who made their living from Luskin's, he wrote.

"The Court paints an incomplete picture of wife's role as perfect mother and housekeeper, giving up her career and taking care of the house and the children. What the Court fails to mention is two full time maids Marie had . . . She was hardly the long-suffering hard-working mother the court portrays her to be."

Entin referred to the money the judge awarded Paul as the "non-existent cash hoard."

"Surely the husband's current assets and income cannot support the Court's award in alimony and child support. In effect, the Court is *deliberately* guaranteeing that the husband will be found in contempt. Mythical money cannot pay the bills."

Four days later, Nutaro denied Entin's motion.

SIX

"No Other Florist"

The criminal trial began Tuesday January 19, 1988, with jury selection. The next day was opening argument, beginning with Gregg Bernstein for the prosecution.

Bernstein began by detailing Cohen and Manley's arrest at the train station. When police pulled them aside, they expected to find drugs, but instead found a cache of guns.

"Oh, and the smell of the narcotics that the dogs had found. But contrary to what the defendants and their counsel may try to distract you into believing and focusing on throughout the trial, this case is not about drugs.

"What it is about, is this man, Paul Benjamin Luskin, the defendant in this case, and how he hired and conspired with the other defendants in order to murder Mr. Luskin's wife, Marie Luskin, to end what had become a bitter and contested divorce proceeding."

Bernstein discussed some of the low points of the divorce. "Finally, in late 1986, with no end in sight to his domestic problems which had caused the demise of the family business, unable to find a job, unable to even see his children or visit with his parents in Florida without risking the fear of being arrested, the defendant desperately sought a way out of his problems by eliminating who he perceived to be their source, and that is his wife, Marie Luskin."

This was the same day the FBI interviewed Charles

Kokes, so Bernstein skirted whether Marie was hit or shot. He said Cohen "brutally attacked her" and fled.

"Does this sound like some movie script, television murder mystery? I wish I could tell this is all it is, but unfortunately it's the truth.

"Now at the outset, I want to be very up front with you. This is not a case in which a witness is going to walk into this courtroom and point a finger at Paul Luskin and say, 'I saw that man try to kill his wife'—what we call the so-called smoking gun.

"The defendant, you will learn, is an educated, intelligent businessman. He was far too smart and suspicious to leave an easy trail of guilt for people like you and me to follow. People who plan to murder their wives seldom leave a road map for others to follow.

"Instead, what we will present to you over the next few weeks are the many pieces of this puzzle, which through great effort we were able to collect, and it will be your job to put those pieces together.

"And at the end, the picture you will be left with will not be a very pretty one.

"But your job is not as difficult as it may seem because there is someone who will help you put these pieces together, and that is James Manley. Mr. Manley was there. He is the top of the puzzle box, the one to provide you with the overall picture of the criminal intent of these defendants.

"Now let me just say something very briefly about Mr. Manley. As you might expect, he has a criminal record. Mr. Manley has entered into a plea agreement, which in return for his plea of guilty, he has agreed to cooperate with the government and testify.

"The defendants and their lawyers may make much of Mr. Manley's prior record and the fact that he has entered into this plea agreement. Watch them. They will argue to you that Mr. Manley is lying to you, that he made all this up in order to spare himself.

"It is important that you carefully judge the credibility of the testimony of Mr. Manley just as you should judge the credibility of all the witnesses who may testify in this case both for the government and for the defense,

and what motivations they may have to tell the truth or
to lie."

Next came Alvin Entin, for Luskin:

"Ladies and gentlemen of the jury, what you're going
to hear in this case, at least as it relates to Paul and Marie
Luskin, is an American tragedy. There are two victims
in this case. Marie Luskin is clearly a victim. Somebody,
we don't know who and we certainly had nothing to do
with it, but somebody hit Marie Luskin on March 9 of
1987. Nobody is going to dispute that.

"The other part of the tragedy is that Paul Luskin had
nothing to do with it and the evidence will establish that
he had nothing to do with it, and the tragedy is he is here
being forced to answer for charges with which he had
nothing to do. Circumstances have conspired to bring
Paul Luskin to this court, no act of his own, and no act
that the government will be able to establish."

Entin said the evidence would show that the codefendants were involved in drug trafficking, which explained
Cohen and Manley's excursions to Florida.

"You will understand that the purpose of the trips
back and forth had nothing to do with hurting Marie
Luskin but had to do with drug traffic, and you will
begin to understand, when you look at the records of
James Manley, that he is a thug and a thief and that he
was in fact persuaded to go down there and rob the rich
lady living in the biggest house in Emerald Hills.

"One thing Mr. Bernstein didn't tell you that the
evidence would prove—and I suggest to you it won't—
is that there is any connection or any phone call, any
meeting, any getting together that he can put Paul
Luskin in with regard to this case. All Mr. Bernstein's
evidence will show as it relates to Paul Luskin and this
case is he's known Joe Liberto, who may have had loose
lips and talked about the divorce, and that he was going
through a difficult divorce. That's it. That's the total
evidence you're going to hear about Paul Luskin, not a
thing more."

Entin called the March 9 assault a robbery. He conceded Bernstein was right that Cohen wanted to murder
Marie after it.

"Why? Because of the fact that she might recognize Mr. Cohen. He wants to eliminate the witness to the robbery, and he wants to eliminate Mrs. Luskin. Why? Because he's constantly back and forth to Florida, and if he's down there again on one of his drug deals, maybe somebody will recognize him and have him arrested for the robbery and assault.

"Mr. Manley will tell you he has never met Paul Luskin, he has never spoken to Paul Luskin, he has never seen Paul Luskin, he has never received a nickel from Paul Luskin, not one penny from Paul Luskin. As a matter of fact, the evidence in this case will not establish Paul Luskin paying one cent to any individual for doing any kind of damage to Marie Luskin.

"You will hear evidence from Mr. Manley about what Mr. Cohen allegedly told him, and His Honor, the Judge, will tell you later on in his instructions, dealing first with Mr. Manley, that he is an accomplice, and accomplice testimony, the Judge will tell you, has to be received with caution and great care because there is a motive to testify untruthfully in regard to an accomplice statement."

Entin said that after Manley was caught, he didn't "immediately get religion and go to the government and tell them about this terrible thing he was involved in. No, the evidence will establish that he waited eight weeks in the jail putting this tale together to try and implicate Paul Luskin, the businessman from Florida, in an effort to get a free ride here in Maryland because he was already a two-time loser and was looking at life without parole.

"Secondly, ladies and gentlemen, Marie Luskin will testify. Granted she was hit over the head. Granted she was hurt. Granted she was the victim of a robbery. But, ladies and gentlemen of the jury, the evidence will establish that she has a motive to come into this courtroom and have her husband convicted."

Entin said he would enter into evidence what Marie was asking for in the divorce. "She's not asking for 10 percent, not 20 percent, not 50 percent. Ladies and gentlemen, what she's asking for is one hundred percent of the marital assets, and on top of that, she wants

$4,000 a month in child support and $4,000 a month in rehabilitative alimony. And not content with that, she has sued Joe and Mildred Luskin for an additional three and a half million dollars.

"Marie Luskin knows if the jury here convicts Paul Luskin, she is going to be a very, very wealthy lady, and the evidence will establish that hell hath no fury, hell hath no fury."

Jimmy Liberto's attorney Howard Cardin also attacked the credibility of James Manley.

"Let me point out to you what you haven't heard. On May 20 of 1987, right during the heart of everything, Jimmy Liberto and his common-law wife Darlene Armstrong, who have been living together for many years, were sitting at home, and you'll hear that Jimmy gets up in the morning and he reads the sports section, loves the sports, drinks a cup of coffee, and was so doing when there was a knock on the door.

"Darlene Armstrong gets up. She answers the door and there's a man there and the man says, 'Is Jimmy here?' And she says, 'Wait a minute,' and she walks back into the living room. Jimmy walks to answer the door, and the man takes a gun and goes to shoot Jimmy Liberto. A stranger goes to shoot Jimmy Liberto. A struggle ensues, the gun goes off, the bullet is in the floor—the police recover the bullet—the man runs away.

"Think of that. Scared? Absolutely. Darlene Armstrong and Jimmy Liberto, people stalking them. He doesn't know who the person was. The government does. Mr. Connolly does. He knows it's Jimmy Manley who came to kill, came to shoot Jimmy Liberto. Does he tell them? No. Lets them walk around, petrified.

"This is James Manley. This is the person that the prosecution would rest its case upon.

"The government pushes off or pushes aside his criminal record for armed robbery, burglary, you name it, James Manley who comes to murder Jimmy Liberto. If I might adopt comments that were made by other counsel, after a person commits a crime, he is fearful of being recognized, he is fearful of being caught, he has a motive to get rid of that person.

"What do we see here? This man, James Manley, is the person who is going to be marched up to a chair, to point a finger at someone, the person he needs to get rid of, because he tried to kill Jimmy Liberto. In case you have any doubt, let me tell you the evidence will not only show that once we were given a photograph of Mr. Manley he was identified, but Mr. Manley went and told Agent Connolly and everyone else, 'Yes, I'm the guy that shot him.'

"Just think how wonderful it is for Mr. Manley under the circumstances that have been presented. And you know the worst part? He should be charged with attempted murder, carrying a life sentence here in Maryland, and you will find and the evidence will show: Has he been charged? No. Has he been arrested for the offense? No. But other charges against him in Baltimore County have been dismissed or stetted. Charges pending against him in Baltimore City will be put aside."

Cardin said Jimmy Liberto was one of the nicest guys around, and that his restaurant, Palughi's, probably served the best food in Baltimore's Little Italy.

"You've heard that Mr. Manley wants to kill him and I suspect Mr. Manley will tell you the reason was because Sonny Cohen wanted him killed.

"Sonny Cohen wants him killed. Manley wants him killed. Luskin wants to make him a drug dealer. The government wants to put him in jail.

"James Manley, I suggest to you, is the name that should be on the indictment papers before you today. You heard the clerk read *United States versus Paul Luskin.* I suggest to you, ladies and gentlemen, what we're really talking about is James Manley."

Later that day, testimony began with Baltimore City Police Detective Dorsey McVicker, present at the arrest of Cohen and Manley.

In cross-examination, Steve Allen began the assault on Manley's credibility.

"Now let me ask you this. Is it your testimony that while you were all together in the lobby at Amtrak, that you or someone in your presence asked Mr. Cohen and Mr. Manley whether or not the dogs would be permitted to sniff their luggage?" Allen asked.

"Yes, Officer Burns," answered McVicker.

"And Mr. Manley, along with Mr. Cohen, said yes; is that right?"

"Yes."

"All right. Now, let me ask you; if Mr. Manley were to deny that and say he did not give consent, would he be lying?"

"What's that?"

"If Mr. Manley were to say under oath that he did not give consent to have the luggage sniffed by the dogs, would he be lying?"

"Yes."

Allen also asked if any of the police officers looked inside Manley's guitar case before the search warrant was obtained.

"Absolutely not," said McVicker.

"If Mr. Manley, to the best of your knowledge, said that any police officer before the search warrant was obtained peeked in, would Mr. Manley be lying?"

"To my knowledge, sir, I typed the warrant in the presence of Mr. Cohen and Mr. Manley, the guitar case was on the table next to the left of me, and when I left that office to get the warrant signed, no one had even touched the guitar case."

"Have any of the police officers who were with you that day ever told you that anyone peeked into this case?"

"No."

"Okay. Well, now based on your knowledge, based on what you saw and what the other police officers told you, if Mr. Manley were to testify that someone peeked into that, would he be lying?"

"To the best of my knowledge, no one looked inside that guitar case."

"So he would be lying?"

"Yes."

"That's all I wanted," said Allen.

* * *

Allen then honed in on another Manley inconsistency. He gave McVicker a Luzerne Avenue address, but later that day he gave a different address to the Baltimore City Jail.

"He gave an address of 190 Westcott Road in Baltimore; is that correct?" Allen asked.

"Yes, sir, it is."

"Okay. So on July 30, Mr. Manley gave two conflicting addresses; is that right?"

"Yes, sir, he did."

"Do you know if 190 Westcott Road exists in Baltimore?" (It didn't.)

"No, sir."

"If it didn't exist, that would be a lie again, wouldn't it? If there is no 190 Westcott Road in the city of Baltimore, that would be a lie that Mr. Manley said when he said, 'That's my address.' "

"I guess it would be," said McVicker.

"Now in your experience, what's a rip-off?" Allen asked. "Do you know what a rip-off is in the context of drugs? Does that term have any special meaning?"

"I guess it's when you're supposed to purchase drugs and someone either takes your money or your drugs."

"Does that happen from time to time in drug transactions?"

"I would guess it does."

"Okay. And based on your experience, is it unusual for drug dealers to have possession of guns?"

"No."

"Drugs and guns go together like love and marriage, don't they?"

"Objection," said coprosecutor J. Sedwick "Wick" Sollers III.

"They're something that is found often together; is that right?" Allen asked again.

"At times."

"Okay. It's not unusual to have drug dealers who are doing a drug transaction to have weapons with them at the time the transaction occurs; is that right?"

"That's correct."

* * *

The next day, Thursday, January 21, the government called Barry Franklin to talk about the divorce.

. After arguing against Franklin in the divorce trial, Alvin Entin relished the chance to confront him on the witness stand in cross. Almost immediately, the two went after each other.

"Mr. Franklin, isn't it a fact, sir, that as of the fifteenth day of January 1988, you on behalf of Marie Luskin are asking for one hundred percent of the identifiable marital assets?" Entin asked.

"Of those remaining, that is correct," said Franklin.

"You're asking for him to pay $4,000 per month child support?"

"Yes."

"And $4,000 a month alimony for at least five years; correct?"

"Yes."

"Is it your testimony, sir, that he was making $8,000 a month from Mr. Lipsitz? Is that your testimony?"

"No, I never said that."

"Was he making $5,000 a month from Mr. Lipsitz?"

"Not that I know of."

"Was he making $4,000 a month from Mr. Lipsitz?"

"Not that I know of."

"Was he making $3,000 a month from Mr. Lipsitz?"

"He may have."

"So you're asking that he pay approximately $5,000 a month more than he was making in the last job that you've been able to identify he had, isn't that correct? That calls for a yes or a no."

Franklin turned to the judge. "Your Honor, I cannot answer that question with a yes or no."

"If he says he can't answer with a yes or no, that's fine," Entin said. Then he continued:

"Now isn't it a fact that you and Mrs. Luskin have a vested interest in getting or in having it determined that Paul Luskin is somehow responsible for the attack on his wife?"

"Objection," said Gregg Bernstein.

"Wait, wait. Say that again," said Franklin.

"Doesn't your request for a hundred percent of the

marital assets depend on convincing someone that Paul Luskin was behind the attack on his wife?''

''No.''

''Didn't you say in your closing argument—you cited to the court a case called *D'Arc versus D'Arc,* did you not?''

''Absolutely.''

''In justification of asking for one hundred percent of the assets?''

''Yes, that's partial justification.''

''Yes. And wasn't the basis of that case that you cited in your own closing argument that it was all right to deprive the husband of all marital assets where he attempted to murder his wife; isn't that what you put in there?''

''That was one of five cases cited in that same context,'' Franklin said.

Marie Luskin testified against her husband on Monday, January 25.

In direct examination, after she described her assault, Wick Sollers asked her if she could pick out the person who committed it.

''I don't know. I'd really have to look around,'' she said.

''Would it be helpful for you to get down and look around?''

''I'll try.''

Marie walked around the courtroom slowly and dramatically, looking at every face in the room. Then she stopped in front of Paul, seated at the defense table.

''I can't tell who it is. I can't,'' she said.

At the grand jury, Marie volunteered that she had been hit during her assault. But at trial she didn't. Sollers asked if she had ever found any fragments in her dressing area, and Marie said she found one little piece of metal on her vanity. She didn't know how it got there, or if someone had found it and put it there.

''About when, do you recall?''

''I'm not sure how long afterward it was.''

"What did you do with that fragment?"

"I remember looking at this funny-shaped piece of metal. It was dark brown, about the size of a dime, and it had like a little lump in it. I can remember fingering it, wondering what it was, I had no idea what it was, and I kept it on my vanity where I keep all my little tiny perfume bottles and samples, and I kept it there for the longest time and then one day when I was dusting and everything, I threw it away."

"Why did you throw it away?"

"I didn't know what it was, just an ugly piece of metal."

"Mrs. Luskin," said Sollers, "is it fair to say that you were under the impression that you had been struck in the head?"

"Yes," she said.

Cohen's attorney Paul Weiss cross-examined Marie first. Noting Marie had testified that her assailant wore a short-sleeved shirt, he asked had she noticed anything unusual about his arms. She said no.

Next was Alvin Entin's turn. After they had faced each other in the divorce trial, Entin privately groused that everything he threw at her came back line drives. As a result, his criminal trial cross was somewhat milder.

At least Entin had managed the best line of the divorce trial during Marie's testimony, but this time, Marie was even the winner of that. When discussing the meetings of the Single Parent Support Group, Entin asked, "And in all candor, you had no desire to get to know Susan Davis any better, did you, ma'am?"

"Oh, I already knew Susan Davis well enough."

"And probably she had no desire to get to know you any better either, correct?"

"She already had what she wanted, she didn't need to know me any better."

On Thursday, January 28, James Manley testified all day. But two nights before, he threatened to renege when he learned that Jim Liberto had filed a $180 million civil suit against him for attempted murder.

To rescue his case, Gregg Bernstein offered Manley another deal—he could have immunity for anything self-incriminating he would say in court about the attempted murder. That way, no other court could use his testimony. Manley accepted, and Judge Motz signed the agreement.

Bernstein began by asking Manley to outline his original deal with the government. He said by pleading to possession of an unregistered silencer—which exposed him to a maximum penalty of ten years and a $25,000 fine—and promising to testify truthfully, the rest of the counts against him would be dropped.

In regard to his pending Maryland state charges, Manley said, the U.S. Attorney's office didn't have authority to drop them, but they had promised to use their influence to help him.

Next, Manley testified to his 1978 conviction for post office burglary, and forgery of postal money orders. But because Judge Motz had ruled earlier to exclude everything more than ten years old in Manley's record, that was the only specific conviction the jury would hear of. Nor would they hear that he had been arrested twenty-eight times since age sixteen.

In the remainder of his direct examination, Manley repeated what he had told the grand jury, some of it in greater detail. However, in reviewing his earlier testimony, he said there was a transcription error where it read that after he and Sonny failed to kill Marie in July, they went back to the hotel "and did some drugs."

"Do you do drugs?" Bernstein asked.

"No, sir," Manley answered. He hadn't done drugs since 1970, when he did heroin.

The fireworks were in cross-examination, beginning with Russell White, for Luskin.

He began with Manley's pending case in Anne Arundel County. "You skipped bail, didn't you, on that case?" White asked.

"That was my father's property, yes, sir, I did," Manley said.

"So you knew you were a fugitive at that time, is that correct?"

"Yes, sir."

A little later, White asked about the attempted murder of Jimmy Liberto.

"Sonny told me that we wouldn't have to go to Florida, we wouldn't have to do no more killings, if I'd kill Liberto, he'd give me $10,000 cash the minute it was done, and do it before Sunday night.

"So I questioned, 'What if I do it Monday morning?' He said, 'No, because I already paid him for my week's supply of drugs and I'm out 20, sometimes $25,000.' So he said, 'Don't touch the man until the following Thursday, only look for him on weekends unless I tell you otherwise.'"

Manley said he didn't really want to kill Liberto—Manley said he himself wasn't a killer—and that's why he shot at the floor. He did that much because he wanted Cohen to think he had made an effort.

"Were you afraid of Sonny?" White asked.

"In a way, yes, sir, I was."

"Why?"

"Because at any minute he could change his mind and have me killed or kill me himself. I was very vulnerable."

"Did you think Sonny was very reliable?"

"Sonny's reliable, you know, he'll give his word, he'll keep it, but if it benefits him to have me killed, I would have been killed."

Next, White asked about Manley's August signed statement swearing that the drugs and guns he and Cohen were arrested with were strictly Manley's. Manley had testified earlier it was supposed to help Cohen get a bail reduction. In return, Cohen promised him $5,000, which he would have used to get a lawyer.

"For that amount of money, you were willing to make a false oath?"

"With the understanding that when I gave that to the lawyer's clerk, that if Sonny didn't appear in court, we were going to retract that statement," Manley said. But when Sonny didn't give him the money or get a lawyer for him, Manley said, "I knew I was being tricked. I didn't know what was going on and decided to get out of it the best way I could."

"Do you know how much time you saved yourself by agreeing to testify?"

"That would be up to the sentencing judge. I know what the maximum sentences are. Anywhere from thirty-five to ninety years."

"So you made a pretty good deal, didn't you?" White asked.

"Yes, sir."

Cohen's attorney Paul Weiss asked Manley whether Maryland's new career criminal statutes had influenced his decision to make a plea deal. Manley admitted that Anne Arundel County had served him with papers showing he was eligible for at least the three-time loser penalty.

"And you were aware of that when you signed your plea agreement, is that true?"

"Yes, sir."

"And you wanted to do everything you could to avoid the possibility of then spending the next twenty-five years of your life in prison; isn't that true?"

"There was enough right here in this case to give me twenty-five years in prison."

"You wanted to do whatever you could?"

"The best deal for Jimmy, that's what it's called," Manley said.

Weiss noted an apparent contradiction regarding the attempted murder of Jimmy Liberto.

"If Sonny is taking a contract, as you say, for $30,000, is it your testimony that he wanted you to kill the source of his contract?"

"Not kill the source of his contract, he wouldn't have to do it, whatever money he'd collected was his already, plus he don't have to pay for the drugs. He was going to make out any way it went."

"Well, how was he going to make out any way?"

"Make out, if he owed Liberto $20,000 and Liberto comes up dead, he don't have to finish the contract and he's got that $20,000 in his pocket."

"So is it your testimony that he didn't want to finish the contract?"

"I don't think it mattered either way. One of them had to be finished, Liberto or Marie Luskin."

Manley had testified on direct that he and Cohen were worried about being caught with the sawed-off shotgun among their arsenal of four weapons, so they threw it off the William Lehman Causeway—the bridge near the Marco Polo between the beach and the mainland. After Manley told the FBI about it, police divers in Miami found it.

"And the murder, you know, carries the death penalty in Florida, correct?"

"Yes, sir."

"And you became nervous because you heard that there was a ten-year penalty on having a sawed-off shotgun?"

"That's an automatic penalty," Manley answered. "We were both worried about that shotgun. We get stopped on a spot check, you can always make a deal with the government or whatever for a minor sentence or a lesser sentence for a handgun, but a sawed-off shotgun, it's mandatory."

"Isn't it true, Mr. Manley, that Mr. Cohen stopped giving you money and stopped supplying money to your wife because you were using that money to buy cocaine in the jail?"

"That's not true," he said.

"Were you shooting cocaine—"

"No, sir."

"—in the Baltimore City Jail?"

"No, sir."

"When was the last time you took cocaine?"

"I can't remember the last time."

"Well, within the last two years?"

"Longer ago than that."

"Three years?"

"I have used cocaine, but I was not addicted to it."

"Well, I'm asking you when was the last time?"

"I don't remember."

"Was it within the last five years?"

"I have used cocaine in the last five years, yes, sir."

"Didn't you testify on your direct examination or cross that you hadn't taken any narcotics in the last ten years?"

"To me it wasn't narcotics," Manley said.

"Cocaine is not a narcotic?"

"Well, it is legally and all that, but like I said, I wasn't—I think the word was addicted. I haven't been addicted since 1970."

"How'd you use the cocaine when you used it? Did you shoot it in your arm?"

"Yes, sir."

"But it's your testimony that while you were at the Baltimore City Jail, you did not shoot any cocaine into your arm?"

"That's my testimony, yes, sir."

Manley's second day on the stand was Monday, February 1. But first, in sidebar, the Court addressed Ruth Walters, who was very upset that Luskin's defense had quoted love letters Manley had written to her in 1982.

Walters told the judge, "I don't know how they got my letters, I don't know who told them they could read them, but I think they've put my life in jeopardy with this Manley person. He's sitting there admitting that he was trying to kill somebody. And I used to go with him. I live in his neighborhood. I don't want him to stalk me."

Steve Allen tried to explain to the judge that he had gotten the letters from one of Walters's friends. "I think one of Ms. Walters's major concerns is that somehow Mr. Manley be told that the letters did not come from her."

"Well, he wouldn't tell the truth anyway," Walters said.

"No, the government could say that the letters—"

"He wouldn't do it. I know him too well."

"Judge, what happened was—"

"He's a habitual liar."

Motz told Walters that Manley would be informed she didn't turn over the letters voluntarily.

"And that's supposed to protect me?"

"We'll do the best we can."

"They're protecting him. Is somebody going to protect me from Mr. Manley?"

"No, that certainly is not within the authority of this Court," Motz said.

"Mr. Manley is in jail," volunteered Steve Allen.

"That doesn't mean anything," she said.

When testimony resumed, Howard Cardin bored into Manley's story of the murder attempt on his client.

"Mr. Manley, isn't it true that in your own mind, you believed that you would never be charged with the attempted murder of Jimmy Liberto if he were convicted in this case?"

"I never thought about it. I never thought I would be charged with it, period, whether I testify here or not. Until this trial started, I wasn't identified as the assailant."

"You are indeed guilty of the attempted murder of Jimmy Liberto, aren't you?"

"That's your opinion."

"And if you are convicted of the attempted murder of Jimmy Liberto, you are then eligible to be convicted as a four-time loser, aren't you?"

"I guess it's four, I don't know."

"And as a person convicted of felonies or crimes of violence, the sentence that must be imposed, is it not, is life imprisonment without parole; isn't that right, Mr. Manley?"

"I have no idea what the penalty is."

"And isn't that all the more reason why you said you made the best deal you could for Jimmy?"

"Objection, Your Honor," said Bernstein.

"Sustained. He said he didn't know," said Judge Motz.

In recross, Russell White asked "What kind of a person are you, Mr. Manley? You're not a killer, you're just a person who assists other people in killing, or what?"

"Very first time I've ever been involved in anything like that," Manley said.

"Mr. Manley, each time you were asked to kill, you never said, 'No, I can't do that, I'm not a killer,' did you?"

"I did say that, I told Sonny I wasn't a killer."

"Well, did you give Sonny the impression then that you believed you just weren't going to, you know, take any part in this killing?"

"I agreed to help Sonny, to go down there and help him out."

"Help him what?"

"Help him with the murder of Marie Luskin."

"So then that seemed to be all right with you, as long as you didn't have to pull the trigger, it was okay; is that what you mean by you're not a killer?"

"That's—maybe that's what I mean, yes."

"Okay. But you don't have any reluctance to see somebody else kill them and assist them in killing them?"

"Objection," said Bernstein.

"Overruled," said Motz.

"Correct?"

"It meant nothing to me one way or the other," Manley said.

Howard Cardin got in the last lick in his recross. He recalled Manley's testimony that he knew someone else had been arrested for the attempted murder of Liberto.

"That was my understanding, yes, sir."

"And you were going to let him go to jail?"

"Yes. If he was innocent, he would have been found not guilty."

"That's what the courts are for, right?" Cardin asked.

"That's what it's for," Manley said.

Charles Kokes testified on Wednesday, February 3, that in his opinion, Marie Luskin had been shot.

Alvin Entin's cross-examination pointed out that Kokes had drawn that conclusion without examining Marie in person. Entin also called attention to the emergency room doctor's report that he had looked for black powder around the wound, and found none. The presence of black powder would have proved that she was shot.

Then Entin suggested some alternative explanations for how lead fragments might have gotten into her scalp.

"Now, doctor, are you familiar through your experience with how a blackjack is made?"

"Just generally," answered Kokes.

"Isn't it a fact, sir, that it's usually some sort of leather or leather-type container that contains lead fillings and lead shavings?"

"Yes."

"Okay. And a blackjack is a weapon that is used to hit people over the head, isn't that correct?"

"That is correct."

"And a faulty or a torn blackjack might leave a lead fragment in a scalp, correct sir—not that you've seen it, but it could?"

"Yes."

"What about a lead pipe, have you ever been familiar with people using lead pipes as a blunt instrument to hit somebody else over the head with?"

"It's not common nowadays, lead pipe not being commonly used."

"More often used in the game of Clue where Colonel Mustard hit Mr. Scarlet over the head with a lead pipe in the conservatory, correct?"

"Yes."

"Okay. But it has been used?"

"Oh, yes, sure."

"And if it was jagged or cut or torn, it could leave a fragment?"

"Sure."

Kokes reiterated that the cause of the wound was still most likely a gunshot.

"But your opinion does not exclude other possibilities which might also have left lead in a scalp wound. Correct, sir?" Entin probed.

"That is correct."

"Okay. And if there was some basis other than the gunshot which would have left the lead, it certainly would have been consistent with the trauma that you've identified to Mrs. Luskin's head, correct?"

"That's possible, yes."

"Thank you," said Entin.

Later, Entin recalled Marie's testimony that she hadn't lost consciousness during her attack, nor that she had heard a gunshot.

Kokes responded: "People who are struck in the head by bullets seem to have a temporary disruption of their neural pathways, if you will, the biological wiring in their head, that sort of makes them lose track of what their other sensory apparatus are relating to their brain. It's not uncommon for people to have been shot, or injured in any other way, and not be aware of it."

"Okay," said Entin. "Would these additional factors, that there was a young child about six years old in the house that wasn't awakened by any sound of the weapon, and that there were people outside the house, including one watching cactus grow across the street, who heard nothing, would these add any facts to your making your determination?"

"No," Kokes said. "It's not an unusual situation for bystanders not to notice gunshots if they are indeed present."

Thursday, February 4: As it did at the grand jury, the government brought FBI Special Agent Charles Hedrick to testify as a summary witness, and introduced in evidence through him a book of phone calls that were relevant to the alleged murder-for-hire conspiracy.

Since October, Hedrick had added a number of calls to his list, but most significant was a one-minute call at 9:34 A.M. on November 24, 1986, from a room rented by Jimmy Liberto at the Marco Polo to Paul Luskin's apartment just across the water.

Hedrick also compiled telephone evidence showing Paul Luskin had been in Baltimore in May and July 1987, which coincided near the dates Manley said he and Cohen had gone to Florida to make attempts on Marie Luskin.

In cross, Steve Allen gave the jury members copies of his own book of phone calls, which included the government's selections plus more. Then he spent hours going over it with Hedrick, attempting to show that the government's book had left out evidence of a drug conspiracy between the other codefendants and the three Miami Hispanic women.

Allen had compiled a consistent calling pattern in which there were 123 calls from one of the women to Jimmy Liberto's home number, plus another forty-six calls to his restaurant over ten months of 1986 and 1987. One of those calls was at 8:09 on the morning of March 9, three hours before all the phone traffic began that the government said proved the murder-for-hire.

In addition, he showed, there was a correlation between the calls and Jimmy Liberto's frequent trips to Florida.

"Did you have, when you prepared this book, access to an FBI 302 regarding an interview with James Manley in which Mr. Manley indicated that there was a source of drugs in south Florida who was a woman?" Allen asked.

"Yes," said Hedrick.

"And in fact, you had already interviewed Mr. Cohen before you prepared the book, in which he told you that the source of drugs was a woman in south Florida; is that right?"

"That's right," he said.

To further point out the government's selectivity, Allen showed that Paul Luskin was on his car phone at the same time Jimmy Liberto's room called his apartment. Liberto's room called at 9:34 A.M. for one minute, but Luskin began a fifteen-minute car-phone call at 9:31 A.M.

During a break, Jim Liberto's counsel Howard Cardin complained to the judge he needed a severance.

"The amount of evidence now coming in is becoming, in my opinion, overwhelming. I mean, when the defense evidence against my client exceeds the government's evidence in length, I firmly believe it is unfair and it is prejudicial."

Judge Motz disagreed and once again denied a severance.

In redirect, Bernstein asked if Hedrick had any knowledge that Paul Luskin knew the Hispanic women.

"I have no information to that regard," Hedrick said.

"Do you have any information at all in the records or your investigation that Paul Luskin is involved in narcotics?"

"No, I don't," he said.

None of the defendants took the stand.

In closing argument, Gregg Bernstein discussed the idea of conspiracy. He told the jury to look at the defendants and think of "the single thing that brings them all together, and that is the murder of Marie Luskin. No other single event links all four defendants together.

"Paul Luskin and Joe Liberto, they both worked at Luskin's. Joe Liberto, the loyal employee, the right-hand man, as one witness testified, who would do any dirty job that was asked.

"And what about Joe Liberto and Jimmy Liberto? Well, of course, they're brothers, so there's a link there. And then of course there's Jimmy Liberto and Sonny Cohen. You've heard ample testimony as to the association that existed between them from Denise Spring, Sonny Cohen's girlfriend, who testified that she had seen them together both in Baltimore and in the Marco Polo Hotel."

But above all there was the issue of motive.

"Who else but Paul Luskin would have had the desire or the motive to murder his wife? You heard the testimony of the acrimonious nature, the bitter divorce proceedings, proceedings that forced Paul Luskin to leave his home, forced him to stop working, resulted in numerous contempt citations because of his failure to pay the temporary support to his wife and children, that resulted in his arrest on at least three occasions and forced him to flee the state of Florida to avoid further incarceration.

"And if that is not evidence enough, you saw with your own eyes the effect that this divorce case has had on the various parties. Do you recall the hostile exchanges that took place between Barry Franklin, Marie Luskin's lawyer in the divorce case, and Mr. Entin, who also represented Mr. Luskin in the divorce case? You saw that.

"And if there is any doubt that that's just the lawyers battling among themselves, think back to November of 1985 when Mr. Luskin was first served with the divorce papers and what he did, as evidenced by the housekeeper, Ms. Valdes. He went into the house, caused about $10,000 worth of damage, breaking all kinds of perfume bottles and slashing paintings."

Bernstein thought it noteworthy "that during each of the critical periods when the defendants traveled to Florida to carry out this plot, how Paul Luskin mysteriously seems to be lurking somewhere in the Baltimore area. Is that just a coincidence, ladies and gentlemen? I submit to you that it's not."

But most suspicious was that "Sonny Cohen and James Manley are told that Marie Luskin on July 28 is going to be at Bennigan's restaurant at a dinner. How else would these men know, living more than a thousand miles away, that this woman would be at this restaurant on this particular evening?"

Bernstein said the conspiracy began on November 24, 1986, with the phone call from Jim Liberto's hotel room to Paul Luskin's apartment. At that point, Joe Liberto was still working for Luskin's.

"No matter what the defendant tries to show you, ladies and gentlemen, to indicate that Paul Luskin may have been somewhere else on that day, that he may have been in Pittsburgh, that he may have been in Washington, that all the car-telephone records for Paul Luskin point him in another place, and no matter what he tries to show you during his closing argument about narcotics, there can be only one purpose for that call, ladies and gentlemen, and that call wasn't to buy narcotics, that call wasn't to talk about business, that call started the plot to murder Marie Luskin.

"The defendants were careful. Paul Luskin in particular was careful. Remember this is a man who is an attorney, who was the chief executive officer of a very successful business, who was running a thirteen-store chain before he got embroiled in this divorce controversy. He knew that calls from his car phone could be traced to any of the other defendants and that would leave a trail of guilt that anybody could follow, so he was careful and he made sure that his contacts with defendants were carefully masked so no one would find them.

"That is why, I submit to you, you don't see a whole trail of telephone calls from Paul Luskin to each of the various defendants but instead what you see are calls to the Luskin's store, for example, from Paul Luskin where someone might think that all he's doing is calling his parents or calling to check on the business but in fact he could easily be talking to Joe Liberto in furtherance of the plot to murder his wife."

Bernstein anticipated the defendants' argument that the March 9 assault on Marie was a robbery.

"In fact, not a single thing was taken from that house, so ask yourself: If it was a robbery, why was nothing taken? If Sonny Cohen went into that house on March 9 to rob her, why didn't he take those things offered? I submit to you because it wasn't a robbery, it was because he had gone there at the request of the other defendants in this case to murder this woman."

Bernstein then argued that Charles Kokes's testimony proved Marie was shot, not hit.

"Ask yourself: Where is the expert testimony that she was hit on the head? Where is the expert testimony that some type of lead object was used that would have fragmented? There is none, no testimony at all. Instead there is the uncontroverted testimony from Dr. Kokes that in fact she was shot, and I don't think there can be really any doubt at all about that."

Bernstein responded to Allen's cross of Agent Hedrick regarding the early-morning call on March 9 between Jimmy Liberto's phone and his alleged drug connection in Miami:

"And this shows the real fallacy in the defendant's argument, the real smoke that he's trying to create in this courtroom to get you not to focus on the true events in this case, because, first, no one would believe that it was simply a coincidence that on the same day Marie Luskin is shot, Sonny Cohen just happens to be in Florida; but more importantly, what it shows is that even if the other defendants in this case are involved in narcotics trafficking—and I'm not for one minute suggesting that they are, nor am I suggesting for one minute that the evidence shows that—it is nothing more than a red herring because there is nothing to stop the defendants from doing both. The two are not mutually exclusive.

"And even if we accept Mr. Luskin's theory that Sonny Cohen and Jimmy Liberto and Joe Liberto are perhaps involved in narcotics trafficking, that wouldn't prevent them from trying to make some extra money in killing Marie Luskin.

"Remember the testimony of Mr. Manley. How could he have made this up, ladies and gentlemen? How could he have provided the details that he provided? Look at his corroboration. In a day of cross-examination of Mr. Manley, none of the defendants ever attacked the facts that he testified about. Remember that?

"Think about what they asked him about. They asked him about the deals that he made, of the crimes he may have committed, other sentences he may have been receiving, what he thought he was getting out of his plea bargain, whether or not he was a drug addict or other prior criminal activity, but they never cross-examined him about the facts. And ask yourself why they didn't do that.

"And I submit to you that the reason they didn't do that was simply because it was true, and they knew it was true, and instead what they tried to show you is simply that somehow he made a deal and, therefore, he's making all this up."

Then Bernstein invoked a powerful recollection Marie had told the grand jury and repeated at trial.

"Ladies and gentlemen, since March 9, or at least since the mid-part of April, Marie Luskin has been living with the nightmare that maybe the next knock on her door, the next person that's standing outside—maybe that will be another florist, because remember the remarks of her husband in the middle of April, to remember there are always other florists. Since then, Marie Luskin has been haunted by that nightmare and wondering if maybe perhaps there are other florists waiting out there.

"Ladies and gentlemen, this is your chance to end that nightmare for her."

Next was Steve Allen, delivering closing for Luskin.

He began by pointing out that the government had brought no direct evidence against his client. "This is an entirely circumstantial evidence case, and when you go back into the jury room, you're going to have to piece together these circumstances, and what you're going to have to say at the conclusion is: Does the picture which the government says this evidence paints, is it painted, or are things missing? I submit to you that you're going to conclude that there's something missing. This case is built on conjecture and supposition.

"If the government has proven anything, I guess, it is that Paul Luskin, beginning in November 1985, was involved in an unpleasant divorce, an acrimonious divorce, and we have never denied it. And the government has proven there was distrust and that the lawyers for Marie Luskin were extraordinarily aggressive and they made hundreds of thousands of dollars doing it.

"Well, frankly, ladies and gentlemen, he had a motive. Everybody who's going through a divorce, who is not happy with their spouse, has a motive, has a motive to castigate them, has a motive to abuse them, has a motive to yell at them, has a motive to potentially, I guess, even hurt them, and the government has proven the motive.

"If you go back to Mr. Bernstein's closing argument, he spent the bulk of his time talking about motive because, frankly, that's where he's strong. Where he's weak is Paul Luskin's participation, if any—and we submit none—in any assault upon Marie Luskin on March 9 of 1987."

Allen argued the government had theorized that Paul's "other florists" statement to Marie was tantamount to an admission. Not so, he said.

"Paul Luskin, in a moment of anger and trying to, I don't know, inflict some emotional hurt on Marie, knowing that she had been assaulted, knowing that that was an event which she was sensitive about, made an inappropriate comment, 'Don't forget, Marie, there's other florists.'

"Now ladies and gentlemen, the government has told you that Paul Luskin is a smart, savvy businessman. The government theorizes that he is so smart and so savvy that he didn't leave a single trail, a single piece of paper tying him to this case. Now, is he going to stand in front of his wife in April and tell her, 'Hey, I'm the guy behind the March 9 assault?'

"Frankly, it's the only evidence in this case after November 29 of 1985 that he ever did anything to harass Marie Luskin, and he said it in a moment he shouldn't have, and everybody knows and common life experience tells us that everybody sometime in their life has said something they really shouldn't have said, to get a little dig in, and that is what the April 1987 statement was. We've all done it. He made a mistake, he said something he shouldn't have said, and that's the long and short of it."

And talking about motive, Manley had one equally— to lie, Allen said.

"To convict Paul Luskin, you have got to buy the testimony of James Manley, because he is the only witness who tells you that Paul Luskin was involved in this crime.

"James Manley is about forty-five years old, folks. Twenty-five years without parole, he's history, he's seventy years old when he walks out of jail. He's got as much motive any human being can have to try and sell you a story, and he's been given the opportunity.

"Who is James Manley? James Manley has been convicted of a variety of crimes, including forgery and counterfeiting. Forgery and counterfeiting are crimes involving planning. They are crimes involving willfully taking the money of other individuals by deceit and fraud. That's the guy who they tell you you can believe. That's the guy they tell you is wrapped in the flag and he's the guy that brings it all together.

"Manley, ladies and gentlemen, has learned how to manipulate the system. He is a bright guy, he is a smart guy, he is a dangerous guy. It is guys like Jim Manley who manipulate the system, who accuse innocent people of wrongdoing to serve their selfish purposes."

Allen conjectured that Manley got his story merely

through the loose lips of others. "Did Joe Liberto at some point tell Jimmy about Marie Luskin, you know, 'Hey, boy, I got this crazy boss and let me tell you this divorce is killing us down there, let me tell you what's going on.'

"And does Jimmy one day while he's having a couple at the bar say, 'You ought to hear about these crazy rich people down in Florida?' And does Sonny Cohen pick up on that and maybe Manley hears it?

"And after March 9, does Joe Liberto one day in conversation say, 'You're not going to believe what happened to Paul Luskin's wife, and I bet you they think he did it because he was the husband.' And does Manley hear that, and does Manley, who's a bright guy, start putting together a story?"

Allen even suggested that Manley might have been Marie's assailant on March 9. But he conceded a major point concerning the fragment taken from her head: "I'm going to give it to the government, it was probably a gunshot."

Allen tried to show that some of Manley's "inside information" that was supposed to have come from Paul Luskin, was plain wrong.

"Misinformation. Manley says, Our information was that she would be alone at Bennigan's. With ten or twenty of her closest friends? The JCC Single Parent Support Group was meeting there that night. If this information came from Paul Luskin, it's flat out wrong.

"Now, how does Manley know that they went to Bennigan's? All right, I'm going to tell you how. And by the way, my guess is as good as the government's, and that's frankly what it is, a guess.

"I think that Manley and Cohen were down there in July on a drug deal, and I think they had heard about the diamonds and jewels at the Marie Luskin house because that word had filtered up because of the unsuccessful March 9 assault. I think Joe Liberto had told his brother about it because he had heard about it at Luskin's, and I think that Cohen and Manley decided to do a robbery and they went to the Marie Luskin house.

"I think they went to Marie Luskin's house looking for her to rob her and they saw her Mercedes driving out and they followed her to Bennigan's and they saw a tall blonde get out."

Allen said that until Bernstein's closing earlier that day, the government had always maintained that Cohen and Manley were in Florida for one purpose alone, and that was to murder Marie Luskin. They kept insisting that even after Luskin's defense turned over the telephone toll records of the three Hispanic women in Miami.

"It's like a lightbulb is going off. The government is finally willing to concede that there's evidence of drug dealing in this case. It's been a long fight, but we finally got them to concede it.

"And by the way, I don't expect any of the other defense lawyers in this case to concede that. It clearly is not in their clients' best interest. It's my job because my client's got nothing to do with drug dealing, and frankly, my client's got nothing to do with this case.

"And by the way, Jim Manley told (the FBI) that these people were drug dealers and that the source of supply was a woman in south Florida, but they chose to ignore that information and they chose not to subpoena the tolls for one of two logical reasons: they didn't believe Manley—I can't imagine that—or, because they were trying to hide something because it didn't meet their theory.

"Now analyze carefully these telephone records. The Hedrick analysis, ladies and gentlemen, is with blinders, and it's incomplete."

Allen closed with a parable—the TV series *The Fugitive.*

"There was a fellow by the name of Dr. Richard Kimble who hated his wife, and they fought like cats and dogs, and Dr. Kimble had affairs on his wife and couldn't stand to be with her.

"And one night Dr. Kimble goes home and he walks in the house and his wife is dead, and he sees going out the back door a one-armed man. And he calls police and he says, 'Please help me, my wife is dead.'

"'Why'd you do it, Mr. Kimble?' 'I didn't do it, the one-armed man did it.' 'Well, Dr. Kimble, you certainly had a lot of motive to kill this lady, we think you did it.'

They took him to a jury and the jury believed it beyond a reasonable doubt because of motive and Dr. Kimble was convicted.

"As the story goes on, on his way to jail he's in a train wreck and he escapes. For the next three seasons, Dr. Kimble chases all over America looking for the one-armed man, and Lieutenant Gerard looks for Dr. Kimble, and finally, on the last show of the series, they found the one-armed man.

"The point of the matter is Dr. Kimble had motive and the government put on blinders, it put on tunnel vision. They didn't go looking for the one-armed man, even though there was lots of evidence pointing to a one-armed man, which is what the government had done in this case.

"Now I don't know who that one-armed man is, but I know who he's not, and he's not Sonny Cohen."

Howard Cardin's close, for Jim Liberto, homed in on Manley's credibility.

"He is an architect of deception. This man knows how to deceive, how to defraud. Does he care? He has no concern for the innocent people who are going to lose their hard-earned dollars day in and day out.

"Concern for innocent people? James Manley? Somebody was charged with the attempted murder of Jimmy Liberto. Did he care that man might go to jail for life? No, because he only cared what was good for James Manley.

"That's James Manley. That's the person this case is all about, who seeks to extricate himself from going to prison for years and years and who has enlisted the aid of the prosecution to do so.

"He is a portrait of a liar and a killer. James Manley said, 'I am not a killer, I just went along for the ride.' Do you believe that?

"I'm sure each of you have seen in your daily lives people who have deceived you or lied to you. Once they lie, they keep lying, because as one thing happens, they have to keep lying in order to try to convince you—to confidence you, if you will. Manley shows us a picture, a portrait of deceit, a liar, a killer."

Cardin pointed out a final irony. "If James Manley hadn't tried to kill Jimmy Liberto, we wouldn't be in court today, because Jimmy Liberto wouldn't have needed to buy a gun, wouldn't have needed to ask Pat (Widerman) Liberto to help him.

"If Jimmy Liberto and Darlene Armstrong had known who their assailant was and known that he was not a danger to them, we wouldn't have been here, because he wouldn't have had the fear, the fear shared with Darlene Armstrong, that required him to go out in violation of the law and get a firearm."

Next was Mike Libowitz, for Joe Liberto.

"We've learned that Paul Luskin is a friend to Joe Liberto. Friends like that Joe Liberto doesn't need. Luskin says that Joe Liberto is involved in a drug conspiracy. With friends like Paul Luskin, Joe Liberto doesn't need any enemies.

"Joe Liberto doesn't have many enemies. He's described by Marie Luskin as a nice, warm-hearted individual. He's described by other witnesses as an addict to corny jokes.

"Joe Liberto does, however, have one enemy that we've heard from. That enemy never met him. That's James Manley. James Manley says that Joe Liberto is a contract killer. We beg to differ.

"The government says Paul Luskin is guilty, Sonny Cohen is guilty, Jimmy Liberto is guilty. The Government needs a link to tie these people together. The link, the government suggests, is Joseph Liberto. The government, however, can't prove a lot of things. They can't prove that Paul Luskin knows Jimmy Liberto, but they can't prove that Paul Luskin doesn't know Jimmy Liberto. They take the easy way out, they throw in Joe Liberto, and there's your link."

"Ladies and gentlemen of the jury, I'm not going to stand here and ask you to believe that Sonny Cohen is a nice guy," began Paul Weiss, Cohen's attorney. "I'm not asking you to like Sonny Cohen.

"Everybody from start to finish in the trial has been pointing the finger at Sonny Cohen. To Mr. Luskin's lawyers, Sonny Cohen is a drug courier and a robber. But this case is not about drugs.

"To Mr. Cardin, he's pointed a finger at Sonny Cohen and said, 'That's the man who tried to kill Jimmy Liberto.' But this case is not about that either.

"To James Manley, Sonny Cohen is, quote, unquote, the way out. Every time Mr. Manley commits a crime, it was Sonny's idea, it was Sonny's plot, I was just along for the ride.

"I think that if the evidence has been clear, I mean really clear on any one particular point in this case, then that is that Sonny Cohen was not, in fact, the person who assaulted Marie Luskin on March 9."

Just before closing arguments began, Weiss had paraded his client before the jury so they could see the tattoos on his arms and even one under his eye. Since Marie Luskin testified that the assailant was wearing a short-sleeve shirt, she should have seen them, he said.

"Marie Luskin got off the stand, she walked around, she looked at the people in the front row, and she walked around to the people in the back row, and she looked, and she looked at me, she looked right at Sonny Cohen. And then do you remember what she did? She turned around, she walked away from Mr. Cohen, and she started looking out into the audience."

The same thing happened when Denise Keltz, the owner of Emerald Hills Florist, testified, he said. "She looked around and she said, 'I don't see him here.'"

Weiss admitted that Cohen traveled to Florida five times, although he only admitted he traveled with Manley once—in July, when they were caught.

"But none of these trips to Florida had anything to do with a plot to kill Marie Luskin. Why did he go? We don't know. Some possible explanations have been presented in this case and you, I guess, can consider those possibilities along with all the other evidence in this case.

"There are two tragedies that are arising out of this case. The first tragedy is the assault on Marie Luskin and what she had to go through, and the second tragedy is that the government is allowing James Manley to be unleashed on the streets of our community again.

"When you go back to the jury room, consider: What would you do to stop from going to prison for the rest of your life? What would you do? Would you lie? Would you cheat? Would you fabricate a story that would buy your freedom?

"Would you tell them what they wanted to hear? Because they believe him. Officer Hedrick said, I believe him, I didn't ask him any questions, didn't probe too deep. They believe him because they want to believe him."

But the last word belonged to the government, delivered by Wick Sollers.

"The defendants got what they deserved when they engaged in a conspiracy to kill somebody. They got criminals to do their dirty work. They got Mr. Cohen, who in turn got Mr. Manley. Who else do you hire to kill someone, ladies and gentlemen? It's not the government's fault that Mr. Manley is a bad guy. Murder-for-hire is a nasty business. You don't go up the street and get Sister Teresa to go out and take on a hit on somebody. It's the James Manleys and the Sonny Cohens of the world who perform the hits.

"Given our choice, we would select other witnesses, people without criminal records to prosecute the case. It is a fact of life that the government must rely on the James Manleys of the world to prosecute people such as these four defendants.

"When Mr. Manley gave a proffer concerning the murder attempts, the government was as skeptical as anyone would be, but the circumstances of the July 30 stop spoke for themselves." Holding up the AR-15 rifle with laser and scope, Sollers continued: "Ladies and gentlemen, this is not the type of weapon you carry on a drug deal. If they were on a drug trip, you don't want to be conspicuous carrying this guitar case with an AR-15 rifle with a laser scope.

"And three and a half ounces of coke is not a significant amount, despite what Mr. Allen would like you to believe. That is not the amount of cocaine that you go to Florida for.

"There's an old saying: If you're weak on the law,

argue the facts. If you're weak on the facts, argue the law. If you're weak on both, you attack the government. And that's what the defendants have done.

"There are plenty of cases out there to prosecute, ladies and gentlemen, and I ask you: Who has the motive to lie, to make up a story? It certainly isn't the FBI.

"The tattoo argument. You saw the tattoos. They are not blatant tattoos. Marie Luskin was absolutely terrified, obviously, when the person came in with a gun. She said she was staring at the barrel, looked at the guy's mean eyes. That doesn't mean she's going to see the tattoo.

"Mr. Allen's suggestion that it was a frustrated robber who shot Marie Luskin is ridiculous. A frustrated robber would have taken the loot, ladies and gentlemen.

"Now remember in opening, Mr. Entin told you that you might be able to conclude that Sonny Cohen committed the offense on March 9, and then later Sonny Cohen and Manley stalked Marie Luskin because Cohen was worried that Marie could recognize him.

"But that didn't make sense. So now the theory changes. When Mr. Allen gets up, he runs another theory by you: How about the theory that Sonny Cohen didn't do March 9? But because the evidence is pretty strong on July 28, to say the least, maybe Sonny and Manley were down there on a combined drug deal—robbery.

"Do you know why this Luskin sort of fluid defense theory makes no sense? Because what makes sense is that Paul Luskin wanted to get rid of his wife. He was under unbelievable pressure in the divorce proceeding. Paul Luskin was in serious trouble.

"Mr. Weiss does not want to pass the composite of the person that shot Marie Luskin on March 9. I want you to look at it carefully and I want you to put your hands over the hair because I submit to you, it is quite similar to Mr. Cohen.

"Ladies and gentlemen, Sonny Cohen is a predator. He's a cold-blooded killer. He did not give Marie Luskin a chance when she bent over desperately trying to hand him money and jewelry. Do not give him a chance. It is only by dumb luck that Marie Luskin is alive to testify before you.

"Ladies and gentlemen, this case is about greed, it's about arrogance, it's about violence. Mr. Allen claims that Paul Luskin would not plot to murder his wife in the family house. Paul Luskin has lived his life without regard to others, without regard—"

"Objection!" shouted Steve Allen, who asked the judge to strike the last line. He did.

Sollers continued: "Paul Luskin has flaunted the laws of society. When his wife caught Mr. Luskin during an affair, he told her that she couldn't tell him who to be friends with. However, when he was served with divorce papers, he had this colossal temper tantrum, doing $10,000 worth of damage in the house.

"Look at how he conducted his financial affairs, the $4,000 a week in cash, the hoards of cash he kept. Look at how he conducted himself in the divorce proceedings, repeatedly ignoring court orders, other sanctions, and being arrested.

"Ladies and gentlemen, I submit that Paul Luskin is capable of anything. That is the evidence of this case. Ours is a civilization of laws, and that's what makes this country a great place to live in, and until now, Mr. Luskin has done his best to circumvent those laws.

"The other defendants were just plain greedy. Money was their motive and they were willing to snuff somebody out for money.

"Tell Mr. Luskin, ladies and gentlemen, that there will be no other florist."

Just before five o'clock, Wednesday, February 17, after eighteen days of trial, the jury got the case.

They stayed out that night, Thursday, and Friday. At 3:40 on Saturday afternoon, after deliberating more than twenty-two hours, they came back with a verdict.

Guilty on all counts.

A reporter for the Baltimore *Sun* wrote the next day that Luskin closed his eyes briefly as the jury forewoman read the first verdict. Then he turned and gave a wan smile to his family and Susan.

The *Sun* reported that deliberations were stormy at times. One juror wiped away tears after the verdicts were read.

Another juror told the newspaper there was ultimately one holdout. The most difficult issue was whether or not Joe Liberto had participated in the plot.

SEVEN

The Wreckage

Immediately, Paul's attorneys announced they would appeal.

When they filed the appeal on March 7, it included affidavits from both Paul and Steve Allen, and a request that the statements be kept under seal. Both claimed that just before Luskin intended to introduce the Western Union money transfers as evidence, Jim and Joe Liberto threatened them.

Allen said Jim Liberto was angry because Luskin was playing prosecutor and discovering evidence of his drug trafficking. Because of that, he expected the government to indict him for it after the trial ended. If that happened, he threatened to falsely implicate Paul in his ring.

Paul said Jim Liberto threatened to hurt him, his family, and his attorneys if he introduced the Western Union evidence. If not for the threats, he would have taken the stand in his own defense.

Then just before sentencing, Paul claimed yet another threat; Marie had told him during the divorce trial that she would testify in Baltimore to "anything that would put me behind bars, unless I paid her one million dollars before the trial."

Between conviction and sentencing, Paul's attorneys asked his friends, relatives, and business associates to write letters to the judge appealing for a light sentence. Marie offered to write one as well—for $750,000, according to correspondence between Barry Franklin and

Alvin Entin. Joe and Mildred would pay it as the lump sum cash settlement between all the Luskins and Marie, and further, it would end all the litigation.

In the end, the deal collapsed. When it did, Paul entered copies of Franklin's proposals into the federal court record, and highlighted another letter:

In May 1986, in between divorce attorneys, Paul had hired West Palm Beach attorney Daniel Blackman to see if, as a fresh face, he could break the impasse with Marie. He found there wasn't much common ground.

Blackman wrote to Judge Motz: "I was made aware via conversations with opposing counsel that Marie Luskin had stated on more than one occasion that she intended to see Paul Luskin behind bars for the rest of his life, to keep him away from his children permanently, and to take everything away from him that he ever had."

At sentencing on April 29, Paul spoke before the Court:

"I feel sorry for Marie and her experience with the robber or assailant. I had no part in it. I did not associate in it. I did not solicit anyone to harm my wife. Anything that would harm my wife would harm my children, and anyone who knows me knows that my love for my children transcends any motive that I would ever have.

"I have confidence that my appeal in this case if I do not get a new trial will be granted because the issues are compelling and the evidence, I believe, is not against me.

"I ask for clemency. I ask for vindication. I ask for a chance to start a new life as soon as possible."

Judge Motz was unswayed. He sentenced Luskin to thirty-five years. Sonny Cohen got fifty years, Jim Liberto got thirty-three years, and Joe Liberto got twenty-two years. All of the sentences carried fifteen of the years without possibility of parole. Cohen got thirty years nonparolable because he was a career criminal in possession of a firearm.

In addition, Cohen was brought to trial in Baltimore City Court and convicted twice more—for attempted escape from jail and cocaine smuggling. He got twenty more years in state prison on top of his fifty in federal.

According to the U.S. Parole Commission's schedule, Paul was made eligible for parole in 2008.

In June, James Manley was sentenced. He faced ten years, and got seven.

Later, Judge Motz denied Luskin's motion for a new trial.

After the conviction, Joe and Mildred Luskin began packing up to move offshore. In mid-March, they began selling their real estate, closing on the Hollywood store location for $1.2 million.

On May 12, Judge Nutaro wrote it appeared the Luskins were placing their assets out of reach of Marie, despite the 1985 court order preventing that. They were also concealing their whereabouts. On May 25, she signed a warrant for the arrest of both Joe and Mildred for failure to appear in court.

Also in May, a U.S. Bankruptcy Court judge ordered Luskin's into liquidation. In mid-June, an auctioneer held a two-day sale of the stores' remaining TVs, video equipment, and stereos.

In mid-July, *The Miami Herald* carried a social note: the treasurer of the Broward County Democratic Club, who was also the president of the county chapter of the National Organization for Women, was married to a Democratic party activist. The ceremony was performed in the chambers of Judge Constance Nutaro.

Paul Luskin, and his counsel Alvin Entin, were active Republicans.

Next month, the *Herald* ran the annual attorneys' ratings of judges in Broward County. Eighteen percent said Judge Nutaro was "Not Qualified" in terms of judicial temperament. That ranked her thirty-fifth out of forty-two circuit court judges.

Since Judge Nutaro had ruled that Joe and Mildred Luskin were in contempt of court for failing to produce the business's financial statements, they were sanctioned from defending themselves until they did. That meant when their case came to trial, in September 1988, the Luskins couldn't present witnesses, evidence, argument, or cross-examine Marie's witnesses.

Considering those odds, the Luskins didn't even show up. Alvin Entin called it a "sham trial."

On September 14, 1988, the jury gave their verdict: Joseph and Mildred Luskin did intentionally cause monetary damage to Marie Luskin with criminal intent and caused civil theft. They awarded Marie $3,275,600 in compensatory damages.

Two days later, Judge Nutaro trebled the amount, then added interest and attorney's fees. That made the bill $10,929,555—and counting.

On September 26, the Luskins began moving money into the Bank of Montreal, Bahamas. Those actions triggered years more of litigation Marie would bring against them.

On December 23, 1988, Barry Franklin subpoenaed Paul's former attorney Steve Glucksman. Glucksman, who was now suing the Luskins himself for $130,000 in fees unpaid, testified that Paul, Joe, and Mildred Luskin had told him when he took their case in October 1986 that the family net worth was $5–7 million—the majority in real estate.

"Joe Luskin made it clear to me there would never be any property available for Marie Luskin to execute on for any judgment she might procure," Glucksman said. He added that the Luskins had told him back in 1986 they had already made tentative arrangements to sell their holdings if need be.

EIGHT

The Bullet That Didn't Shatter the Mirror

I got to the story, as always, late.

In the summer of 1990, I visited Baltimore for the first time in five years. At the end of the trip, my brother-in-law Jeff Hines, an attorney, suggested I look up the Luskin file in federal court.

I thought of *The Miami News* headline the day after Luskin was indicted, but the Miami papers hadn't covered the day-to-day of the trial. I knew he had been convicted, but not much more.

Almost the entire file was at the Fourth Circuit Court of Appeals in Richmond. About the only thing in the clerk's office in Baltimore was an October 12, 1989, appellate decision. I read the case facts as the Court reviewed them:

"The first attempt of Mrs. Luskin's life occurred about 10:00 A.M. on March 9, 1987. Within the hour, a telephone call was forwarded from the Marco Polo Hotel, where Sonny Cohen was a registered guest, to Pellucci's [sic] Restaurant in Baltimore, owned and operated by Jimmy Liberto.

"Five minutes later there was a call from Pellucci's to Joe Liberto's home in Florida. One minute after that call ended, there was a call from Pellucci's to Paul Luskin's home in Baltimore. Shortly thereafter, Luskin placed a call from his car telephone to his home in Florida, where his wife's aunt answered the phone.

"Although Marie Luskin had at this time already been

shot, the aunt who answered the telephone did not so inform him. Luskin then immediately placed a call to Pellucci's Restaurant. Again, the reasonable inference to be drawn from this evidence when coupled with the events of the day is that Luskin was in fact involved in the conspiracy."

Based on those facts, that conclusion was hard to argue.

When I returned home to Miami, I called Barry Franklin, who was listed in the court papers as Marie's lawyer. He invited me to lunch with Marie.

They bought. Marie was polite but didn't want to talk about the story with me; she preferred to put it behind her. I had brought a notebook but took no notes. I dropped interest.

Next summer, 1991, I saw a headline in *The Miami Herald:*

MURDER-FOR-HIRE CASE MAY BE REOPENED; CONVICT SAYS HI-FI EXEC WAS FRAMED.

The convict was Sonny Cohen. Silent at trial, three years later he was talking up a storm—a two-hundred-page sworn statement.

Cohen said there was no murder-for-hire—it existed only as his and James Manley's invention so they could offer it as bait for a deal to the feds after their arrest for drugs and guns. It worked, too, but Manley crossed him.

The *Herald* reporter wrote:

"The legal troubles of Paul Luskin are a convoluted tale of intrigue, infidelity and torment. Precisely where the truth lies is buried beneath a ton of court documents. Maybe."

Perhaps like the feds themselves, I was hooked. I called Barry Franklin for a copy of Cohen's statement. He had it, but didn't want to give it to me. He suggested I call Alvin Entin, Paul's counsel.

Entin was most genial. He referred me to Benjamin F.L. Darden, the attorney who had gone to Lewisburg federal prison in central Pennsylvania and taken the statement. Darden had recently moved from Miami to Ithaca, New York. He first told me to get a copy from the court file in Baltimore, then finally I convinced him to send it to me.

Although Cohen had argued at trial that someone else assaulted Marie Luskin, he admitted to Darden it was him. But, he said, he was there to rob her, not kill her. The assault had nothing to do with Paul Luskin.

Cohen said he was in Florida to run drugs. He went there about once a month to buy a few ounces of cocaine for $800 per, then he'd sell it in Baltimore for a 300 percent profit.

Cohen said he was friends with Jimmy Liberto, but wasn't part of any alleged drug ring of his. Sitting around the bar at Palughi's one night, Jimmy told him he had just gotten off the phone with his brother Joe, who he said worked for Luskin's in Florida.

Joe was angry because he had worked twenty years for the Luskins, and a few months earlier, Paul Luskin had fired him. However, when Joe Luskin fired Paul he rehired Joe Liberto, but for less money.

> "Paul Luskin got fired because of a divorce, he wasn't running the business, they were losing money. And Joe was just saying how pissed off he was, he said Paul has got money stashed all over his house, and that him and his wife are being divorced, he knows that Paul keeps like a hundred grand in his home all of the time. And he knows that Paul ain't going to come back to work. Paul don't have to work, he has got all of this money stashed."

Cohen lit up when he heard about $100,000 cash. He asked Jimmy where the Luskins lived, and he said Emerald Hills.

Next time Cohen was in Florida to buy drugs, in February 1987, he found Emerald Hills on a map so he could try a burglary. Jimmy Liberto had no idea what he was doing, nor did Cohen want him to.

Cohen said he rode throughout Emerald Hills and hung out in the center of it at a 7-Eleven. There he drank coffee and sat on the curb in front of his parked car, which gave him a view of the entire street. Over the course of a couple weeks, one morning he saw a cream-colored Mercedes. When it passed he saw the vanity license plate "P-L."

"When I saw the P-L, automatically I thought, Paul Luskin, got to be the car."

Cohen said he didn't see who was driving, and it was too late to follow. With nothing else to do, he sat in the same place long enough to watch it come by again in the other direction. This time he jumped in his car and followed it home—just a few blocks. He saw a woman get out alone.

Cohen was impressed with the neighborhood:

"As soon as you drive in Emerald Hills you see you don't got a few million, don't even go in there. The homes look like they are out of reach for the average person. It is like you see on the rich and famous on TV."

Now that he knew where the Luskin home was, he watched it to observe its daily schedule. At 8 A.M., the school bus picked up the kids. The maid didn't work on Sunday and Monday. Neighborhood security patrol didn't go on duty until the afternoon. The husband was nowhere to be found.

Cohen described his assault on Marie and it matched what she had said. The major discrepancy was that Marie told police the assailant had hit her over the head with his gun, and Cohen said he had used a blackjack.

Cohen said he hadn't intended to hit her, but he had to knock her out once she began screaming. He knew the front door was open and there were people outside, so he got nervous and left without even taking anything.

"Why didn't you hit her with the gun?" Darden asked.

"It might have went off. I didn't want to hurt her.
Well, it sounds a little ridiculous, I don't want to hurt
her but I hit her with a blackjack. Well, I knew I would
hurt her, but not thinking I would do real damage to
her, I just hit her on the head."

Even after Marie pleaded there was no cash in the
house besides the hundred-dollar bill, Cohen still believed she had the hundred grand. After all, he had seen
the neighborhood and the inside of the house. He
wanted to take another chance next time in Florida; but
since he was sure she had seen his face, he needed
someone to help. He asked Manley, a B&E man—
breaking and entering. Manley even had experience
robbing houses in Florida.

At trial, Cohen's position was he had only made one
trip to Florida with Manley. Now he admitted Manley
told the truth they were together on the May trip, too,
when Manley dressed up in a security guard outfit so he
could knock on Marie Luskin's door. But it wasn't to
murder her; if someone answered, he was to say something about some vandalism. If no one answered, he was
supposed to break into the house. Manley told him an
old lady answered.

But there was also a June trip together that Manley
didn't even mention. On it they burglarized a drug
dealer's room at the Marco Polo and stole jewelry and
guns—including the sawed-off shotgun they later threw
over a bridge.

Cohen explained why he had all the guns and drugs
with him on the July trip, when they got caught: Jimmy
Liberto had showed him his AR-15 rifle with the laser
and scope, and Cohen offered to calibrate it in the South
Carolina woods since he planned to drive down to
Florida.

But just before he was to leave, he had a fight with his
girlfriend Denise and he moved in at his mother's house.

"I didn't want to leave any of the guns or any of the
drugs at my mother's house, so I took all the guns and
drugs with me."

"Why did you not want to leave them?" Darden
asked.

"Because I didn't want my mother to find them. Whenever I stay there she roots through all my stuff just to see what she can see."

"How old is your mother?"

"Right now, sixty-eight. She has been rooting through my stuff all of my life, I know that. She goes through everything."

Then Cohen decided to take the train because he had just bought a new 1987 Chevy Monte Carlo a week before to replace the Mercury Cougar whose engine he had blown out on the June trip with Manley.

"It was a week old and I didn't want to drive it two thousand miles on the highway. I didn't want to test the motor that way, I didn't want to put too much pressure on it. And the fact that Jimmy and I were both riding to Florida in my car just didn't get it with me because of dropping cigarettes on it and burning holes in it, just being dirty on the trip, so I just decided not to take the car."

After Manley's trial testimony that he and Cohen were in Florida strictly to kill Marie Luskin, Bernstein argued there could be no good reason besides attempted murder why they had all that firepower. Yet jurors who believed Manley also had to swallow something illogical that he said: the drugs they were caught with on the train north, Cohen hadn't bought in Florida—he had brought them with him from Baltimore. That was the basis on which the government had insisted this was not a drug case.

So although Cohen now agreed he did bring drugs with him from Baltimore, he also contradicted Manley. He said he had a drug connection to meet at the Marco Polo the day they arrived. That was the primary purpose of the trip.

While they waited, he said, he and Manley talked about the Luskin house and decided to go there. They sat in the 7-Eleven parking lot for half an hour, then they saw the Luskin Mercedes pass again.

Cohen said they followed it. It went up a back road to a shopping center where Bennigan's restaurant was.

They watched as Marie went into the restaurant with another woman, then he and Manley decided to drive to her house to burglarize it. But when they got there they saw another car in the driveway and decided not to chance it.

With nothing else to do for the rest of the evening, they returned to Bennigan's, waited until Marie left, then followed her back to the house to see what would happen. When both women entered the house, the men gave up.

After their arrests, Baltimore City Jail put them in cells next to each other. They knew they were in big trouble; they both faced thirty to fifty years because of their prior records. That's when together they came up with the murder-for-hire story.

"And you were serious, did you actually think that federal officials would buy this story?" Darden asked.

"Yeah, well, they did," said Cohen.

"What was your thinking? Where did you come up with this plan? I mean, is this something you heard about happening before?"

"Well, we know it happened before, we've seen it happen before. Jimmy Manley especially knew, I know now that he knew how to deal with it. All right, he had been making deals all of his life, and I didn't know it.

"We knew we were going to jail, we couldn't get out of it, so what you got to do is you got to offer something to the Government that is worth more to them than just putting a couple of guys in jail with handguns, or drug dealers, whatever you want to call us. That is what they got us for at Penn Station.

"So the first thing we thought of, we were hired by Paul Luskin to go down there and scare his wife out of divorcing him, went in, hit her, told her don't file no more divorce, back off of the divorce things, and that we were paid $50,000 for it by Paul Luskin. So then we come to how did Paul Luskin know us."

Cohen said he told Manley that the AR-15 belonged to Jimmy Liberto, from whom Cohen had told Manley to steal drug money the month before.

"Now this AR-15 is coming into it and he knows Jimmy Liberto is going to see him and he knows he is going to get busted for that crap at Jimmy Liberto's house.

"So we hook Jimmy Liberto in it as Joe Liberto telling Jimmy Liberto that Paul Luskin wants somebody to beat his wife up to tell her to back off the divorce.

"And then we thought about it, thought about it, and it's just an assault charge. It is nothing, they are not going to give us deals or no breaks for just somebody paying to beat up their wife, it's not worth it. The most anybody could get out of it would be a couple years. Paul Luskin would probably get probation, and they are not going for that for that kind of a charge.

"So then Jimmy said, 'Well let's make up a story that he hired you to kill her.' So we discussed it, same scenario, Paul Luskin asked Joe if he knew anybody that would kill his wife. Joe said, I will give you my brother and see if he knows anybody up in Baltimore. Jimmy Liberto approached me about it and I said yeah, and that's how we came up with the whole story.

"But it was just something to get us out of jail, get us off the charges we were on.

"It took two or three weeks to really try to figure out every angle. We finally got it together and the more I thought about it, the more I just said to myself, you know, I can't do it. I have never ratted on anybody in my life, never informed or never put anybody in jail. I just told Jimmy Manley I couldn't do it, just back off of it, and he said okay.

"The next thing I know he uses the story. He didn't even try to cut me in on it because he knew that I would probably tell the truth once we got on the stand. He knew that I would tell that this whole thing was a lie.

"If I was a hired killer like they said, it is kind of stupid to go down there for one day, try to go down and kill her and not be able to do it because I don't know where she is at and then come back to Baltimore. I would have stayed there for a month or two months until I got the job done.

"If you are in jail for a minor crime and you can come up with a better story, the feds jump right on it, even if it is not true. They love it, they just love it. They will take a deal in a minute, they are known for it. I mean they actually believe but they believe too hard, I don't think they investigate fully enough."

At the same time Darden filed Cohen's statement, he also filed one from Paul Luskin.

"I'm absolutely 100 percent innocent and there is no basis whatsoever for this indictment," he said.

Luskin also explained his "other florist" remark:
It was mid-April 1987, and Marie had had him arrested on the contempt order. He had spent eighteen nights in jail, missed Passover, and had just been released. He wanted to see his kids, and picked them up for the weekend.

"When I returned the children, Marie Luskin was waiting outside the house. She and I had a discussion, not a very happy one, in which she threatened to take away everything I owned, including my children, and to harm my parents in any way that she could, and that she wanted to go so far as to dig up my grandmother, who was buried in a plot that was owned by Marie's grandfather.

"My grandmother died in 1982 or 1983, and she wanted me to dig up my grandmother and transport her from the cemetery because she wanted nothing to do with any member of the Luskin family, dead or alive. And at that point, I probably made the comment, or I did make the comment that, in that case, there's always another florist."

"By that, you did not mean that you had sent a florist?" Darden asked.

"No. It was just an angry remark on my part."

After Darden entered both statements into the record as "newly discovered evidence," he asked Judge Motz once again for a hearing that could lead to a new trial.

"If I ever got Manley and Cohen in the same courtroom, Paul could make his reservations home," Darden told me.

Talking to Alvin Entin again, he offered to let me read through Luskin's files and photocopy anything I wanted. I took him up. Most of the next month I spent in his conference room in North Miami Beach, rummaging through boxes and asking questions.

Paul lost the case because "the jury looked at the case and concluded if he didn't do it, he should have," Entin wisecracked.

"I do not believe that with a gun two inches from her head, Cohen could have missed. Not even for a Jewish hit man."

Beside that, two things went wrong for Paul at trial: First, the wrong attorney cross-examined Manley.

Paul's Baltimore cousin Steve Miles had told him he needed a politically connected attorney in Baltimore to win, so they hired Russell White. Paul insisted White do Manley's cross, but he didn't know the case nearly as well as Entin or Steve Allen.

Second, Liberto's threat kept him off the witness stand. Paul took it very seriously.

"I deal with criminals every day of the week. Paul as an attorney did corporate work, and was much more likely to be scared by a threat from a thug."

Entin said he and Steve Allen advised Paul "to hell with the threat, let us introduce the evidence." But Paul decided not to go forward.

"Some decisions you have to leave to the client. He was scared for his family. I don't know it was a wrong decision. He would have gladly spent seventeen years in prison to save his parents, his sisters."

On the other hand, had Paul testified, Bernstein would have gone over every little detail of the divorce case, which would have added even more fuel to motive.

The divorce case was an even worse horror story, he said. It should have been uncontested and cost $1,500, but Marie's attorneys saw that the Luskins had deep pockets and so engineered all of the meanness in the case. He figured Marie and her lawyers got $2 million each.

Plus, "Judge Nutaro was the most unfair judge I've ever seen. She made off-the-wall rulings. Not only we, but Paul's lawyers before us never won a motion more important than 'Can we go to the bathroom?'"

Entin conceded Marie was right to go after Paul's shielded one-third ownership of Luskin's, but the cash value Nutaro assigned it was far from reality.

Joe and Mildred Luskin hadn't voluntarily paid any of the $11 million she ordered them to give Marie; everything Barry Franklin recovered he had had to sue for. Entin guessed the Luskins had managed to salvage $2–2.5 million from sales of their real estate and were probably in the Bahamas.

Although Entin wasn't their attorney, he defended their flight. Had they stayed and appealed, they would have been in contempt unless they posted a hundred percent of their bond. Since they didn't have $11 million, they would have sat in jail indefinitely.

"What did they do? They were just the parents. They treated Marie like an empress, gave her gifts, and then for her to turn around and sue them?

"The case was a pig fuck. And we were the pig."

I found Gregg Bernstein in Baltimore. He had since left the U.S. Attorney's Office and had entered private practice.

The entire case was circumstantial, he said. We talked about the phone calls on March 9, 1987, and the call from Jimmy Liberto's hotel room to Paul's apartment.

"To believe Luskin's defense, you have to disbelieve what Manley said," he said. "I spent a lot of time with Manley, the FBI spent a lot of time with Manley, and the assistant prosecutor spent a lot of time with Manley. We agreed that it was inconceivable that he could have made it up. There is no way he could have had all those details."

Then I asked him why Marie was still alive. He laughed. "Cohen is not a competent hit man. He had never done it before. Luskin hired the wrong guys to do the job."

Bernstein conceded that the assault might have been a robbery instead of a murder attempt. "It's within the realm of possibility—that's what trials are for. But personally I don't believe it."

Nor did he insist that Marie was shot. Police didn't find a bullet at the crime scene, but probably because they weren't looking for one.

Then he said something surprising.

"The evidence we had was not all the evidence. There may have been more evidence out there." He compared the prosecution of the case to my investigation; he had to get it ready for trial in a few months, and I, as a reporter, had the luxury of time and perspective. It was certainly possible I could turn up new exculpatory material. But, he added, that wasn't to say he had found it first and withheld it at trial. That would be illegal.

Bernstein said that all the defense attorneys, save for Joe Liberto's attorney Mike Libowitz, felt confident and even cocky throughout the trial that they would win.

Ending the conversation so he could go into a meeting, I read from my 1990 notes about the calls between "Pellucci's" and Paul's home in Baltimore on March 9. "What?" he said. He didn't know what I was reading from, and whatever it was, it was wrong.

I told Entin about the interview with Bernstein. He said the calls in evidence "don't prove a damn thing. Jim Liberto's call from the Marco Polo—that could have been from Joe Liberto, calling from his brother's hotel room. And it was to Paul's answering machine.

"On the two subsequent attempts there was no pattern of calls like the government alleged on the first. This causes me to believe the pattern on the first set wasn't there either.

"You can have the story both ways. Robbery or murder."

At trial, Steve Allen conceded Marie was shot, but it wasn't a murder-for-hire. Bernstein told me it could be a murder-for-hire if Marie was either hit or shot. I reasoned still differently.

First, the government went months believing Marie was hit—as she testified. It just made sense if Cohen had a gun at Marie's head and was there to murder her, he would fire it and not hit her with it. In fact, there recently had been a very similar flower delivery assault in Palm Beach that was during a divorce, too. In that instance, the deliveryman shot and killed the wife in the doorway. He didn't bother saying "Give me all your money."

If I could determine Marie was hit, I thought, that would help convince me that Cohen was telling the truth. The first step was to find Dr. Charles Kokes, the government's expert witness who testified Marie was shot.

Kokes had since left Maryland, and was now working in the coroner's office in the San Francisco Bay area—Contra Costa County.

I told him Cohen had just given testimony that he hit Marie with a blackjack. At trial, Entin had theorized the lead fragments had come from a blackjack that split open on impact.

That wasn't likely at all, Kokes said. "I've never seen an instance where a blackjack deposited metal like this." And if it did, he asked me, "Why wouldn't it leave fragments all over the floor?" Surely the crime scene technicians would have seen that.

Second, he said, "The fact the metal fragmented showed that a great deal of force was used—much more than one would expect from a blunt force injury." The fragment was flat and deformed, not round like a lead shot that would be in a blackjack.

Marie's doctor wrote in his medical report that the fragments might have come from a barrette Marie was wearing at the time; however, she had discarded it before she got to the hospital. Although Entin hadn't brought that up at trial, I asked Kokes about it.

Paul and Marie Luskin in 1983.
(Courtesy Paul Luskin)

Paul, always a big contributor to the Republican Party, posed with President Reagan at a Senator Paula Hawkins re-election dinner.

(Courtesy Susan Davis Luskin)

Joe Luskin relaxes in 1985.
(Courtesy Susan Davis Luskin)

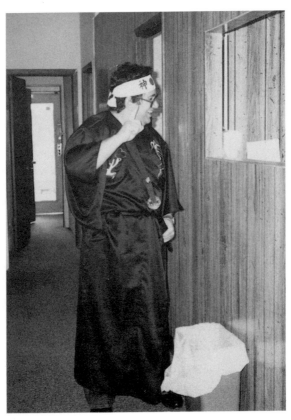

Joe Liberto mugs for the camera in the Hollywood, Florida, branch of Luskin's.

(Courtesy "Goldstein")

The scene of the assault. Note the flower petals strewn around the marble lobby.

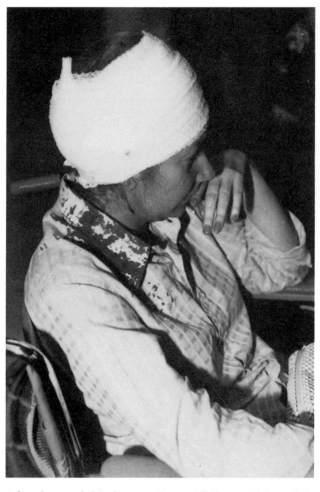

After the attack Marie was taken to Hollywood Memorial
Hospital.

(Courtesy Hollywood Police Department)

Sonny Cohen taken
in November 1994
at Lewisburg
federal prison.
(Author's photo)

Jim Liberto at
the Allenwood
federal prison.
(Author's photo)

Paul and Susan Luskin in a recent photo.
(Courtesy Susan Davis Luskin)

"I'm not aware that any barrettes are made of lead," he dismissed. "That would be for health reasons. Lead is very toxic."

However, "If you didn't know this was a lead fragment, I wouldn't be able to form as strong an opinion on this injury."

"But the police found no bullet hole, and Cohen said he was carrying a .38. How do you explain that?" I asked.

"If there was a .38 slug, there should have been more slug elsewhere, and more damage to her head. I can't address the thoroughness that the scene was investigated. Unless the police investigation was extremely sloppy, if it was a .38, there should have been a slug somewhere."

"What about the fact that if she was shot, she didn't even spend a night in the hospital?"

That was because the bullet didn't penetrate very far into the skull. If she had taken the whole bullet, yes, then it would have been unusual for her not to stay in the hospital for the night.

If a .38 was unlikely, we talked about what caliber the bullet might have been. Kokes suggested a .22. To illustrate how a person could survive a shot to the head with a .22, he recalled an autopsy he once did of a suicide:

A man shot himself point-blank in the head with a .22 five times. Then he used his sixth and final bullet to shoot himself in the chest, with less frustrating results.

"I don't get it," I said. "If Cohen was a lifelong criminal going back to age nine, and was hired as a professional killer, why would he use a .22?"

"Well, it would make less noise than a .38."

I was making some inroads, and Kokes realized it. He felt incumbent to explain the rationale for his findings:

"Given the amount of available information I had, I hope you can see how I came to form an opinion in this case. The simplest explanations are almost always the correct ones. It was consistent with a gunshot wound; there was lead, bullets have lead, it was a gunshot wound.

"It is far less likely, but an admittedly possible explanation is some such blunt object was used."

Afterward I consulted a local expert, Dr. Jay Barnhart, a pathologist for the Dade County Medical Examiner's Office. Was it logical that a .22 bullet would shatter after contact with a skull, but the skull itself wouldn't show any damage?

Barnhart said that was somewhat unusual. "Most of the time a .22 bullet doesn't break up going through soft tissue—unless it was a hollow-point bullet."

None of the bullets taken from Cohen's arsenal were. That was a dead end.

I also asked his opinion on Kokes's explanation at trial why Marie didn't hear the gunshot but stayed conscious. Barnhart said that kind of blacking out does happen, but only rarely.

Kokes had failed to dissuade me from the barrette theory. I began shopping women's notions.

My first stop was a chain drugstore. I bought a plastic barrette for about two bucks. Its metal clip was attached by glue.

That wasn't liable to be it. The fragment couldn't have come from the shiny metal clip.

I had been told Marie liked to wear expensive barrettes, so next was a trip to a department store, Burdines, at the 163rd Street Mall in North Miami Beach. I'm sure I looked a little suspicious examining womens' jewelry so closely. For eight dollars I bought a barrette with a gold-plated metal ornament attached to its metal clip.

This time the clip wasn't glued on. I walked to a jewelry kiosk in the middle of the mall with an unusual request.

"I just bought this at Burdines. Here's my receipt. Can you help me deconstruct this?"

The woman behind the counter laughed. All it took was a screwdriver and a flick of the wrist—too easy, frankly—and the ornament and clip separated. They had been connected by solder.

I borrowed a jewelers' tweezer tool. It was only a soft, easy cut to remove the solder and I stuck it in a little Ziploc bag. Under a magnifying glass, there was a definite similarity between it and the pictures of the metal taken from Marie's head.

Solder, I knew, is made of lead. So are bullets.

I had a new working theory. Maybe it was even right: Were the fragments in Marie's scalp remainders of lead solder when Cohen crushed her head with either his gun or a blackjack?

I asked Entin. "It never crossed my mind," he said.

Part of the problem was that the government didn't make an issue of the fragment until the eleventh hour, he said. The defense was busy with the divorce up until the week before the criminal trial. In addition, since the FBI lab couldn't prove it was from a bullet, he didn't think Kokes's testimony would stand up.

A month later, I reached Kokes again. He told me that since we had first talked, he had called someone in the government to discuss the case.

He referred to Marie's trial testimony that perhaps the remaining piece or pieces of the bullet were left at the scene, concealed in the carpet. Possibly, others were later picked up by a vacuum cleaner.

I ran past him my lead solder in the barrette theory. We'd been having an agreeable conversation up to then.

"I'd rather not comment," he said. Soon after, he excused himself from the phone.

Considering Marie's reaction that she didn't want to recall bad old memories with me, I wondered if I'd get the same thing from Susan. The file had her phone number and address in Hollywood, and for a while, I thought I'd just go there, knock on her door, and show my Pikesville High School class ring. I was '74 and she was '68, but my middle sister Gail had graduated that year. Maybe Susan remembered her.

As it turned out, I called. She had just returned from an Israel trip with her two boys to celebrate the oldest's Bar Mitzvah. At the Wailing Wall, she had stuck a scrap of paper into a crack between the stones, as is custom. It was a prayer addressed to God:

> My husband has been imprisoned in an American jail for a crime that he did not commit. Please help me get him out.

Unlike Marie, Susan was very pleased to talk to me.

We talked about home. She did know Gail; they had been in second grade together. In addition, she grew up around the corner from and knew one of my best friends, Hal Schenker.

She had numerous ill things to say about Marie. She expected that once Paul got out of prison, Marie would chase him for all the back child support and other monies the court had ordered but he hadn't paid since he went to prison. Rather than let him fall back into the same cycle of contempt of court and jailings, she thought they'd move to Israel together.

Paul was in prison in Jesup, Georgia, about fifty miles northwest of Savannah. She visited him every month or so and they talked on the phone three times a week. He hadn't lost his sense of humor behind bars, as evidenced by the well-drawn greeting cards he had sent her:

One was a Garfield the Cat wearing a decorated military uniform, smoking a corncob pipe, captioned "As Douglas McGarfield once said, 'I shall return!' "

Another was *Peanuts* characters. In the first panel, Woodstock the yellow bird walks behind a prison fence laughing, "How big is my sentence?"

The second panel was Charlie Brown, Snoopy, and Lucy behind a table with the logo of the U.S. Parole Commission, arms outstretched: "So Big!"

The logo was clever too—a hand with a thumbs-down. The commission's motto was "You Don't Go 'Til We Say So!"

I asked Susan to have Paul call me—collect, of course. Immediately, I found, it was hard not to like him.

He was charming, intellectual, witty, and playful. I was sorry I hadn't met him under different circumstances. I figured we would have been friends.

I didn't hear any rage from him, but there was definitely a little desperation; he would say puppy-dog things like "Can I go home now? I'm not having any fun anymore."

I had lots of questions and he answered them all, about the criminal case, the divorce, and himself. He said losing all his money didn't really bother him that much, but what did was losing his kids. He hadn't seen them since the day his divorce trial ended in January 1988, nor even talked to them by phone for a year because Marie had blocked all incoming calls on the children's line. He said he wrote them constantly, but he suspected Marie had been short-circuiting his letters, too. Replies were rare.

But in May, he got two letters, and he was beaming. Shana, fourteen, wrote:

> *Well I got and read your letter today and I really don't know what to think. If you really didn't do it, then I'd really like to see you come home soon. But when? The letter was very interesting, but was it all true? I hope!*

Diana, nine, wrote:

> *Dear Dad,*
>
> *I miss you a lot. When I'm pasted college I will see you. I love you a lot.*
>
> > *Love,*
> > *Diana, your kid*

"What keeps me going is I know I'm innocent. It's resting on Marie's conscience. She knows I didn't do it. She realizes the effect it's having on the kids. But it's her conscience versus her bank account."

Meanwhile, the stress of prison had led to a forty-pound weight gain.

Almost immediately, I became a regular on Paul's phone rounds. I also got a tremendous amount of mail from him. In his first letter he wrote:

*The horror of jails and being innocent hits me when
the door gets locked at night as well as the rest of the
family disaster that has occurred as a result of the
conviction.*

He told me that if he ever got his conviction overturned, he expected to get his law license back. His new
career would be federal criminal law.

Paul talked about a number of issues that didn't come
out at trial, but the most interesting to me was that the
small dressing area where the assault took place was
mirrored on three sides. One wall was mirrored floor to
ceiling; the area above the vanity was mirrored from
counter to ceiling; and the wall behind it had two
mirrored doors that led to bathrooms.

If the metal taken from Marie's scalp was a small
bullet fragment, might not the remainder have struck
glass?

Sherlock Holmes had solved the case of the curious
incident of the dog that did not bark in the night. My
curious incident involved a bullet that had failed to
shatter the mirror.

I called Hollywood Police and got interviews with
Barbara Alleva—the first officer on the scene on March
9—and her superior, Lieutenant Gregory Brand. Although Hollywood had investigated the crime as a home
invasion robbery, they were now convinced it was a
murder-for-hire.

However I detected a slight reluctance to admit that
the feds had shown them up. They said their investigation had touched all the bases, and Alleva recalled Marie
telling her that she hadn't heard a gunshot. The story
was plausible either way—Hollywood's robbery or the
feds' murder attempt, they said.

Later I talked to Leo Soccol, the investigating detective.

"Paul got stupid guys to do this," he told me. He said
he "heard through the grapevine as a rumor that Luskin
set it up—or his friends—and they were there to kill
her. She was shot, and she got real, real lucky."

Since I knew that courtroom rules of evidence kept out "through the grapevine" testimony, I asked Soccol where he got that from. The best he would say was it came either from Marie or someone associated with her.

Then Soccol admitted Marie's injury didn't look like a bullet wound, and that "If a guy wants to kill you, he'll pull you over and shoot you five or six times.

"For all we knew, it was a robbery."

Hollywood Police showed me the crime scene pictures, taken by crime scene technician Marjorie Hanlon—whose name had been mentioned at trial, but had not been called as a witness. She had since taken a job as a lieutenant at Plantation P.D., another suburban city police force in Broward County.

In 1987, Hanlon had been a crime scene tech for ten years. It had been another four years since the Luskin investigation, but she remembered it well—it was the largest house in Hollywood. She, too, was convinced Paul was guilty. But she didn't think Marie's wound was from a gunshot either.

"If there was a bullet hole, we would have found it," she said. The same for fragments, considering how confined the area was. Further, a gunshot would have been too loud in that room for no one to have noticed it.

"Most likely, there was not a shot fired."

Now that I was this far, I needed to interview Marie. I felt reluctant asking Barry Franklin, but he graciously had her call me. At eight-thirty on a Saturday morning, she did. It was obvious from the beginning she didn't want to be on the phone with me. When I had met her, she carried herself with confidence, but I didn't hear that from her this time.

I asked if she was wearing a barrette on the day she was assaulted, reminding her that the emergency room doctor had written so. In a very soft voice, she answered she couldn't say either way because her memory was hazy.

"I'm trying to forget the events of that day. Dredging it all up makes it worse."

She said as an aftereffect of the crime, she no longer

watched movies with guns in them. Now, she preferred Doris Day movies.

The ordeal had been hard on her kids, too. Neither had talked about it, but Shana, the oldest, seemed about ready to. Marie knew that their father wrote to them and said they replied once in a while. She said she didn't screen their mail.

I could tell my time was running short, and small talk wasn't getting me anywhere. I knew I might not get another chance, so I asked if she now believed she was hit or shot during the assault.

When she answered, she sounded like she had regressed into a six-year-old. She singsonged her words so they danced in the air, as if she were Peter Pan:

"Whatever the government says."

After we hung up, I realized that in our twenty-five-minute talk, Marie had not said Paul's name once.

I asked Barry Franklin, at his office, whether he thought Marie was shot or hit.

"My opinion, for whatever it's worth, to my knowledge there was no credible evidence to contradict the case that was presented by the U.S. Attorney's Office as to what happened. Yes, she was shot."

After I deciphered that quote, I realized he had just said, *Whatever the government says.*

Franklin believed Paul was guilty because he had made a pattern of lying in the divorce action. Therefore, he felt his statements denying the murder scheme were tainted.

He also thought Paul was capable of murder after seeing how he had played "Charlie Manson" at his own home on the day he was served the divorce papers.

"Even if he had appeared for years well balanced, this could have brought him over the edge," he said.

I asked Franklin how much of the $11 million judgment against Joe and Mildred was collectible. More than half, he said, but Marie had decided not to pursue them any farther. She had just settled for $975,000 with three real estate title companies who had let the Luskins sell their properties although they were legally encumbered by the court.

At the end of the interview, I showed him Paul's attorney Daniel Blackman's letter that Marie's counsel had told him she "intended to see Paul Luskin behind bars for the rest of his life, to keep him away from his children permanently, and to take everything away from him that he ever had."

"What?" Franklin said, grabbing the paper to read it. He marked it up, then said he didn't even remember Blackman. If he was in the case, it was just for a blink of an eye.

"That is so far removed from the truth that it sounds like it was written by Paul Luskin, which wouldn't surprise me. Amazing."

To make sure, I found Daniel Blackman. He had written the letter.

"That was accurate. That woman went out to frame her husband. The system didn't catch her, and in fact helped her along. It was horrible."

It was true he was Paul's counsel only briefly—two or three months. On his own, he said, "I decided it was time for a conversation one-on-one to find out what they wanted."

He couldn't remember if he talked with Franklin or Burton Young, the senior partner in Franklin's firm. "This was the response: She wanted blood; more than the law was going to provide. He said they were going to be the tool to do it.

"Paul had no chance of a fair trial with that judge and that law firm."

Since Gregg Bernstein had left the U.S. Attorney's Office, a new assistant U.S. attorney, Maury Epner, had been assigned to answer Paul's appeal. He was totally unimpressed with Cohen's confession under oath to attempted robbery and assault.

"Cohen has nothing to lose," he wrote. "We rather doubt that Cohen, who was in his mid-forties when he was sentenced to fifty years imprisonment in this case, is losing too much sleep over the risk he runs of additional jail time in Florida.

"Cohen is trying to jerk the system around that jerked him around. Who knows what agreement he and Luskin have?"

I got Epner on the phone. He admitted he wasn't familiar with the facts of the case, and that I probably knew it better than he did at this point. Given that, I asked if he thought the assault could be a murder-for-hire under the circumstances if the gun wasn't fired.

His first impression was "I wouldn't think so." But then he added "The issue is intent. Did they intend to murder the victim? If they used a gun or a sledgehammer, it doesn't matter."

Slowly, unapologetically, I came to speak out—based on the original case and the new evidence plus my gatherings—that Paul Luskin deserved and could win a new trial. I couldn't attest as certainly to his innocence; that carried a different standard, but it looked likely too.

However, the man who mattered was not equally convinced. In September, Judge Motz denied Paul's motion, refusing even to hold a hearing to listen to its merits.

When Paul told me, he grumbled that the fix was on against him. Look at how the Fourth Circuit Court of Appeals had ruled in 1989, citing prejudicial facts that didn't exist.

"I feel as low right now as I can get. I don't know if I'll ever get out of here alive.

"The Fat Lady hasn't sung yet, but I can hear her humming."

But there was a bit of new hope. In late August, Darden had received an envelope without a return address, postmarked Baltimore. Inside was a copy of a September 1987 letter on stationery that a Baltimore City assistant state attorney had written to Bernstein:

"The state will ultimately dismiss the charges it currently has against Mr. Manley at such time as his cooperation, which includes testimony in state court, is completed."

Darden called it the "Andrea Smith letter," after the assistant state attorney. He checked with Alvin Entin and Steve Allen, who told him they couldn't remember seeing the letter before. Darden concluded it was proof of a never-disclosed secret deal the government had made, further proving Manley's overwhelming incentive to perjure himself. It was also grounds for a new trial, he wrote again to Judge Motz.

When I reached Maury Epner again, it sounded like he considered Luskin an albatross around his neck: "I haven't researched the file, but I'm sure there's a very simple answer that completely blows his theory sky-high.

"These defendants have a lot of money. They're in jail, and they can't enjoy their money. They're wasting my time and the Court's time. They're like insects; they're real pains. How many times will these guys keep filing motions?"

In September, Joe Luskin entered a hospital in Los Angeles for an ulcer. He was diagnosed with cancer, and died in six weeks.

Paul was desperate. He wanted to say good-bye to his father but the Bureau of Prisons wouldn't let him go, not even with armed guards that the family offered to reimburse the government for.

Susan asked me to call the warden at Jesup, R.E. Honsted. I left a message, and a few minutes later he returned the call and very politely listened as I pleaded for Paul. But the answer had to be No. Because Paul had been convicted of a murder conspiracy, he was too dangerous to extend that courtesy to.

On November 24, *The Miami Herald*'s Sunday magazine, *Tropic,* ran my work as their cover story. The art was a watercolor of a broken pot of pink flowers on a parquet floor, and a pool of blood underneath. It was titled:

FLOWERS FOR MRS. LUSKIN
Money And Passion, Violence and Vengeance, Crime And Punishment. The Saga Of One Of The Nastiest

Divorces In South Florida History Has Everything.
Maybe Even An Innocent Man.

Inside, the headline was:

The Divorce From Hell
A Millionaire Has An Affair. His Wife Throws Him Out.
She Gets The Mansion, The Business, The Cash. His
Parents' Business. His *Parents'* Cash. She Gets Shot And
Doesn't Know It. The Bullet Disappears. He Goes To
Prison. His Parents Flee The Country. He Weds The
Other Woman Behind Bars. Has There Ever Been A
Case Like This?

On December 15, the *Baltimore Sun Magazine* reprinted it as their cover story. Getting published in the
old hometown newspaper was too much fun to stay
home for, so I flew to Baltimore that weekend.

When I arrived at the airport Saturday afternoon, I
bought a first edition of the Sunday paper. Besides
enjoying first seeing it in print, I nearly doubled with
laughter when I spotted a half-page ad on the back of the
Travel section. It read:

"The cover story in today's *Sun Magazine* concerns
Marie and Paul Luskin of Hollywood, Florida.

"They have no connection with the Luskin's stores of
Baltimore."

Under that was the logo of the Baltimore *Sun,* and its
motto, "Light for All."

I had never seen anything like it. Obviously Jack
Luskin—a major advertising client—had demanded its
printing. During trial coverage, the *Sun* had frequently
mentioned that the Florida and Baltimore Luskins were
not the same. Once, a story even referred to "Jack
'Cheapest Guy in Town' Luskin."

Later, an editor told me that Jack didn't know about
the story until it had come back from the rotogravure
printer. He then threatened to end his business with the
paper if they didn't pull it, but it was much too late for
that. As a compromise, top brass offered the half-page

ad. Nothing against me, the editor said, but the *Sun* would run no further stories about Paul and Marie Luskin.

And in fact, there weren't.

When I stopped in at the paper, the episode was the buzz of the newsroom. Someone showed me a satire that had been posted on the bulletin board, and he let me copy it:

By Lord N. Taylor

BALTIMORE—Longtime Maryland crime figure Jimmy "The Weasel" Macy turned himself in to federal marshals yesterday, as U.S. prosecutors unsealed an indictment charging Macy and 17 others with conspiracy to distribute cocaine, racketeering, money laundering and operation of a continuing criminal enterprise.

Macy, 39, is unrelated to the national department store chain that spends $5 million a year on *Baltimore Sun* advertising. Prosecutors say he is a distant cousin to the retailing family and actually shops at K-Mart.

Also indicted in the case were Benny "Three Fingers" Hecht and Louie "The Mouse" Riteaid, both known associates of Mr. Macy. Neither man is, in fact, related to the retailers so very dear to this newspaper.

Prosecutors say the three-year investigation into Macy's ring stems from the 1988 slaying of Johnny "The Giant" Foods, an FBI informant and low-level drug trafficker who has nothing whatsoever to do with the supermarket chain that, by the way, is running a remarkable sale on ground round and tenderloin this week.

"These arrests have created a real gap in the underworld," said Special Agent James K. Lee of the Baltimore office of the FBI. "And by that, I'm obviously not referring to the casual wear shops responsible for such a significant share of the area's retail advertising."

Darden had hoped people would crawl out of the woodwork after the *Sun Magazine* story appeared, and while I was still in Baltimore, one did. He was Phil

Caroom, who had prosecuted Manley's Anne Arundel
County burglary case. He called Darden and described
how Bernstein and Connolly had come into county
court—a month after Luskin's federal trial ended—
asking the judge to give Manley a break. Caroom,
somewhat insulted, had opposed them; Manley had
jumped bail and had a terrible record. The judge gave
Manley a suspended sentence.

The day after Darden told me, I raced to Annapolis
and met Caroom. He was now a Master—akin to a
judge, but not quite. He looked Lincolnesque; when I
walked in he was listening to an untranscribed court
reporter's tape of the proceeding. Later, he helped
Darden obtain a transcript of it.

He referred me to Manley's case file. Inside I found a
reference that he had been placed in the federal Witness
Security Program. I hadn't heard that before, and as it
turned out, Paul, Entin, and Steve Allen said they hadn't
either.

It became the basis of yet another motion for a new
trial. Putting Manley in Witness Protection was tantamount to compensating him for his testimony, Darden
said. The program offers stipends, new housing, and
jobs. He wrote that the jury never heard about it because
the government had failed to tell the defense.

NINE

1992–1994

Paul wanted to meet me, and in January 1992, I made arrangements with Susan to drive to Jesup.

First I talked with Diane Yariv. "To see them together, you can tell they love each other. It will carry them through everything," she said. "They think alike and sometimes they have private jokes they think of simultaneously. It takes a while for them to be able to explain the logic of them to me. You should see them play Scrabble together."

Diane said Marie is probably even more miserable now than before. "No matter how much money Marie gets she'll never know the happiness Paul and Susan know."

Before we left, Paul told me the Scrabble game had lost half its tiles. I offered to buy a new one and donate it to the prison visiting area. He suggested which toy store to go to.

"Daddy, buy me a toy," he said.

It broke my heart.

During the ride, I recalled I had come close to meeting Paul in 1984, during Luskin's Expo sale. It wasn't the year Marie had served him the divorce papers, but it was when Marie testified she saw the half million in cash in the store. Both my parents and I bought stereo receivers and speakers that day—by credit card. My parents spotted Joe Luskin, then Mildred and their daughter

Donna came over. I don't think I had seen Donna since we were in kindergarten together in 1962.

Joe sent a message upstairs to Paul to come meet old friends from Baltimore. We waited, but he never showed up.

I remembered my parents and me looking at each other, thinking, *What a jerk.*

Susan told me about their wedding, in October 1989, at the prison in Marianna, Florida. She asked me to refer in print to it as "a traditional Jewish ceremony" although it obviously had its quirks.

Paul had called Susan's parents from prison, collect, to ask for her hand. They blessed the wedding. "My parents would not have let me marry someone who had tried to kill his former wife," Susan said.

(I had already met Susan's mom Gloria, who told me she had known Paul just as long as Susan had. She told me: "I just have two things to say about Paul Luskin. I think he's innocent, and I love him.")

Dress took more thought than usual. Prison guards can deny visitors entry if they're clothed provocatively or inappropriately—and their judgment seemed arbitrary—so Susan had to pick out something "pretty enough to be a wedding dress, conservative enough for the guards to let me in." She chose an ivory lace V-neck gown and high heels.

Paul's problem wasn't getting in. His friends in the prison's food service specially tailored and monogrammed him a white outfit. He wore a white yarmulke and new white leather Reeboks Susan had bought for him. "He looked real nice," she said.

Another problem; Marianna had no rabbis. Susan found one in an unlikely place—Dothan, Alabama. He was willing to travel, and brought a silver goblet and kosher grape juice—no wine is allowed in prison.

Diane Yariv came, too. Susan was so nervous on their way from the hotel room to the prison that her knees shook so hard they kept bumping the steering wheel.

It was a pretty day and the ceremony was held outdoors, but no pictures were allowed.

They wrote a wedding announcement together.

Paul and Susan of Hollywood fame
Would like to announce and proclaim
That in spite of the distance
*   and all the resistance*
They decided to use just one name.

The wedding was nice—
But no wine or rice;
So the bride and the groom were both sober.
The weather was sunny—
The rabbi was funny;
All on the 24th of October.

Proud parents are Gloria and Irv
Who wonder how we got up the nerve.
Then there's Mickey and Joe
*   Of Turnberry, you know.*
Wish them naches—they all deserve.

The wedding was never an if . . .
Just a question of when
We'd share all our joys
With our girls and our boys
Shana, Jeremy, Diana, and Ben.

Though now things are not ideal
The love and commitment are real
We hope you're elated
*   though the news is belated*
And this is the end of our schpiel.

On the evening they were married Paul had a florist
take roses to Susan's hotel room.
Flowers for Mrs. Luskin.

There must be a rule here against holding the same
kiss too long. Every few seconds they had to stop and
start again. Finally when they were ready to acknowledge the rest of the world, Paul's first words to me were:
"Hi, how are ya, get me outta here."
We talked about the case, but mostly I just watched

the two of them together for most of the next seven hours. They were barely separable. In the rare moments they didn't have anything to say, they just made direct eye contact with one another, burning the exposures in their minds. It must be how they possess each other after the prison doors shut.

"People tell me when I leave for here 'try to have a good time.' But I do have a good time," Susan said.

On the way from Miami we had stopped and Susan found a sweatshirt that read "Princeton." She bought it to wear inside the prison as a proud Scarlet Letter.

Paul laughed. "Marie didn't care. Poor Marie was in Delaware, with her boyfriend," he said.

I reminded him the *Sun* had highlighted his quote that he liked Marie because she was "pretty, intelligent, and *not* from Baltimore." Paul cleared his throat, and the record, for Susan's sake:

"I have a slightly jaded view of girls from Delaware right now. Girls from Baltimore look pretty good compared to girls from Delaware."

"How could you be so stupid to marry her?" Susan ribbed.

"Well, my intelligence improved with age."

"Oh yeah? Look at the surroundings."

Inevitably the issue of Paul's weight arose. Paul called his problem "stress eating." His sister Nance had joked that he'd better enjoy his life in prison, because "at Susan's house she'll never let him eat again."

Paul seemed to have junk food on the brain. He fantasized building a "choo-choo" in Susan's house running between the kitchen and the bedroom "so it can bring me snacks." Susan cracked up, wondering whether her two cats Sabrina and Farfel would let it operate.

"Does Paul stay up all night thinking about snacks?" I asked her.

"No. He stays up all night eating them."

"You're unmanageable, Susan," Paul broke in out of the blue. "You're negative and you're argumentative."

"I'm not argumentative," she answered back.

"See! See!"

Realizing she'd been tricked, Susan buttoned her lip, until Paul smiled and winked at her.

At the end of our first visiting day, Susan reflected on the state of her universe:

"What a waste of a life. Not many people could be as productive as he, and they've flushed him down the toilet. Also, they're wasting my life. This is not the life I want.

"I have total bitterness toward the government. It's vicious not to give him a hearing. They don't care about people, just winning. This is not how it's supposed to be. It's unheard of not to even get a hearing. People here get hearings all the time on very small things."

In the almost four years since his conviction, Susan had pretty much lost hope it would get overturned. When she talked about Paul getting out, she referred to parole.

"When he does gets out, I don't want him to make a lot of money. He would get aggravation from Marie. He has someone who he wants to spend his time with. If he starts a new business, he'll have to invest all his time into it, and I don't want him to."

She said prison had broken him somewhat, but not completely. "He's trying to prepare himself for his mother dying. He may die in there. His father's already dead.

"At least he has no regrets for things he didn't do in the first part of his life. He did so much, shared so much with his kids. Paul doesn't have a present, doesn't have a future. He only has a past.

"Tomorrow, it'll be hard for me, because we'll be leaving him there."

The next day we talked about the past. Paul loved to buy toys for his girls, and they would all play together with them. One was a bathtub toy he named "Burton the Bug," after Marie's attorney Burton Young. They also had colored soap in the shape of Crayola crayons which the kids painted all over themselves, then it washed off.

He remembered the messes he let Diana make at his parents' apartment. When they'd leave there'd be Play-Doh buried in the carpet.

"Did he finger-paint with them?" I asked Susan.

"Are you kidding? You think he was going to miss out on that? Paul would be up to his elbows in finger paints, then he'd take his messy fingers and flex them in your face. Marie had rules for finger-painting, like spreading newspapers underneath. Paul didn't do that."

Once Paul threw raw cookie dough at Susan, trying to start a food fight, she remembered. "He's a master at getting other people into trouble. But if you threw it back, he'd tell his mother."

"I threw it at you? What a waste of cookie dough."

Paul said he was now just like Marie: "At 11:30 I'm locked in my room, and I read romance novels."

On the ride back, Susan reminisced some more. "At fourteen I knew who I wanted to marry. He was neat. He looked like a nerd, but I didn't think so at the time. He had exactly the same mannerisms as now. He had a sense of fun, and was funny. He made everything seem special.

"I don't think any different about him now than I did in high school. I still feel very honored—after all the people he could have chosen, he chose me. Even if he was stupid the first time."

The Sunday we traveled home was the day the *Orlando Sentinel's* Sunday magazine, *Florida,* reprinted *Tropic's* story under the title "Hate in Bloom." Driving through Orlando, we picked up a copy.

Gregg Bernstein hadn't responded to the stories in either Baltimore or Miami, but for some reason, a few weeks later he wrote a letter to the Orlando editor:

Mr. Cohen's story is equally implausible when one considers it against the evidence that he and Manley traveled to Florida in July of 1987 to carry out the contract based on information Cohen had received from his coconspirators that Mrs. Luskin would be at Bennigan's Restaurant near her home on Tuesday evening, July 28, at 7:00 P.M. in order to host a single-parent support group dinner.

> *It is inconceivable how Manley and Cohen could
> have obtained this kind of detailed information
> about Mrs. Cohen's whereabouts and the status of
> the divorce case without an inside source.*

I had to admit, if Cohen had told Manley about the single parent support group, that clinched Paul Luskin's guilt.

But Bernstein was wrong; Manley didn't say that at trial or to the grand jury, nor did the FBI report he said it. Manley had the time and place, but only Marie said she was there for the single parent support group. Manley testified his information was she would be alone.

Only the Baltimore *Evening Sun* reported Manley said it. Melody Simmons, covering the trial, didn't quote Manley but did write:

> "Manley said he and Cohen stalked her as she drove to a restaurant for a meeting of a single parent support group."

I had read that long before I got a copy of the trial transcript, and it had bugged me all that time.

On January 23, Judge Motz denied Luskin's motion for reconsideration based upon the Andrea Smith letter. Months later, the same fate befell the Witness Protection motion.

In the next few months, Susan got depressed. She stopped talking to Paul for a few weeks, and told me she had given up because she no longer trusted the courts or Darden. She began talking suicide.

In 1987, when Susan was thirty-six, they had planned to have a child together. But at forty-one, with no immediate hope of Paul's release, it was getting late. "It kills a part of the dream we had together," she said.

She cursed him for doing this to her. Every day, every minute was difficult without him present. At the beginning she couldn't get to sleep because he wasn't there; still now she couldn't go to the beach, to a social dinner, or plan vacations without cursing him.

And it was all his fault because he had had such an

arrogant attitude during the divorce. When he moved
out of the house he took an expensive apartment at
Turnberry, then claimed he couldn't pay all Marie's
support. He infuriated Marie by telling her to sign a loan
document before he left the house. His father firing him,
even if true, looked stupid.

"If the divorce hadn't gotten out of hand, then the
employees wouldn't have talked so much, and Joe
Liberto wouldn't have opened his mouth and told his
brother things. I pay the price for that every day."

Susan said she asked Paul a number of times after
Marie's assault if he was behind it. She told me he was
capable of it, but he wouldn't have hired people who
would do such a sloppy job.

She remembered Paul trying to intimidate Marie on
the telephone after the assault. They were in Susan's
living room, she was sitting on the love seat, Paul on the
sofa.

"He was saying things that made me uncomfortable. I
didn't like it." She motioned to Paul to hang up because
he was getting carried away. He didn't say there were
other florists, but said something similar a few times.

"He was blowing off steam. But it wasn't right. That's
why I get so mad at him. I remember thinking it was one
of the all-time stupid things he did in the divorce. I
thought, you're wrong, you're digging a grave for yourself.

"I was upset that any woman would be subject to that
(the home invasion assault). I am afraid a lot. All I have
to protect me are Jeremy, Ben, and my cats.

"Marie's paranoia is never going to go away. In one
way, I'm thrilled. On the other hand, it's a terrible way to
have to live."

Susan's depression affected Paul. It compounded his
inability to reach Darden, and his mother's complaints
that Joe wasn't around anymore. Susan told me Paul had
written her that he would commit suicide himself if
none of his appeals succeeded.

"Susan thinks she is getting older, but I am not," Paul
told me. "Only one of us is going into middle age."

* * *

Once I got Jim Liberto's address, he answered my letter with a call. He said his brother Joe visited him whenever he stayed at the Marco Polo. Jimmy would go into the shower and Joe would use the phone for business, calling around to the different Luskin's stores. That November 1986 call to Paul's apartment was Joe's, he said.

He told me he considered all the Luskins "garbage." I asked whether he had threatened Paul at trial, and he denied it. Regardless, he was still disturbed that Luskin argued a divisive drug defense.

Was it true? I asked. Jimmy tacitly agreed it was. "If you were here in person, I would tell you more," he said.

"He's innocent of this goddamn thing. But I gotta stay married to this stinkin' bum.

"Truthfully, I don't think we got a shot. I'm innocent. But I'm very bitter. If I would have done this, then I'd have no beef."

In May, Darden told me something big was brewing, but wouldn't say what. Whatever it was he had found out "will definitely make a difference" but he had been sworn to secrecy, able to tell only Paul.

"There are very positive things happening. Things are not what they seem."

Days later, I heard it from Paul. He got Darden's "secret" letter, which said if Paul couldn't keep it secret, then Darden would have to ditch it. It would eventually make a pleading, but first Ben needed to commit the information to paper, with a signature. Ben sounded certain he could pull it off, but Paul was less sure. It would be dramatic if it happened, he said.

Two weeks later, in Alvin Entin's office, his partner Sheldon Schwartz invited me into his office, which was part pinball arcade. None of the other attorneys in the firm had been quite the cheerleader for Paul that Alvin was, but I hadn't expected what Shelly had to say:

Two people had come to him early on in the case and said the government had indicted the wrong Luskin. There was a murder-for-hire, and Joe Luskin was behind it. Paul knew nothing about it, they said.

Shelly offered no details, and added that Alvin didn't believe them. One person was worthy of doubt, but the other was better, Shelly said.

I had already listened to a line of people tell me that Paul was guilty when it was clear they knew almost nothing about the case beyond his conviction. If Shelly wanted to show me something I would listen, but he said he couldn't.

However, Shelly did agree with me that the police evidence didn't add up to a murder-for-hire. Shelly said hit men are precise; they leave 'em dead and don't try to rob the place—not for the $25,000 to $50,000 you pay the Italians. There wasn't a bullet fired in that room, he said, nor was there any linking evidence against Joe Luskin, such as phone calls on the record. If he made any calls, they had to have been local.

On Darden's mention, I called Charlotte Cohen, Sonny's mom. She told me Sonny and Jimmy Manley were brothers-in-law, so she had some insight into Manley and his family.

Yes, Manley was in Witness Protection, she said. He was already out of prison and had been placed somewhere in Wisconsin. His wife wouldn't leave Baltimore and her grown kids, "but she is still crazy about Jimmy." Her phone bills were very high.

Mrs. Cohen, however, never liked Jimmy, and didn't want Sonny hanging out with him.

"Do you think Jimmy Manley has a conscience?" she asked me. It was a good question I hadn't even considered.

Mail call: Paul said someone got a package of magazines from home, and everyone crowded around to see. "I got *Playboy!*" he announced. Paul got a package of magazines from Susan, too.

"What did you get, Luskin?"

"I got *Hadassah.*"

He got permission to teach a mythology class, and it was a success—fifteen enrolled, and more wanted in.

I was interested. "How do I get in?" I asked.

"Rob a bank," he suggested.

Darden had appealed Judge Motz's denials for a
hearing on the merits of his motions for a new trial, and
the Fourth Circuit Court of Appeals granted him a brief
oral hearing. It was a step removed from what Darden
was after; it wasn't an evidentiary hearing, just a legal
argument why Motz should hear one.

The hearing was scheduled for July 9 at the federal
courthouse in Wilmington, North Carolina. A week
before, Darden told me a little bit more about his secret
project.

He said on May 1, 1993, "all of Paul's wildest
thoughts would come to bear." That day, someone was
going to go public with their knowledge. Already he had
some of it on audiotape: it indicated witness tampering,
coercion, and evidence tampering.

A few days later, I talked to Paul about it. "May 1, '93
is exactly five years from my sentencing date, and the
end of the statute of limitations for perjury," he said.

"It's not Manley, is it?" I asked.

"Hmm?" he said.

"Not Manley?"

"Hmm?" he said again.

Wilmington is a small historic seaport town, and its
1910 courthouse at the corner of Princess and Water
Streets was beautiful and in perfect condition. Outside,
its white marble steps and brass handrails were polished
and gleaming. The main courtroom was large and dramatic, with four white Greek columns behind the bench,
and a very high ceiling so the heat could rise.

"Oyez, oyez, oyez," called the bailiff. "The honorable,
the judges of the United States Court of Appeals for the
Fourth Circuit are now in session. God save the United
States and this honorable Court."

As the three judges of the panel came in—ancient
men, all three—Darden whispered to me that two of the
judges were the same as last time, the ones who had
mistakenly stated facts that were not in evidence and
ruled against Paul.

"This is a waste of time," he said.

During Darden's argument, it was clear by the questions they asked that none of them knew even the basic background of the case. They obviously hadn't read the briefs. Early on, when Darden tried to move on to his next point, one of the judges told him to slow down: "We're mixed up enough."

Maury Epner argued for the government. He said Judge Motz had already concluded that the Cohen statement was "utterly without substantive worth."

"There was a rank silliness to Mr. Cohen's statement. This was the most exculpatory confession you're likely to see. It was a confession in no sense of the word. He said there was no murder-for-hire. You have to take with a grain of salt when a codefendant later exculpates a defendant.

"'Manley and I go to Florida to do a robbery,'" he quoted. "Judge Murnahan and I are both Marylanders, and lots of Marylanders have at least as much wealth as Marie Luskin. You don't need to go all the way to south Florida to do a robbery."

At the end of the argument, each of the judges shook hands with both counsel.

Afterward, I had lunch with Darden. He thought he had won. I was hoping he'd talk about Manley, but he wouldn't. He said he wanted to tell me the details, but asked me to be patient.

On the way home from Wilmington, I stopped by Jesup to visit Paul. There I walked in on a family gathering—Mildred, Nance, Donna, and Donna's little daughter were there, too. In front of them was a picnic of junk food obtained with quarters they had brought for the vending machines.

I gave them a blow-by-blow of the oral hearing. We also talked about Manley; Paul said Manley had told Darden that Sonny's story was right, they had made up the murder-for-hire in jail so they could get a deal.

I thought, the prosecution had been able to call Cohen's statement worthless, but what would they do with Manley's? They'd be forced to say he was a liar too—but he had told the truth at trial. How would they get out of that?

September 9 was Paul Luskin's lucky day. A

computer-generated letter said he had just taken "two giant steps" toward winning the Reader's Digest $5 million sweepstakes.

It was addressed to the prison, at 2680 Highway 301 South, Jesup, Georgia:

> *Just imagine the excitement on 301 S. if an armored car were to drive up to 2680 Hwy 301 S. Think how surprised your friends and neighbors in Jesup would be if I were to step out of that armored car and ask you to accept delivery of $167,000 cash!*

Jim Liberto had passed on my address to his brother Joe, and I got a letter from him in November, a little disappointed that I hadn't interviewed him for my magazine article. He was in prison in Seagoville, Texas. I wrote him back and he replied promptly:

> *There is a lot more I can explain about Paul since I basically all but raised him. Yes, we worked together a long time ago. He was a thin, good-looking kid and very smart. His father dominated his life and so Paul became like a brother more than a friend or employee.*

I had asked him if he remembered making the November 24, 1986 call from his brother's hotel room to Paul's apartment.

"I do not remember calling Paul on that date. I don't remember any particular calls to Paul; why would I? Could you remember calls you made last year? I don't think so."

Nor did he remember telling Jimmy how much money the Luskins kept in their house.

"The Luskins kept large amounts of money at the office and I'm sure many times they brought money home. When Paul was having problems with his wife, I was in Orlando (managing the Orlando Luskin's store) in the beginning. Paul was running around with his girlfriend and when it blew up the first thing the Luskins did was to try to hide some of their money and assets. This is why the divorce judge ruled in Marie's favor, because they tried to hide money from her and got caught with their fingers in the cookie jar.

"I was called to come down from Orlando because the business was falling apart. When Paul and I ran the business, it did great. The fact is, I was brought down to Florida (in 1977, from Luskin's in Baltimore) to run the business and transform it from a stereo store to video and TVs and I taught the man how to sell and worked day and night to build the business up."

But then the Luskins brought in someone else to be his boss and exiled him to Orlando to open a store there. Orlando did very well until they asked him to close it "so Marie would not get money from that store." That was the same time Paul left the business, so they asked Joe to return to the main Hollywood store and run it. "The fact is they started closing store after store because of the divorce."

Joe criticized Paul's trial strategy. "He made an effort to bring in the drug conspiracy and that made everyone look bad. After that, all the government had to do was discredit Paul and win the case. I worked for Paul for fifteen years (actually ten) in Florida and his uncle and father over a twenty year time in Baltimore and his antagonistic defense hurt us so badly at trial it was all but impossible to win. A close look at the evidence shows there was not enough evidence to uphold a conviction on me from the beginning."

He said in 1990 he got a sentence reduction, so his twenty-two years had been cut to fifteen years, thirty days. Judge Motz had sympathized with him because his family had been "devastated" by the conviction. Gregg Bernstein had opposed the reduction.

"I'll tell you something. Bernstein's uncle Sid worked under me in the Towson (Maryland) Luskin's store. He told me how Bernstein hated the Luskins when he worked for a law firm and worked for the (Baltimore) Luskins through that firm as a lawyer. Interesting to say the least!"

Joe said he had had a heart attack in 1990. "I grieved so much for my family it all but killed me. You see, my riches in life were my family, the most precious part of my life was taken from me. It was not money. Never was, never could be. That is what makes all this so crazy. I was the most honest person I ever knew and to do what the government said was impossible!"

Darden had been right when he whispered to me in the Wilmington courthouse; it was a waste of time. On February 3, 1993, the Fourth Circuit denied Paul's appeal to force Judge Motz to hold a hearing to determine whether he should have a new trial.

It was denied *per curiam*—they didn't even write an opinion explaining why.

Apparently my story in the *Sun* had something to do with Manley calling Darden, but May 1, 1993 came and went without any news. Frustrating months passed during which Paul couldn't even reach Darden by telephone. Meanwhile, Donna and her husband Henry Gradstein—both attorneys in midtown Los Angeles, practicing together—hired another post-conviction attorney, William Genego, a former law professor at University of Southern California.

In June, Genego had made headlines in the *Los Angeles Times* for winning a reversal of a murder conviction of a former marine lance corporal, Thomas Merrill, in Orange County, California. And a year later, he would turn up on national TV as the attorney representing Kato Kaelin at the O.J. Simpson trial.

Originally, Genego was hired solely to argue Paul's sentencing issues, but as the family put less and less faith in Darden to deliver a Manley statement, Genego took over the entire appellate case.

Genego said Paul was just about out of "bites of the apple," that is, chances to return to the courts and ask for a new trial. This last appeal would be based largely on "newly discovered evidence" Paul had learned when the FBI filled his Freedom of Information Act—FOIA—request.

Paul said the FBI had told him and Steve Allen that the metal fragments taken from Marie's scalp had been destroyed by the lab during their examination; there was nothing left to give Luskin's experts for their own testing. But internal FBI documents in the FOIA file showed the fragments were not destroyed.

Also, Paul said, the FBI had claimed the fragments were composed of lead but hadn't provided documentation proving that.

The second issue was that the government knew Paul's codefendants were under previous investigation for drug trafficking, but when Luskin's defense asked them to disclose it, they denied it.

Frank Liberto—Jimmy and Joe's brother, who testified to the first grand jury, but not at trial—was a mysterious figure to Paul. When Gregg Bernstein took his testimony, he admitted pleading guilty to cocaine smuggling.

I got a copy of that case file from the National Archives. Frank Liberto had been arrested in Washington, D.C., on a northbound Amtrak train between Fort Lauderdale and Baltimore, carrying three kilos. The date was February 26, 1987—eleven days before the assault on Marie Luskin.

The day after he was arrested, his brother Jimmy posted his bond, $50,000.

Paul had alleged Frank and Jim Liberto's drug link once before, in a 1990 motion. In August 1990, Gregg Bernstein responded that the government only learned about Jim Liberto's trafficking during its investigation of the murder-for-hire case. Further, he wrote, "The Government has no information linking Frank Liberto to any alleged drug activity by James Liberto."

I also spotted something in the grand jury testimony—the initial one—of Roy Cheeks, an agent of the Bureau of Alcohol, Tobacco, and Firearms.

"Isn't it true," Bernstein asked him, "that because of the good work of your office and the Baltimore City Police in arresting these two individuals (Cohen and Manley) that it has come to light that the FBI has been investigating Mr. Liberto for some time?"

"Yes. The FBI is definitely investigating Mr. Liberto," Cheeks said.

"Which one?" asked a juror.

"James Joseph."

"Can we ask why they are investigating him?"

"That has nothing to do with the subject of this indictment. At this point it is somewhat speculative, so I would rather wait until we have some concrete information," he said.

"Agent Cheeks, isn't it true that there has been some evidence that indicates Mr. Cohen may know Mr. Liberto?" Bernstein asked.

"Supposedly some rumor has it that Mr. Cohen is an enforcer for Jim Liberto," he said.

Beyond that, I had a private theory.

On March 4, 1987, six days after Frank Liberto had been arrested, Jim Liberto checked into the Marco Polo. Telephone records showed he called his alleged drug connection—one of the three Miami Hispanic women. On March 5, 6, and 7, calls were documented from Marco Polo pay phones that were consistent with Cohen's calling pattern.

On Saturday, March 7, Joe Liberto's home phone called the Marco Polo, then a fancy waterfront restaurant called Martha's not far from the hotel.

Did Jim Liberto, Joe Liberto—and Cohen—have dinner together that night? Did the drug ring—out the wholesale price of three kilos of cocaine—discuss robbing Marie Luskin because they needed a quick $100,000?

At last in July there was news from Darden. Manley had reaffirmed he would make his statement, and in a letter, Darden asked him to pick a place and date between August 1 and 15. That's when Darden had planned a summer family trip out west by car.

After that, the news as Paul told it was contradictory. First Paul told me Darden met with Manley somewhere near Yellowstone National Park and a number of times after that.

Then, when Darden came to visit Paul on the day after Thanksgiving, it changed to they hadn't met but were close to arranging a date. Manley was in Billings, Montana, under a name Witness Protection had given him. He was unemployed, drinking, and getting only $1,200 a month from the government. He was homesick and wanted to come back to Baltimore, but before he'd give Darden a formal statement he wanted assurances that no one he'd ratted on would kill him if he did.

Darden told Paul he would see Sonny Cohen in Lewisburg the next week. After that he planned to see Jim Liberto; Manley wasn't concerned with Joe Liberto.

However, Darden was worried that something was fishy. Since he still hadn't met Manley, he couldn't be sure whether it was really him, or if he was being set up. Since Darden had a relationship with Cohen, he planned to ask him whether the Manley he was talking to sounded like the Manley that Cohen knew.

Still suspicious, Darden asked why anyone would be lonely for Baltimore. Paul laughed.

In December Darden sent Paul a copy of a letter he had written Manley. On the copy Paul sent me, he blocked out Manley's address and new last name.

Dear Jimmy:

A lot of conversation has passed between us over the past months. We have now reached the point where you have an excellent opportunity to right the many wrongs perpetrated on at least four people.

I have verified—to the maximum practicable extent—the many items that you have brought to my attention, e.g., Gregg Bernstein pressuring you to testify as to facts not related by you, the non-involvement of James Liberto, the attempt by you and Sonny to take over the Liberto drug enterprise, etc. Needless to say, some of the information you have made available to me can only be verified by you. However, I have spoken to Sonny and he has partially verified some of the details.

You spoke to me of your personal security and intense desire to return to Baltimore. As you proba-

bly know, I have had personal contact with the defendants in this case. In fact, my last contact was just last week. I have never had any participant or defendant express a desire to do anything other than get out of prison and get on with their lives. No one has ever expressed to me a threat against you or any member of your family.

So if it is your intent to right the record and allow my client, Paul Luskin, extricated from this mess, now is the time. I will personally meet with you at any location of your choice for the purpose of working out a formula so as to achieve this purpose.

Sincerely,
Benjamin F.L. Darden

Once again, Paul got his hopes up.

In late November, at Paul's prompting, I bugged Alvin Entin to see his files again so I could look for Frank Liberto's grand jury statement. By now the files were in a storage warehouse, and I had to agree to pay a fee to have them retrieved.

I found what I was looking for, and more. First, there was a copy of the Andrea Smith letter concerning Manley's plea agreement deal in Baltimore City, but without Darden's "Received" stamp on it. The defense had had it after all.

Also, I found a page of notes dated October 19, 1987—the Monday after Paul had been indicted. It had the initials of two other attorneys in Alvin's office—one was Shelly Schwartz—and was entitled with a name of a Luskin's employee. After I spoke with him, I agreed to give him a pseudonym in print. I'll call him "Jackson":

Joe LaBerto—left Luskin's 8–10 months ago, mngr Hollywood. Was muscle for store, know people to get job done.

Saw him 5–6 months ago in Kendall as personal for Joe and Milly—know what Marie doing to Co.

Joe Luskin asked him (favor to Joe and Mildred) to

come back to eliminate Marie—contact brother and
we are going to kill her.

This was upsetting.

I found Jackson's phone number in the phone book,
but just before I was going to call him, Paul called. I
shared with him what I had just found. He had known
about it at the time.

If his father was involved in a murder-for-hire, "He
never told me, that's for sure," he said. However they
did discuss it after the indictment. Paul asked him,
"Dad, who are they talking about? Is there any way you
and Joe Liberto ever had a conversation?" No, he
answered. Paul also asked him how Manley knew about
Bennigan's: "I don't know, not from me. I couldn't care
what that bitch does."

Rumors were flying. "Everybody in the company
thought I did it. Why not? Of course," Paul said. Joe
Liberto was Jackson's boss. It was true that Joe Luskin
had rehired Joe Liberto in February 1987, and that they
did have daily contact together. It was also true Joe
Liberto talked in language consistent with "Why don't
you knock her off?"

Paul said Alvin asked him about it. He answered then,
"Everybody has suggested this avenue, but it was never
taken seriously.

"My father had always been pretty straight with me.
Either he would tell me the truth or he wouldn't tell me
at all." Just before trial, Paul said he asked him again:
"Will you tell me if we did it?"

Joe repeated No, he didn't do anything with Joe
Liberto, he wouldn't trust him.

"If we had wanted to do it, we wouldn't have needed
the bozos from Baltimore who didn't know the city. My
father knew everybody. That's not his style.

"When you put all the things together, he wouldn't
bother with Joe Liberto. If he knew Joe Liberto was
dealing in drugs, he would have fired him."

Paul said there was no profit to him in trying to
murder Marie because Florida divorce law requires
equitable distribution between the spouses.

But Marie's civil suit against his parents was different,
I noted. No, he said. In 1987, they were trying to settle
the divorce and the civil suit at the same time. The
numbers were between $500,000 and one million.

Paul left me with one last interesting note. The family
was very worried that Joe Luskin would be indicted.
That's why they hired Russell White.

I called Jackson. He had wanted to talk his piece for
the last six years, but no one had asked him. He started
before I even told him about the note.

"Paul and I genuinely like each other. We're cut from
the same type of cloth," he said. If Paul were out of
prison, and Jackson had a business, he'd take Paul in
without hesitation.

Paul had hired Jackson when he desperately needed a
break. But Paul never let him forget it; they fought often
and Paul fired and rehired him many times.

"Paul was the kind of guy who would give you the
biggest slice of the birthday cake, and then push your
face into the rest of it."

However, that didn't make him a bad manager. Paul
knew how to motivate his employees by making them
angry, then focusing their anger.

Jackson confirmed he had said what was written on
the note. At the time, neither he nor Joe Liberto were
working for Luskin's, and they both coincidentally were
at the Kendall store. He asked Liberto what he was
doing there: "I'm helping Mr. and Mrs. L help get rid of
Marie."

"You have to understand Joe Liberto. Whatever was
on his brain was on the tip of his tongue."

When Jackson read about the indictment in the newspaper, he thought Joe Liberto would have been "the last
one in the world" who Paul would have trusted with
something like that.

"Paul knew what Joe was. Joe Liberto didn't have the
brain he was born with. The last one Paul would ever
confide in was Joe Liberto."

When Liberto said what he did, "I told him that was

the most stupid thing I had ever heard, and don't tell it
to any sane person."

Jackson said Joe had been jealous of Paul since they
were teenagers working for Luskin's in Baltimore. When
Joe was hired to come to Florida, he thought Joe Luskin
would realize he was much better qualified than Paul to
run the store, and would give him the job. When Paul got
it, Liberto resented him for it.

"Joe was a yes-man. He didn't have an original
thought in his mind."

Liberto also used to boast he was involved with the
Mafia through his brother in Baltimore, whom he idol-
ized, a big deal Mob kingpin.

"Then what are you doing working here as a flunky?"
Jackson shut him up.

"I tried to listen as little as possible to Joe Liberto."
He remembered that people made fun of his speech: he'd
spit when he talked, or use the wrong word, like "pacif-
ic" when he meant "specific."

Nor did Jackson like Marie. "Marie was out for what
she could get. Paul was her meal ticket." Jackson sensed
Marie put up with Paul because wealth and the feeling of
royalty was more important to her. Once, Jackson remembered, he had to go to their house late at night with
a question. At the door, Marie, wearing a bathrobe,
greeted him as if to say, "How dare you, the hired help,
attempt to visit us at the castle?"

"I had always felt that Marie had disdain in her nature
for him. I don't think Marie could share her concern for
anyone but herself. Paul was like a bear—but he had a
little kid in him. He wanted to cuddle up with someone.
He needed a pat on the head from his wife, and he didn't
get it."

"Who ran Luskin's?" I asked.

"Paul did. Mildred kept the store together when Paul
got too obnoxious. Joe Luskin was treated poorly by his
son and wife, made to seem like he was senile. He was a
nonentity. Time had passed Joe by. Milly was the sharp
one." They'd condescendingly assign Joe meaningless
chores.

That was why Jackson couldn't believe Joe Luskin had

ordered a murder. "There was no way in the world that
Joe Luskin would go to Joe Liberto" for something like
this.

I asked about Paul's "another florist" line.

"That's Paul's cutting sense of humor. If he knew
something hurt, he would attack the wound." But it
wasn't in Paul's nature to hurt anyone bodily.

An incident at the store demonstrated that. A stock
boy had gotten mad at Paul and bloodied him in the
face, knocking his glasses halfway across the room.
Another employee was about to pound the stock boy
when Paul said, "Don't hurt him."

"Paul would rather do something snidely. He
wouldn't hurt you physically. I just know him."

Jackson described Paul as "a business genius with the
personal mannerisms of a kid." He always believed that
if he'd lose his money, he'd make it back. "That was part
of his cockiness."

Jackson said that had he considered Joe Liberto's
statement to be serious, he would have told it to the U.S.
Attorney. It was ironic and a "comedy" to him that the
government used essentially that theory to indict Paul.

I asked him why he wasn't called as a trial witness to
disprove the link between Joe Liberto and Paul. He said
Alvin Entin never called him back.

Jackson said there was no way Paul was involved in
drug trafficking. However, he did concede that the bonus
Manley said would be paid if Marie were killed by July
sounded suspiciously like a SPIF. That was an industry
term for a special incentive manufacturers offered to
motivate dealers and their salesmen to sell a certain
number of products by a certain date. Nor was Jackson
the first to say that to me.

After the Thanksgiving visit and the December letter
to Manley, there was no more news from Ben Darden.
Paul tried and tried to get him to take his calls, without
success. Finally, Paul lost hope and concentrated on
working with Bill Genego.

* * *

In August 1994, I called Mrs. Cohen. She asked me whether I knew that Jimmy Manley had been dead for two years.

"Two years?" I said.

Mrs. Cohen had stayed friendly with Sonny's ex-wife, who was Manley's stepdaughter. She had attended Manley's funeral, in Baltimore.

"The story is, Witness Protection let him go home, and gave him $2,500 and a car. But someone found him so strung out on drugs, he died during surgery," she said.

"But I talked to his stepdaughter a couple weeks ago—she's a nurse—and she said, 'I checked hospital records, and there was no operation on my father.' I don't think he's dead."

In the previous twelve months, Darden hadn't taken any of my calls either. This time I left a message with his secretary:

"Is Manley dead?"

It worked. When I called back, Darden picked up.

Darden had heard the rumor, and thought it had been cooked up by Witness Protection to cool off Manley's trail. There had even been an obituary in the Baltimore *Sun,* he said.

"He's not dead. I talked to him. He died prior to my last conversation with him."

However, Manley had missed his August 1993 appointment in Billings, and Darden hadn't talked with him since. Darden tried the post office to get a forwarding address under Manley's new name, but was told he had moved more than a year before, so they hadn't kept the record. Darden didn't buy it.

He did have a 15–20-minute audiotape of him and Manley speaking. He said Manley told him Bernstein had pressured him to say things.

"Did Manley tell you there was no murder-for-hire?" I asked.

"Not really," he said. But he never met Paul Luskin.

Darden said he would have the tape transcribed, then he'd send it to me. *Fat chance,* I thought. I'd have to go to Ithaca to hear it.

* * *

I called back Mrs. Cohen, designated her a Baker
Street Irregular, and set her out to pump some information that could lead me to a death certificate. If I could
get it, I could send copies to every federal agency Manley
dealt with and demand Freedom of Information Act
material. That might be even better than any statement
he could give to Darden. Federal privacy rules require a
person's notarized authorization before they can send
FOIA, unless you can prove he or she is dead. A death
certificate or printed obituary does the trick.

With a death certificate, even if Manley was alive, it
would be difficult for the federal agencies to decline
FOIA to me. And if they did decline it, at the very least it
would confirm Darden's theory that he was still alive.

A few days later, Mrs. Cohen told me she now believed
Manley was dead. She had talked to someone else who
had gone to his funeral. That person told her his body
was in an open casket, and said, "I saw the body. It was
him."

Manley had had a cardiac arrest, which was consistent
with his prior heart condition. Witness Protection had
given him the $2,500 and a car, and told him he could go
home to Baltimore if he wanted. Apparently he never got
there.

Mrs. Cohen also told me that Darden had visited
Sonny the previous December, and out of the blue,
asked him to admit there was a murder-for-hire, and
that Joe Luskin had wanted it done.

Sonny was apparently as shocked as I was. He asked
Darden, "What's going on? Are you wired for the FBI?"
Then Sonny told him to get lost.

In the meantime, I met informally with Miami FBI
Agent Carlos Costa for an entire afternoon. He had been
peripherally involved with the investigation, and remembered it. I explained a lot of the new things in the
case, including my pursuit of Manley's death certificate.

He said Witness Protection is not for guys like
Manley. He wondered if he had talked more about drugs
than had been disclosed; perhaps he was in protection
from those guys. Also, his twenty-plus arrests left his
credibility wanting.

Costa was further intrigued that Cohen was a bank robber, which he thought made him less likely to be a hired killer as well. He asked to read Cohen's statement. I told him I wasn't confident Cohen was telling the whole truth, certainly not about his involvement in drugs, maybe not that he was even the assailant in Marie's house.

I suggested there was enough for the FBI to reopen the case. Costa agreed, but he didn't have any say. If it was, he thought Cohen should be polygraphed. I mentioned Cohen said in his statement that he would.

Then Costa said Paul should be polygraphed, too. I remembered what Paul had once told me, that early in the case he was offered a polygraph and refused it on his attorney's advice because results could be manipulated. I was also thinking that Charles Panoyan had heeded exactly that advice in the murder case I had written about in my first book, *Until Proven Innocent.*

I hesitated before answering that he probably would.

Costa noticed my pause. Suddenly his perception changed.

"Don't fall in love with these people," he advised me.

Two weeks later Mrs. Cohen found out the details I needed to get started. She had the name of the funeral home in Baltimore. Manley was found dead in his apartment, but she didn't know where it was.

Mrs. Cohen said she asked Sonny why he didn't sing to save himself at trial, like Manley had:

"Mother, I could have talked, I could have gotten myself off. I could have sung a lot of times. But I would never ever want to spend the rest of my life looking over my shoulder. I'm not a stool pigeon, I never will be. Every day, Jimmy Manley had to look over his shoulder if someone wanted to kill him."

I called the funeral home and asked as many questions as I could until they became suspicious. They had a death for James Thomas Manley, Senior, forty-nine years old, on October 29, 1992, in Montana. That was the right age. When they looked farther, they told me that all the information was supposed to be private, and I had to contact the family.

Now I was off to the races. Montana meant Billings, I knew that. I called *The Baltimore Sun*'s library research line to see if they had printed an obit around that date. A researcher called me back; they hadn't, and when she called the funeral home, they denied they had any records of Manley's death.

Interesting.

Next I called the *Billings Gazette* library to ask the same question. They had nothing as well. But they referred me to the Yellowstone County clerk and recorder's office, and they confirmed a record of Manley's death on October 30, 1992. He had lived at 515 $\frac{1}{2}$ Clark Avenue, Billings, died of heart disease at Deaconess Medical Center in Billings, and they told me what home had handled the funeral arrangements. The body had been cremated.

The recorder's office wouldn't send me a copy of the death certificate, but when I called that funeral home, they offered to if I would send them $3. Deal.

Days later I had it. Immediately I sent FOIA requests for Manley's files to the U.S. Attorney's Office; the FBI; U.S. Marshal's Witness Security Program—the formal name of what everyone calls the Witness Protection Program; the Drug Enforcement Agency; and the Bureau of Alcohol, Tobacco, and Firearms.

I made arrangements to visit Sonny Cohen and Jim Liberto in prison in Pennsylvania. After that I planned to see Darden since Ithaca wasn't much farther north; then I'd stay in Baltimore for a bit.

Arranging prison visits was easy compared to getting Darden on the phone again. Susan had told me when Joe Luskin got frustrated trying to reach him, he would just show up unannounced in Ithaca. I decided to leave a number of messages simply that I was coming and when, then just go whether or not he responded. Predictably he didn't.

TEN

November 1994

November 13–15

Susan called me in the evening, frantic. Paul had missed his regular Saturday evening call to her, which prompted her to think something was wrong. It was. When he called Sunday night at 6:30, he told her he might have had a heart attack, that part of his heart muscle had shut down, and he was on blood medication Lasix and Inderal.

Despite what had happened, the prison hospital ward had sent him back to his regular bed Saturday night, promising to have an outside cardiologist see him Monday morning. When he finally called Susan he had numbness in both his hands and both his legs, and barely had the energy or breath to get to the phone, or to speak for the fifteen minutes the phone system allotted before it automatically cut off the call.

The next two days were hell for Susan as well as Paul. When she called the prison Monday morning after eleven, the promised cardiologist had arrived. Whoever answered the phone told her Paul was going to be taken to a local hospital—for security reasons, he wouldn't say which. Nor would he say anything about Paul's condition, because, he said, Paul had to sign authorization to release that information. Regardless, taking a prisoner out of the compound implied something very serious.

On Tuesday, the prisoners' network sprang to action.

A friend of Paul's called his wife, and since she had three-way calling, she phoned Susan. Paul had first noticed a problem Thursday night, and passed out twice Friday. The prison doctor told him he had edema, which meant his body was unable to process liquid, therefore, it bloated in the body. Susan called it a total body shutdown.

"I think he's going to die," she said matter-of-factly, but she couldn't mask how close she was to tears. In the past her defense mechanism had been to steel herself for the worst, suspend hope, then wait to see what would happen.

"He's probably scared to death right now. This is what I was worried about when I did this—that we wouldn't have any good time together."

Three hours later she called me back, relieved. Paul had called, from intensive care. It was against the rules, but somehow he had convinced his two armed guards to let him tell his wife he was still alive.

He had bled internally, he said, and lost most of his blood. He was scared, exhausted, and very weak, but relieved that he was finally being taken care of.

"I thought I was going to die yesterday, when they transported me," Paul told her.

"Don't die," Susan both instructed and pleaded with him.

"Okay. I'll try."

"Whew," she said to me.

November 17

Approaching Lewisburg Prison off the main road, I thought I was entering a campus, or a monastery. In the parking lot, I heard the sound of a military-style drill chorus in the distance. It's a boot camp outside the prison walls for first-time drug offenders, a tough-love alternative to the inside. Pretty intimidating.

Gangster movies labeled Lewisburg "The Big House," and the staff has embraced the reference. I saw it on T-shirts, jacket backs, and souvenir license plates. But I had no idea that the prison would be such a magnificent place, built in Italian Renaissance style, with a campanile tower. Ed Claunch, the prison official who met me at the front, said the English believed that great architecture could have a rehabilitative effect on its inmates, and the feds had imported the idea. After I passed security, we walked into a parlor; it had a mosaic wood ceiling, arches, and crossed keys in relief on the walls. I was right about the monastic effect—a guard told me people notice that all the time.

I was disappointed that the visiting room was nondescript. Sonny Cohen was about my height—5′8″—and although he was lean, he had weightlifter's arms. When he saw mine, he joked to Claunch that if I made any trouble, he could beat me up.

On the subject of Cohen's arms, you couldn't miss his tattoos. Marie had missed them; ah, well. She and I hadn't had the same type of conversation with the man.

I took inventory: the back of his left wrist read "Mom." On his upper right arm, covered by his short-sleeve shirt, was "Denise," a reference to Denise Spring. Below that was "Sonny." On the underside of his upper arms he had a matching set—his left said "Out" and his right said "Law."

But his spectacular tattoos were on his forearms. His right arm had a tiger, his left a lion. Gone now, but present in 1987, he said, was a two-inch hatchet on his right forearm. Tattooing is allowed in prison, he said, but only in monochrome.

There was another identification controversy at trial over whether Marie and other witnesses said the assailant's hair was blondish brown or salt-and-pepper. Almost everyone told Hollywood Police he had blondish brown hair, but at trial the same witnesses tried to say they had seen salt-and-pepper hair. Cohen's hair was not blond or brown in any way. At trial it was salt-and-pepper, and now at age fifty, his hair was even more salt than pepper, cut short and neat. When he put on his thick reading glasses to read Manley's death certificate, he struck me as looking a little like Saul Bellow.

"I have no idea in the world how they got blond," Cohen said. "My hair is gray."

Alvin Entin hadn't totally believed Cohen when he admitted he was Marie's assailant, so I asked him directly.

"No, that was me in the house."

I asked whether he believed Manley was really dead. Yes, one of Manley's daughters had told him she saw his body, and he trusted her. The death certificate didn't mention a drug overdose, but Manley did have heart problems. Once Manley was released, he began shooting heroin again, and that might have aggravated the problem. Although getting drugs inside prisons is not unheard of, Manley probably couldn't get any where he was, in the Witness Protection unit at Otisville, New York, because "they have very tight security there."

As his mom had told me, Cohen has accepted that he will grow old inside these walls.

"I told them we'd be convicted. I know I'm going to get thirty years for the guns, because I'm a convicted felon.

"I'm a thief, I'm a crook, I'm a bank robber, but I'm not a liar, and I'm not a killer. I've stole cars and beat people up—but I didn't shoot Marie Luskin."

He wanted to testify at trial, but his attorney told him not to. Cohen understood the logic—the prosecutors would be able to bring up Cohen's prior record—but instead, he said, the jury was left with the unresponded to allegation that Cohen was a hit man, when he wanted to say he wasn't.

Besides, the lawyers *want* to lose, he said. "They make more money on appeal than they do at trial."

I asked if he thought Darden really had the tape of Jimmy Manley saying the prosecutors told him what to say.

"Naah. I know Jimmy. Nothing exists." When Manley supposedly came forward, Darden had told him, "He wants to help you, Sonny, but he doesn't want to go back to jail to do it." Cohen believed Manley said that, but "Jimmy ain't gonna say more of that (other) shit."

He explained why. Manley had two parts to his deal; although he was clear with the feds on perjury because his five-year statute of limitations had expired, he had a deal on Maryland state charges, too. They were dropped contingent on truthful testimony in the federal case. So if he admitted perjury now, the federal five-year rule wouldn't apply to the state, and he could face those charges again. Further, Manley's exposure to the state was life without parole.

Talking about Darden, Sonny was angry that neither Luskin nor Jim Liberto had tried to help him.

"I've tried to help Luskin. I went on TV ("A Current Affair") and tried to help him." He did it as a good deed because Darden said it would convince Paul's daughters to talk to him. But when he tried to tell the reporter that the codefendants weren't guilty either, they only wanted to hear about Paul.

I asked when he'd be eligible for parole. First he said 2024, then 2018, then 2024 again. The confusion was over state obligations he'd have after finishing his federal time. Even had he been found not guilty of murder-for-hire, he'd still have had state time for drugs and carrying a weapon by a convicted felon.

Then Cohen dropped the first bombshell of my trip: "If he (Luskin) had done the right thing, none of them would be in."

Okay. I had no idea what he was talking about. I asked.

He said Luskin was supposed to help post his bail after he was arrested at the train station. It was $500,000, and there were ten days before the feds stepped in and slammed the window, scared that he'd run.

"I had $50,000, Jim's bar was worth $250,000, my mom offered her home and her car." Luskin was supposed to have matched Jim Liberto's $250,000 in property.

If they had, "I would have left," that is, skipped bail.

It would have crippled the case; Manley wouldn't have been able to testify because all he knew was hearsay from Cohen, and Cohen wouldn't have been there. "Everybody's home free without me."

Did they know you were going to run? I asked, not fully comprehending.

Sure, he said. "They were worried about losing some property."

Continuing his jailhouse lawyer analysis of how the case could have and should have been won, Cohen said a major mistake was not fighting hard enough to exclude the arrest and search at Penn Station.

"If they beat the illegal arrest, we're all out of jail. You can't be tried for the fruits of an illegal tree," he said, sounding like a legal scholar. "I was carrying an AR-15 with a silencer, and eight balls (of cocaine), and I'm going to agree to let those fucking cops search me?"

We talked about Manley. "He's a piece of shit," he said, wasting no words. They had met in 1958 at Cub Hill, the Maryland state reformatory for boys. Manley and another boy jumped him and beat him up. Later they became friends.

"His crowd was junkies. I never did drugs." They didn't hang out together although Cohen saw him in the street occasionally, and their paths sometimes crossed in jail.

"Why did you use Manley when you went to Florida?"

"I knew he was a crook like me." Needing a burglary man, "I knew he did that kind of shit. He's been a thief all his life."

Cohen said he was under the impression from Jimmy Liberto there was $100,000 in the house. I argued with him; that was money Marie said Paul had kept there when they were together, but when he moved out, she said he took it.

All of that was beyond Cohen, who restated simply that he thought the money was in the house. He made a deal with Manley to give him $10,000 of it.

"The bitch lied. There was no jewelry pouch in the

room." When she reached into the vanity, he figured she
was getting the money. Then she screamed and "it
scared me. I banged her in the head with the blackjack,"
expecting to knock her out.

"Are you sure you didn't use the gun to hit her?"

"I wouldn't have hit her with the gun—it might have
gone off." Had she not screamed, he had planned to tie
her up, then search the room himself for the money.

We talked about drug trafficking. Talking in the present tense, he said, "In Florida you can buy an ounce of
coke for $400 to $800. In Baltimore it sells for $2,200 to
$3,000 an ounce. Shit, you can make money this way."

I suggested my Frank Liberto theory that his three-
kilo bust on Amtrak in late February 1987 caused the
need for a quick $100,000 cash, prompting a robbery of
the Luskin house. Cohen recalled that a kilo of coke
wholesaled for $22,000 then, which made the loss about
$66,000.

No way, he said. "I used to make $65,000 off a key in
ten days' time." That loss was "chump change. You'd
make it off the next key."

Not ready to dispose of such a well-contrived theory
so quickly, I brought up the dinner at Martha's Restaurant the weekend before the assault. Cohen knew that
Jim and Joe Liberto had eaten there that night, but
denied he was there with them. He said he hadn't even
arrived in Florida yet.

(Later I checked my notes. According to phone records at the Marco Polo, Cohen had arrived two days
before the dinner.)

"All I know is what Jimmy was saying. Joe was
complaining about Luskin's firing him. He's been such a
good friend to Paul. Paul keeps $100,000 in the house all
the time. That's the only thing I keyed on."

Cohen had pumped Jim Liberto for information without making it appear so, and learned they lived "somewhere in Hollywood, Fort Lauderdale." Cohen told me
there is an informal criminals' code of ethics, which
explained why he had to use subterfuge. Since the ill-
gotten gains would be based on Joe Liberto's information, he was entitled to a share of the loot. It was just like

the way lawyers give referral fees to each other. The way
to beat paying it was to keep the Libertos from figuring
out that Cohen had done it.

Sonny said it was a "freak" that he spotted Marie's
car, even before I had a chance to challenge him on it.

"I rode all through Emerald Hills, looking for something I recognized." Believing that every house in the
neighborhood was a millionaire's home, for a short time
he thought of robbing somebody else's place.

Then, sitting at the 7-Eleven, the Mercedes with the
Luskin initials on its license plate passed, and he went,
"Whoa!"

That was close to what he had told Darden in 1991,
and I wasn't any more convinced by it now than then.
But I didn't want to start a fight with him.

I asked what he had planned to do with the $100,000.
That was easy, he said. "I'd have bought five kilos, and
make a half mill in one shot. Then I'd quit. Or do it once
more, and make a million dollars."

Cohen's role models sold dope. One friend had made
$3 million, and Jimmy Liberto had made "a fortune"
doing the same.

Cohen was careful to say that the drugs he ran from
Florida were his own, not Liberto's. However, in Baltimore he did buy drugs from Liberto and resold them.
Then he asked me not to write he said that if Liberto
denied selling to him. That would be considered "rat-
ting" in Lewisburg, "and you can get killed here very
easily."

(The situation was resolved the next day. Liberto also
talked openly about his drug business, and agreed that
Cohen did buy from him—although, Liberto said, he
never personally handled the drugs Cohen got.)

We talked about Darden. They had been close up until
his visit a year before. He said Manley was still alive,
"then he asked some weird shit"—that Joe Luskin had
hired him to kill Marie.

Cohen said he answered, "You're a fucking asshole—I
got no answers for you," then he asked to leave the
visiting area. They hadn't talked since. Since Mrs. Cohen

had told me that before, and she thought Paul had prompted the question, I suggested to Sonny I didn't think that was so. No, Cohen said, he had also since realized that Darden was acting on his own.

I mentioned that Susan distrusted Darden. He smiled, chalking that up to woman's intuition. Denise was the same way, he said. "She told me, 'Jimmy Manley was a fucking piece of shit. He's a rat—why are you hanging out with him?'"

Cohen said he answered back then, "'You don't even know the fucking guy.' Now she says, 'If you'd have listened to me, you wouldn't be there.'"

I asked if Sonny knew anybody at Lewisburg who was wrongfully convicted.

No, he answered. But there were lots of people who weren't guilty of what the feds had convicted them of. "If they can't get you for one thing, they'll get you for something else. They don't play by the rules." That was what had happened to the Libertos.

"In the whole federal prison system of 100,000 inmates, how many do you think are truly innocent?"

"Maybe a hundred are truly innocent. Maybe 40,000 are not guilty, but are guilty of other crimes. Paul Luskin is truly innocent."

"Do you think the feds were taken in by Manley, or did they realize his long record made him less than fully credible?"

"They're not idiots," he said. They knew Manley was a liar. "They wanted the name Luskin. It's headlines for them."

Cohen remembered a lawyer told him before trial that if the government lost the murder-for-hire case, they'd try him and the Libertos on drug charges. He was ready to plead guilty to twenty-five years, but the government wanted him to testify against Luskin, and Cohen said no.

"There's no way around it, I got to do the time. I can't sit there every day and think about your time," like Paul. Meanwhile, he was concentrating on self-improvement. He'd become a vegetarian in the last seven months, given up smoking, and cut down on coffee. "I figure I'll be here until I'm 72 or 73. I'm trying to stay in good enough shape to make it."

November 18
Allenwood Low Security Correctional Institution
Allenwood, Pennsylvania

I wish I could describe Allenwood LSCI—just ten miles north of Lewisburg—in as much detail as Lewisburg. But Allenwood is a new prison, and these days the feds build prisons like Burger King builds restaurants— they all look the same. There is also a federal prison camp on the grounds. Years ago the press labeled it "Club Fed" because of its well-off inmates who needed the lowest level of security. The LSCI is different.

Jimmy Liberto has only five years on Cohen, but seemed an entire generation older. He greeted me smiling, and didn't have his guard up, like Cohen did at first. He had an unmistakable Italian look—a thin, trimmed blond-and-gray mustache, thick eyebrows, and a full head of hair with a shock of gray. I could picture him as a restauranteur, a cordial maître d' with a Baltimorese accent.

He pointed to his belly and told me his heart problems had inspired him to lose thirty-five pounds. He had become vegetarian, too.

I told him I had just seen Sonny the day before. "He's a nice guy. I like Sonny," Liberto said. "He's a legend in his own mind." Then although his tone of voice stayed the same, he said, "I thought the world of Sonny, but I can never forgive him for destroying my brother and Paul Luskin."

What did Liberto think of Paul?

"I have no bones to pick with Paul. I just don't trust him after the trial." He was still angry that Paul had filed a motion saying Jimmy had threatened him to keep him from testifying. "I feel that gave me an extra ten years. I would have gotten what Joe got. What'd he do it for? We were already convicted."

But did you threaten Luskin, like he said?

"Maybe I was mad at the time, and said, 'You fucker—one of these days . . .' It's possibly got some

truth to it. But I didn't mean it. I wasn't going to follow
through."

Later, Liberto said more. He admitted threatening
Luskin to quit using his drug defense. If he continued,
and the Libertos were subsequently indicted for drugs,
they would bring him down with them.

He said he leaned over and told Luskin at trial, "What
are you trying to do, hang yourself . . . Boss?"

Liberto explained: "You say to yourself, how are they
going to convict? You know you didn't do it, you don't
know the accuser, you never heard of the crime. They
can't convict me here, they're trying to get me on drugs.
So I said to Luskin, 'You want to make it a drug case,
let's make it a big one. We'll testify you're our boss.'"

That was when he might have dished up the more
explicit threats. But it was justified, he said. "How'd you
like to be sitting here with all these rats around?"

Liberto said he and Luskin split the cost of the private
investigator, but Paul "crossed me up" and used the PI
to investigate him and his brother. They found the
Western Union receipts, which he said wasn't evidence
of anything.

"All Joe was doing was holding money for me. I sent it
to him, and I picked it up from him. My brother is guilty
of nothing. He's just as innocent as Paul. His biggest
crime was being my brother. For that, he's lost everything he has, and his family's been destroyed."

Bernstein had offered Joe five years to plead guilty.
Jim said his brother went, "For what? I don't know
anything."

I asked about Sonny's bail. Liberto said he and Mrs.
Cohen were supposed to post property, but when Mrs.
Cohen backed out, Jim's girlfriend Darlene told him to
back out, too. He said he didn't know Sonny planned to
jump bail, and that Luskin wasn't involved in posting
bond because Sonny was arrested before there was any
talk of a murder-for-hire.

"I was leaving for Las Vegas when Sonny called from
jail. Up to before I was arrested, I didn't know there was
another guy with him."

He remembered October 15, 1987. The day started
with Darlene testifying to the grand jury. "I was thinking

drugs, money laundering. When she came home, I said, 'What's the target?' She said, 'You.' "

At six o'clock, Liberto was arrested outside his restaurant. He said "eighteen or nineteen" agents were there, plus the media. He resented that both Luskin and his brother Joe knew in advance they would be indicted and were able to arrange surrender, but he was apprehended with a show of force.

"Everybody knew but me," he said.

He said he was fingerprinted next to Luskin. "I didn't acknowledge him. I didn't know him." He didn't even ask what the charges were until after his photograph and prints were taken and he was handcuffed in FBI Agent Patrick Connolly's car. He thought to himself, *Loansharking?*

"When they told me, I said, 'You got to be kidding me. What the fuck you talking about?' "

"I should be in jail—but not for this." He wasn't directly in the drug business, he said, but people doing drug business borrowed money from him at one hundred percent interest over a week or two. Sometimes he just guaranteed that money would be paid.

He was also in the collection business, for which he employed Sonny.

"Did he beat anybody up?" I asked.

"No, you don't have to beat up people, just be present."

He said he had financed Sonny in the drug business for the six months prior to his arrest, as well as introduced him to his Florida drug source. But the coke Sonny had on the train, he had taken with him from Baltimore.

"That's a fact. He's the only stupid SOB I ever heard of who would take drugs *to* Florida. How stupid can you be? I would swear on my mother's grave—that's a fact. That's how dumb he is."

(By saying that, I later realized Liberto seemed to be indicating there *was* a murder-for-hire. If Cohen wasn't in Florida to pick up drugs, then he was there only for Marie Luskin. Cohen said he wanted to burglarize her home; if he had a murder contract, he would have staked her out for a month, not one night. Of course, that statement didn't address Manley's "inside information" testimony that she would be at Bennigan's on the single night they were there.)

Liberto did praise Sonny for fulfilling his obligations.

"Sonny was very honorable with money. If he owed you a dollar, you got it—and the day he'd say you'd get it. Not ninety-nine cents."

I referred to Sonny's FBI statement that he was going to buy a middleman's position in Liberto's drug ring. Just before trial, Sonny denied saying that, and Liberto disputed it, too.

"Sonny was going to take my position. I was retiring. I was going to turn everything over to him—for nothing. I had the restaurant, a couple condos in Ocean City (Maryland), I didn't need the money anymore. I told him to make your killing, and then retire."

We talked about his restaurant, Palughi's. "We had good food, and lines around the block. When I took it over, it was doing $4,000 a week, and I got it up to $30,000 a week. I put in a piano bar, with singing and dancing—I made it exciting."

Then he added, "What did I need with money to whack this broad?"

Liberto recalled at the end of each day during trial, he got to ride down the elevator with the jurors. "I was chatting, kidding with them, walked with them to the parking lot. They were real nice, smiling, asked me 'How you doing, Mr. Liberto?' We didn't talk about nothing to do with the case"—that would have been a violation of the judge's instructions.

"But the minute drugs were introduced into the case, the jury wouldn't look at me. Stupid, some of the things he's (Luskin) done."

However, Luskin's defense undercut Luskin himself. Liberto said he'd been anxious to take the stand to deny there was a murder-for-hire. But because Luskin's attorneys would have cross-examined him on drugs, he had to keep silent. Same for his brother Joe.

The government alleged Jimmy and Paul met in Baltimore, but had no proof. "I'd take a lie detector test that I never met Paul." Then he said he might have met

Paul in 1966, when Paul and Joe were stock boys at Luskin's.

Bill Genego had come here to see Liberto about two months before I did, and that's when Liberto first admitted his involvement in drug trafficking. (A major reason may have been that by 1994 he was beyond the five-year statute of limitations.) Genego had asked him to make a sworn statement but he had refused.

He explained to me why not: "When you say drugs, it puts the man on them. You have to think about other people. Just because you want to get out, you can't endanger other people."

(But after I got home from the trip, Genego told me Liberto had called him and changed his mind, he would make a sworn statement. Genego never followed through.)

I brought up Frank Liberto. Jim said Frank was dead—which Joe had told me some time before. He had died of a heart attack when he came home from prison.

I asked if Frank was a part of the smuggling operation.

No, he said. He had been arrested with somebody else's drugs. "A guy told him on the train, 'Bring these up the road for me.'" Frank was an alcoholic and out of money, so he said yes. "It had nothing to do with us."

Jimmy agreed that Cohen had the AR-15 rifle because he was supposed to calibrate it in the woods somewhere along the trip to Florida. He had Frank's new wife Pat buy it because he had a criminal record. When Pat testified so emotionally at trial that Jim had "used" her, he was very surprised. He had paid for their wedding and given them money. Then just before trial, they had spent Christmas together at his restaurant.

He had given money to his brother Joe, too. When Jack Luskin fired him in the late 1970s, Jim bought him a bar, but it didn't work out. More recently, Jim had given Joe a few hundred to a thousand dollars at a time "because he was doing for me (picking up money at Western Union) and because I was his brother."

I had asked him two years earlier if he recalled the

phone call in November 1986 between his room at the
Marco Polo and Paul Luskin's number, and now I asked
him again.

He'd been trying to remember it, he said. "Joe had
stopped at the hotel that morning to eat lunch with me.
He called work, he called Luskin's apartment—I don't
even think he got an answer. It was an innocent phone
call." He said whenever Joe would visit his hotel room,
"He used to make all kinds of calls—4–5 calls, he'd call
around to the other stores. Luskin was in Philadelphia
that day (Pittsburgh actually)—he was calling to see if
Luskin was back."

Then Jim gave me bombshell number two of my trip:

His brother Joe had filed another appeal for a sentence
reduction. Jim had a copy, but he had sent it to Genego.

He told me a little bit of it. Joe had alleged that Paul
and his father were trying to cover something to protect
themselves; Jim didn't know what. To those ends, Joe
Luskin had hired and paid for Joe Liberto's trial lawyer.
After the trial, Joe Luskin had gotten someone to kidnap
Joe Liberto's young daughter.

"Go to the courthouse and read it. It will open your
eyes."

For the moment, I would have to leave it at that.

I asked if Jim was convinced by Sonny's admission
that he was Marie's assailant.

No, he said. "I don't think Sonny has got that much
brains to figure out the flower deal. It don't add up."

Sonny wasn't the shooting type. "Some people can
shoot, some can't. He can't." He was the fighting type,
though.

He reminisced. "I enjoyed Sonny—I still consider
him a friend, although I'm still mad at him for what he
did to Joe, Paul, and their families.

"What you do to me, I can handle. Someday, on the
street, we'll have to settle it."

He agreed with Cohen that the law may not get you for
the right crime, but if you're guilty, they'll get you. "Me
and Sonny, we've done things. We belong in jail for
something. Well, you win one, you lose one."

"But I would have gotten fifteen years for drugs. This

conviction is a death sentence for me. Nobody's ever lived over sixty-two in my family, and I'll be sixty-seven when I'm paroled.

"I'm bitter—but not enough to fucking rat on somebody."

It was pushing three o'clock. I had only spent two hours with Cohen, so I hadn't expected to do five hours with Liberto. I figured it was more than a two-hour ride to Ithaca, and I needed to catch Darden before he left his office. I had his office address but not his home address. If I got there too late, I might lose the whole weekend, since it was Friday. I excused myself, and hurried out onto the road north.

At five-thirty I rolled into Ithaca, then took another twenty minutes to find 407 State Street. It was a turn-of-the-century two-story wood shingle house. In the window was a child's hand-drawn brightly colored sign reading "Benjamin F.L. Darden." I rang the bell and was relieved when I heard loud footsteps descending stairs, and then a familiar face responded.

"I was just now thinking that you were supposed to be here sometime this afternoon," greeted Ben Darden.

Hah! I thought.

In fact he was very glad to see me.

I told him I had just been to see Cohen and Liberto, and that the mystery of the story was growing deeper. He gave me a look of disappointment, that I hadn't figured it all out yet.

"It was Joe Luskin," he blurted.

I hadn't even gotten my coat off. The past two days had already begun to shake some of my strongest-held positions on the case, and now Paul's own attorney was telling me it was a murder-for-hire after all?

Please, I said, let me sit down first.

I had really come here to talk about Manley. I raised Cohen's point that Manley wouldn't talk on the record because admitting perjury would leave him exposed to his Maryland state charges. No, said Darden, Manley's state deal was iron-clad. He had no problems at all.

I told him I had brought a copy of Manley's Montana death certificate under his true name. Darden was dubious. He said not only had he talked to Manley after the date of the supposed death, but he had made a car payment for him. To do it, he had selected a lawyer in Billings, called him, and had Manley go there to sign for the money. Manley had told Darden what Witness Protection was paying him wasn't enough to support himself.

It was getting late, and Ben and his wife Birthe had theater plans, so we adjourned to meet later at Hal's deli a few blocks away. In the meantime, I walked four blocks to one of the country's most celebrated vegetarian restaurants, the Moosewood. It was in the basement of the same building where Darden's office had been until recently.

The meal gave me a chance to collect myself. Later that evening, over the Dardens' breakfast table, we talked about his Joe Luskin theory. I called it a "theory," but Darden said it was the truth. "I know so," he insisted.

Everything went back to the bankruptcy case, he said. In early 1985, when divorce was first in the air and Paul wanted to hide his one-third ownership in Luskin's from Marie, Paul simply gave his stock back to his parents, without receiving any compensation.

That was stupid, Darden said. What he should have done was sell it back to the corporation in exchange for a promissory note. It doesn't matter for how much. Then when the divorce comes, you give the full promissory note to the wife, take the business into bankruptcy, and wife gets zip. After the divorce, the company reorganizes and issues new stock. The only requirement afterward was that Paul would have to be kept out of a supervisory role in the business for ten years.

Had they done this, almost everything could have been avoided. It would have cost $2,500 in legal fees. But the Luskins figured since Paul was a lawyer, why waste the money?

Darden said the Luskins looked guilty and greedy for doing it the way they did it. Everything that followed was a cover-up for this blunder.

Then Darden argued why Joe Luskin was the guilty man, not Paul Luskin:

"Joe Luskin had more to lose than Paul." Paul only had a third of the business at risk, but Joe and Mildred had the remainder. There wasn't any connection between Joe Liberto and Paul—"they disliked each other. Paul fired him, Joe Luskin rehired him.

"Joe Liberto and Joe Luskin go back thirty years. Joe Liberto knows it all—and isn't talking." For a while, Joe Liberto did talk over the telephone to Ben, but "somebody got to him" by the time he went to see him.

It was going to take more to convince me that there was a murder-for-hire, and that someone was guilty whom I hadn't considered. Darden could see I was resisting. Knowing how I felt about Paul Luskin, he gave me words of caution, wisdom he said gained from years of dealing with criminal defendants. Oddly, they were virtually FBI agent Carlos Costa's words:

"Don't fall in love with the people and what they're saying."

I knew that a few days after Paul's conviction, Joe Luskin had hired Darden to represent both Paul in his appeal and the family in the divorce case. Darden said Joe Luskin had expected to be indicted, and that's why Russell White was hired—repeating what Paul had told me a year before. "By a fluke, he wasn't indicted, and Paul was." Since White wouldn't refund the fee he had already been paid, the Luskins decided to use him in Paul's trial.

After the conviction, Darden said he asked Joe Luskin to admit his guilt. He wouldn't. Then Darden asked him to take a polygraph, just to prove to him that he was telling the truth.

Darden dramatized Joe Luskin's answer: He shrank back in shock, cupped his hands to guard his face, and insisted, "Oh no, no, no!" Then in late 1991, dying, Darden asked him again. Still he wouldn't.

"As a lawyer, I don't care if they're guilty or not," he said.

"How often are they guilty?" I asked.

"They're always guilty," he said.

What about Cohen, I asked. In 1991 Darden took his sworn statement that there was no murder-for-hire, but now Darden was saying there was one. I kept to myself that Cohen was sore at him for suggesting he admit it, and that Joe Luskin was involved.

Darden conceded that Cohen would not change his story. Then he added that Cohen had no contact with Joe Luskin. Only Joe Liberto had contact with him, and "If Joe was not Jimmy's brother, Joe would be dead now."

I said I didn't believe that, and frankly, it diminished the whole Joe Luskin theory.

Darden said the proof was in Joe Liberto's 1990 sentence reduction. But Judge Motz had sealed it, and Darden hadn't been able to think of any way to get it unsealed.

What about the crime scene evidence, I asked. How about the solder theory?

Darden said I wasn't the first to suggest that. In fact, Joe Luskin had. When I later thought about it, Joe Luskin had grown up building radios and TVs, and therefore had worked with solder.

How about that police never found a bullet in the small room?

"Hollywood Police didn't find a bullet because they didn't look for one," he said. Marie said she was hit— but Darden recalled when Dallas Cowboys quarterback Troy Aikman had suffered a concussion during a playoff game in 1993. Afterward, someone asked him a simple question to check his alertness—where the Super Bowl would be played. He answered, Henryetta—the name of the tiny Oklahoma town where he grew up. By the same reasoning, Marie might have gotten it wrong that she was hit and not shot.

"Crime scenes are rarely definitive. Nobody looked under the carpet for a bullet." Then, to prove his point, he asked me to name the most famous crime scene in history.

The Kennedy assassination, I said. Right, he said, and

no crime scene has been more studied and less agreed
upon than that one.

But whether a murder-for-hire was truly carried out or
not, that's not important, he said. "Either way, Paul is
not guilty. The Joe Liberto connection is to Joe Luskin."

"Have you discussed this with Paul?" I asked. Yes, he
said, in 1993, when he last went to see Paul at Jesup.

That reminded me why I had come. Darden must have
realized it too. Without prompting, he said, "Maybe I'll
let you listen to the Manley tape."

I told him Cohen's story that Luskin and Liberto were
supposed to put up bond so Cohen could jump. That was
true, Darden said.

Later I realized that was the moment the story
changed for me.

It had taken two days to hit, because it had been
contrary to so much else I had. If Luskin (I hadn't asked
which) was going to post bond for Cohen in the first
week of August—but remember, Luskin's name only
surfaced a month later, when Manley squealed to the
feds there was a murder-for-hire—then clearly, obviously, truly, Cohen was sent to whack Marie.

And in the past two days, Cohen had let it slip, and
Darden had confirmed it. Could it be?

From there on in, I would take a new philosophy:
listen to everything, fall in love with nothing.

I was a victim of love.

Darden picked up on my angst. Trying either to
salvage my beliefs, or clean them out entirely, I mentioned Cohen's claim that it had been a robbery. Of
course, as I had pointed out to Cohen myself, the logic
that he was looking for the Luskin cash didn't follow
once you realized Marie had been crying to the divorce
court that Paul had taken the money with him when he
left the house.

Darden criticized me for discarding parts of the story
that didn't fit into my coherent whole.

My mind raced back. What hints had I tossed into the
trash?

Jackson.

When I had found the page of notes about Jackson in

Alvin Entin's file, it spoke quite clearly that Joe Luskin had paid Joe Liberto for a murder-for-hire. But when I spoke to Jackson I had let him talk me out of it. I thought now, *This guy was an appliance salesman—and obviously a good one.*

November 19

Reason number two I was in Ithaca was to see the Luskin file. Darden's file warehouse was his office basement, down wood stairs guarded by an ankle-high metal rod placed there to trip an intruder in the dark. Each time up and down the steps I had to remind myself about that rod.

Darden showed me his eight or nine boxes crammed full. Within it was all of Steve Allen's files, which he had sent north. With only the caveat to leave it the way I found it, Darden gave me a key to the office and permission to read and copy anything I liked. The office copier was on the fritz, but Kinko's, open twenty-four hours, was only a few blocks down the street.

Later, we talked again about Manley. Darden said he had talked to him about fifty times, and believed he was telling the truth. Although Paul had told me that Manley had said there was no murder-for-hire, Darden said Manley told him there was—just that he never knew who Paul was, that is, until Bernstein took him aside and told him. Bernstein threatened Manley that if he didn't say what he wanted, he'd send him back to jail for the rest of his life.

I asked Darden if he had made notes of his conversations with Manley. He said he had some, and could reconstruct the rest. He also said he had the receipt for Manley's car payment he had made.

We revisited Joe Luskin. Darden said he had had suspicions from almost the beginning that Joe Luskin was involved, but when he asked Joe directly, his denial led him to believe he was right. Darden told him, "It doesn't matter to me, I'm not the police." He explained to him how defense attorneys use polygraphs: "If you flunk it, it never sees the light of day. If you pass it, you parade it in flying colors." Still Joe Luskin refused to be polygraphed.

The whole murder-for-hire thing, Darden said, was Joe Liberto's idea. "He went to his mentor—Joe Luskin—and suggested he could take care of it. He called Jim Liberto, who got Sonny, who got Manley because he knew he'd be recognized if he went in a second time." Joe Luskin, Darden said, paid Joe Liberto $25,000 in cash.

I declined a theater invitation from the Dardens for later that evening and spent until three in the morning in the basement, which had long since become uncomfortably cold. As I finished reviewing each box or two, I took the documents I had picked out and shuttled them back and forth to the self-serve copiers at Kinko's.

I figured I'd copy first, read later, but a few things stood out.

Steve Allen had jotted notes of his conversation with Alvin Entin on November 5, 1987, regarding what Jackson had told Alvin. Allen wrote: "Conversation with Joe Liberto—Joe Luskin brought him back to set up a hit on Marie Luskin—gets piece of business in return."

Next were Allen's notes from talking to a man who I will refer to as Goldstein, another store employee: "One time Joe (Liberto) opened his briefcase and showed (Goldstein) a large amount of money—before he quit." Joe Liberto had left in December 1986. Speculating, I guessed it could have been Jimmy Liberto's money, but I knew that Gregg Bernstein would have insinuated it was the cash payoff for the murder-for-hire.

Then I found a whole file full of FBI crime lab documents and charts concerning their testing of the metal fragments. Here was all the stuff Paul was trying to say the government had denied him.

I was getting deflated. Maybe Paul had never seen the stuff, or had forgotten it over the years, but it had been there the whole time.

On a typed document labeled "Shift Commander's Daily Log" dated Monday March 9, 1987, Hollywood Police wrote: "Victim Marie Luskin W/F reported that an ukn W/M 40 yrs., 6', thin build, light colored hair (possibly salt & pepper or sandy in color) . . ." So it was not true that witnesses at trial had changed their identification to salt-and-pepper hair because that matched Cohen's appearance.

Next: Steve Allen's notes from a conversation with Paul on October 17, 1987, at Baltimore City Jail. Among other comments, Allen wrote, "Manley in witness protection program." So when Paul said in 1992 that he had never known Manley was in witness protection, that was not true.

The Andrea Smith letter was there, too.

Then the worst of all: another set of Steve Allen's notes from a conversation on October 28, 1987, with Paul's cousin Steve Miles, the Baltimore attorney.

> Joe (Liberto) can tie up whole case. Hired by Paul. Price tag $65,000 to be paid by Paul. Plot struck before he was fired. He pointed out the house . . . Plot to kill. Originally Joe involved. Make him a part of the business . . . Joe originally going to get bad guy. Jimmy said let me do it. Jimmy gets Sonny Cohen. Jimmy made large loan to Joe—$10,000 or so after March incident.

When I finished my work photocopying, I drove in the rural darkness toward the Darden home, looking for the side street off the main road that led to their house. I missed it the first time and realized I had gone too far when I hit the county line. I turned around, then found two firemen by the side of the road of whom I could ask directions. I got to sleep at about four-thirty.

November 20

I was now ready to believe the murder-for-hire story.

Back at the office, I asked again—did Manley say there was, or wasn't, a murder-for-hire?

No, Darden repeated, Manley didn't say there wasn't a murder-for-hire, he only said that Paul wasn't involved, and that Bernstein had made him insert Paul's name.

"Did Manley know Joe Luskin's name?"

Darden didn't know that, he hadn't asked him. "Remember, my role isn't to solve the crime, it's to help my clients."

So if Cohen was there to murder Marie, I asked, why didn't he?

Here Darden admitted he didn't have a good answer. "When did you first think it was Joe Luskin?"

Early on, he said. "It didn't add up that it was Joe Liberto and Paul Luskin together. They really didn't like each other. I know how it is in a small firm—there are always petty animosities. Paul would dock Joe for taking a bad check, or underages at the cash register."

I pitched in that I had seen references to that in the files, and it had bothered me, too. Small amounts like $12, $20, once $120 had been deducted continually from Joe's paychecks—which were only $650 a week.

And Paul fired him a few times, Darden said, but "each time, Joe Liberto would go back to his mentor, Joe Luskin, and get his job back.

"Paul and Joe Liberto—impossible," he said.

Darden said he put together his first suspicions after he learned the characters of both Paul and his father, then discovered from Steve Miles that Russell White had been hired as criminal counsel for Joe Luskin. "I had been wondering, why all these lawyers?"

He confronted Joe Luskin: "It was either you, or your son," he told him. "You're an old man—give your son some life. Take a polygraph test, so I can dismiss this idea. You can trust me, it doesn't matter to me who did it."

That's when Joe Luskin cringed and went No, no, no, absolutely not.

Maybe Joe Luskin was suffering from Alzheimer's disease, Darden thought. "I'd spend hours explaining something to him, and the next day he wouldn't remember, and I'd have to do it all over again."

I could see the frustration on Darden's face. Joe Luskin never admitted anything, much less signed a sworn statement. Now Manley was missing, if not dead.

"What do you do now?" I asked.

That was the million-dollar question. "You got to wait for someone to crawl out of the woodwork." And that someone was Joe Liberto. "He's getting out soon," he said.

"But he doesn't like Paul—and if he talks, he'd be admitting the murder-for-hire," I said.

"And he'd have to give up his brother," said Darden.

We went back to Manley. Manley called him because he wanted to return to Baltimore. Manley was in Montana, but his wife Doris wouldn't join him. "Baltimore—this wonderful place where no one wants to leave," said Darden.

"It does have its peculiar charms," I deadpanned.

He said Manley was afraid that either Sonny or Liberto would have him killed in Baltimore if he returned.

"True?" I asked.

"Probably," Darden said.

I hadn't shown Manley's death certificate to Darden, and now I pulled it out. He conceded it was a real document, but he still didn't believe it meant that Manley was dead. It didn't make sense to him that he died under the name Manley. "He had his name under Ford. I know, because he picked up the car payment money with that ID. How would the hospital know his real name?"

He also pointed out how convenient it was that the death certificate said Manley's body was cremated.

We moved our discussion to a Mediterranean lunch restaurant in College Town, just off Cornell's campus. I asked how he knew the murder-for-hire was Joe Liberto's idea.

"From a number of sources. Joe Liberto, Joe Luskin, Paul, Jim Liberto."

"They told you?"

No, he said, he pieced it together, partly by listening to how they denied his suggestions.

Manley told him that money was paid—$60,000— "perhaps more." But Manley only knew what Sonny told him.

Manley learned more in Baltimore City Jail, when they did cook up a story together, he said. But Sonny planned to rat, too. "Sonny was going to help Manley if

Sonny got out and Manley stayed in. He'd give Doris money, pay for Manley's lawyer." But when Manley got into a spot, he took the government's deal instead.

I asked Darden to describe Manley. He paused. "Reasonably intelligent. Working-class. Cunning. A bigot."

"Do you mean he was a racist? I'm sure he didn't realize that here you are trying to help him, and you're a black man."

Darden seemed temporarily put off by my observation. Had I made a *faux pas?* I wasn't the only person to recognize that Darden's personality was more Jewish than black.

"I wouldn't call him a racist," he said slowly, thinking about it. "He's a bigot. He made anti-Semitic comments, too. This is not someone you'd want to break bread with."

Manley hated Montana, he said. "There was nothing to do, no good jobs, and Witness Security didn't provide enough money."

"Wasn't he able to get drugs there?" I asked.

That Darden didn't know. Every time they talked, Manley denied he shot heroin.

When they had first begun to discuss making a sworn statement, Darden said he told Manley to check for himself when his statute of limitations would expire. Darden didn't want to give Manley legal advice, because it was a conflict of interest.

"I said, 'Don't risk your neck for Paul Luskin.'"

"When you wrote the letter to Paul in December '93," I asked, "was the deal still on?"

It was, he said. He hadn't spoken directly to Manley since November or December 1992, but Manley had a friend in Annapolis who stayed in touch with Darden through November 1993.

"Then they both disappeared. Then I hear that Manley is dead."

He wondered if the feds had been listening to their conversations, and got nervous. Any wiretapping probably would be legal, he figured, because it would have been included in Manley's release agreement.

"It's a high-profile case, and the feds don't want the

embarrassment. But a signed statement from Manley would have shaken things up."

Darden wondered again how he got into this. "Why did he call me? People in Witness Protection don't usually call me to say they testified wrongly." Was the FBI trying to set him up? But when Ben went to Sonny to find out things to ask Manley that only he and Sonny would know, Manley checked out.

It was getting late Sunday afternoon, and I hadn't heard the famous Manley tape. I hadn't pushed it, considering the volume of other material I had gotten. But now I raised it, and Ben said he wanted to listen to it again alone first, to make sure there was nothing on it that could hurt his client. Then he pulled a microcassette tape from his pocket and announced that he'd brought it along. After we were finished eating, we'd go off to a Radio Shack whose owner he knew, and would let him use the equipment.

Darden had already given me the impression that he had no love for his client, Paul Luskin. "Paul is difficult because he thinks he's smarter than everyone else." After Darden took Cohen's sworn statement in 1991, Paul demanded to make a statement, too. There wasn't any legal reason for it, and despite putting him off for months, "the client insisted" so the statement was made.

"There was no reason to bring the drug defense. But Paul ran the defense strategy. There might have been cooperation otherwise—they all wanted to testify, but couldn't."

And by keeping the defendants off the stand, they almost guaranteed their convictions, he said. "To get acquittals, nine out of ten times you have to put your client on the stand."

"What do you do when you don't like your client anymore?" I asked.

"You don't ever like your clients," he answered.

In the month before, I had cataloged all Paul's mail to me since mid-1991—maybe two hundred pieces. Revisiting it all at once—copies of all his demanding letters to Darden, long presumptuous letters to public officials asking for help, endless case law for me to read, legal

documents he narrated in the margins, threatening letters to FOIA bureaucrats, administrative problems with
two prisons—I got the impression for the first time that
he'd acted guilty ever since I'd known him. I suggested
that to Darden, and he agreed. "He's acted guilty even
before that—when they did the stock transfer."

Of course Paul had been complaining about Darden
for the previous two years. Paul had wanted me to ask
Darden why he hadn't returned his communications,
but once in Ithaca, I didn't want to ask. In fact, Birthe,
alone, volunteered an apology for her husband. She said
that all his clients—especially those in jail—call and
want to chat, and Ben's inclination is to chat with them.
If he took the calls, he wouldn't get anything done. They
call the house phone number as well, which I noticed,
never got picked up until after the answering machine
had screened it. And rarely after.

Yet I liked Ben. As the weekend went on, I got the
feeling he was lonely in upstate New York, he was
friendly with everyone in town, but wasn't close with
anyone. I think he was very glad that I had come—and
crashed.

He wore the same outfit all weekend: a black turtle-
neck, blue jeans, a worn-out beige corduroy jacket, and
old tennis shoes. Like a lot of trial lawyers, he could have
been an actor.

On the street outside his office, he told me a story that
described his courtroom procedure: his client was arrested in a drug sting and accused of buying $2 of
cocaine. "I know you only ask questions you know the
answer to," he said. But the arresting officer had already
identified his client, so he fished and asked if any
pictures existed of the bust. In fact there were, and he got
the judge to order the state to turn them over.

He got a recess to show them to his client. The picture
wasn't him. On the back was written someone else's
name. Darden covered the name with a sticker, on which
he wrote "Defendant's Exhibit A."

Returning to his cross-examination of the officer,
Darden asked if he could identify his client in the
picture. "He says, 'It's your client.'"

"Officer!" Darden's voice rose dramatically as he

retold the story. "Are you *certain* of your identification?"

"The officer looks again, and repeats, 'Yes, it's your client.'

"Now the jury is starting to wonder, Is this attorney crazy?" His voice went up another pitch and got louder still. "Are you *certain,* Officer, the man in this picture is the defendant?

"Now the officer gets haughty. 'You *fool!* I told you, it's your client!'

"The jury thinks I'm out of my mind. I ask the officer to read what's on the back of the photo. He reads, 'Defendant's Exhibit A.'

"No, no, what's *underneath* the sticker, I say. He pulls it off and reads the other name.

"The jury acquitted. It's all dramatics, all bullshit."

It was getting dark. Now I pressed him for the Manley tape, and we left for the Radio Shack at the Triphammer mall, which stayed open until six. There, he borrowed a player and earphones and began searching for the recording.

I checked back every five or ten minutes. He hadn't found it yet. He was almost sure it was the right tape, although he hadn't labeled it.

After about a half hour, he gave up and handed me the tape. He'd let me search for it on my own microcassette player when we got back to his house.

At the house, I changed batteries, checked to make sure my machine was working, then listened end to end, both sides on the Manley tape.

There was nothing but static.

I gave it back to him. "There's nothing there."

"No, there's definitely something there. I'll take it to a shop and get it enhanced," he said. Then he'd send me a copy.

At that point I knew I would never hear it. And I wasn't sure it was even important anymore. I also realized that Darden hadn't shown me any hard evidence that he had ever spoken with or dealt with Manley.

* * *

November 21

Each morning I had slept in the Darden house I had been awakened by the screech of the metal door to the boiler downstairs opening as Ben loaded fuel for the day into it. This morning I noticed it was five-thirty or so. I was to meet him in Ithaca city court later that morning.

Today was definitely my last day there, but on the ride between the house and downtown, it began to rain—which would make my drive to Baltimore miserable. At ten I got to the courthouse and asked a bailiff which court he might be in. There's only one, he answered.

After he was through with city court, it was on to Tompkins County court, where he argued a resentencing while I watched. When he was done, we went into an attorney-client area and spoke for a few minutes before I had to go.

I had a short list of questions. "How did the FBI know to investigate Joe Luskin?" I asked.

"They may not have," he said. "You have to remember, Joe Luskin is just my theory. I don't know that it's so."

"When did Cohen tell Manley it was a murder-for-hire?"

He wasn't sure. "Sonny really didn't tell him that much. He never trusted Manley. He was a junkie." But Manley swore to Darden that he had intended to shoot Jimmy Liberto—on Sonny's orders.

I had some questions about Cohen's sworn statement, especially what I had considered the most suspicious part—that Cohen had seen Marie's car from the side when she passed the 7-Eleven. Darden admitted that was not true. "Sonny had information from Joe Liberto—through Jimmy—where the house was."

"Then the sworn statement wasn't entirely true," I said. I followed that with a not-too-confrontative version of the question "Did you tell him what to say?"

"Sort of," he said. He admitted "shaping" the statement, but "I didn't put words in his mouth."

Following up, I thought of the three major filings Darden had made in 1991: the Cohen statement, the Andrea Smith letter, and the discovery that Manley was in Witness Protection. I told him I had found a reference in the files that Paul had made early in the case that Manley was in Witness Protection; and also that I had found a copy of the Andrea Smith letter—as I had in Entin's files.

"It's possible the Andrea Smith letter was placed in discovery, but remember, both Steve Allen and Alvin Entin said they hadn't seen it," he said. I considered mentioning the FBI crime lab charts I found which Paul was claiming had been denied to him, but I kept it to myself. As if to answer my unasked question, Darden said, "Paul doesn't remember seeing things, but his attorneys said he was there for everything."

In the car the rest of the day, I tried to grasp what had happened. In a weekend, I had found that three and a half years of research was all wrong. And if I hadn't have made the trip, I'd have still believed it.

The family's ground zero in Baltimore is now my oldest sister Helene's place. Arriving after dark, my parents were there. They had flown in for Thanksgiving while I was gone.

My parents had known Joe and Mildred Luskin as social friends since the 1950s. I told my mom there probably *was* a murder-for-hire after all, but Paul might not have been the one behind it. Showing an incredible prescience, she filled in the blank.

"Joe Luskin," she guessed—but who am I to use the word "guess?" "Now you've got the real story," she said.

I thought how disturbing to be beaten on a story by your mother.

Darden had mentioned that Joe Luskin "was lucky, not smart" in business, and my dad agreed.

"Jack Luskin had the brains. Joe didn't do anything," he said. Jack threw Joe out of the Baltimore Luskin's business in the mid-sixties because "Jack was going to expand, and he didn't need his brother."

I called Gloria Pruce, Susan's mother, hoping *Oh, God, I hope she can't tell, too.* I asked about Paul, and she said he was okay and was out of the hospital and back at the prison. He had been bleeding internally from

his esophagus. They didn't know what had caused it,
maybe a puncture from a fishbone or a chicken bone he
had eaten. He had just called the day before, to wish
Gloria a happy birthday, and sounded cheerful and
ebullient.

November 22
Baltimore

I expected that Joe Liberto's 1994 motion for sentence
reduction would be in the clerk's office in federal court
in Baltimore, but that I would have to go to federal
archives in Philadelphia to see the rest of the case,
including what he had filed in 1990. When I got to the
courthouse, I found I was wrong—happily, the whole
case file was there.

Darden had led me to think that the judge had sealed
all of Liberto's pleadings and government responses, but
that was not so either. For both the 1990 and the 1994
sentence reductions, there were docket entries marked
"SEALED" which undoubtedly were either hearings or
the judge's decisions.

But the pleadings and responses were public record.

The 1994 motion was stunning. It was filed *pro se*—
that is, by Joe Liberto himself without benefit of an
attorney, although knowing Joe Liberto's spelling and
grammar, it seemed obvious that a jailhouse attorney
had written it.

"On, or about, September 1987, the Movant, Joseph
Liberto, was approached by agents of the Federal
Bureau of Investigation. At that time, the Movant was
taken to a motel and questioned for approximately
two hours concerning his knowledge of a murder-for-
hire scheme. The target of which was the daughter-in-
law of his employer, Joseph Luskin.

"The agents released Joseph Liberto and he went to
his employer, Joseph Luskin, and related what had
occurred. Joseph Luskin's son, Paul, also an employer
of Movant Joseph Liberto, had been implicated in the
murder-for-hire scheme.

"Luskin threatened the Movant, saying that if he gave testimony against his son, Paul, or against him, he would see that harm came to the Movant's family.

"At that time Joseph Luskin contacted his deceased brother's son, Steven Miles, formerly Steven Luskin, obtained counsel for the Movant, one Mike Libowitz. Joseph Luskin paid Libowitz $20,000 to represent the Movant.

"Joseph Luskin was a multi-millionaire who owned a large chain of electronic/stereo stores throughout Florida. As such, he was a powerful man with many political contacts and alleged underworld connections. The threat was not taken lightly by the Movant. He knew that Joseph Luskin had the connections and the means to implement his threat.

"Movant's fear were well founded; in April 1989, Movant's 12 year old daughter was abducted and sexually assaulted as a warning to the Movant not to testify or cooperate with the authorities in any way.

"The attorney representing the Movant was acting on behalf of the person holding the purse strings, Joseph Luskin and codefendant Paul Luskin. Movant had been employed by the Luskin family for over twenty years. Joe Luskin was fearful that the Movant knew things about him and his son, Paul Luskin, which could result in criminal prosecution.

"It has been a long established maxim that an agent cannot serve two masters. An inherent conflict of interest existed in the present case. The gesture of Joseph Luskin paying the attorney fees for the Movant's criminal representation was anything but magnanimous. It was a self-serving manipulation that directly affected the course of the criminal investigation, as well as the trial."

The government responded a few months later with a sworn statement from Mike Libowitz denying any conflict of interest.

"In these proceedings, I represented Joseph Liberto and no one else. I was not paid by Joseph Luskin to represent Mr. Liberto. I was paid by Joseph Liberto, who, along with his wife and members of his family, executed an engagement agreement whereby any balance of the fee due was to be paid."

Liberto had also alleged that it was the Luskins' idea that he not testify, nor enter into a plea agreement with the government. Libowitz disputed that.

"To the contrary, on Mr. Liberto's behalf, I attempted to negotiate a plea agreement with Gregg Bernstein, then assistant United States attorney. Initially, on Mr. Liberto's behalf, I sought a dismissal of charges in exchange for full cooperation from Mr. Liberto. Mr. Bernstein was not inclined to so offer."

Libowitz continued that on the eve of trial, Bernstein suggested Liberto plea to five years, considering that the government had developed the money transfer evidence. "I recommended to Mr. Liberto that he accept the government's offer. Mr. Liberto declined. He indicated that he would not accept any plea bargain which would require incarceration."

As for not testifying, Libowitz said, "For tactical reasons, Mr. Liberto chose not to testify. . . . I believe Mr. Liberto's honest testimony would not have advanced his position."

In Liberto's counterresponse to the government's answer, he included copies of agonized handwritten letters he had mailed to Judge Motz. The first was dated January 10, 1989, postmarked from the El Reno, Oklahoma, federal prison, asking for a transfer to a lower-level prison closer to his family:

Your Honor:

I am writing this letter in the hope you can help me with the desperate situation I've been placed in. I was convicted from the statements made by a drug addict facing life imprisonment in a trial that sentenced me to 15 years for his weapons and 7 years for conspiracy. At 47, father of 5 children and (with) a wife of 25 years, this amounts to a possible death sentence.

Never having ever committed a crime and no record, how this could happen (has) left me devastated. Since the sentencing I have not seen my lawyer and have found it impossible to contact him. I have called at least 50 times but always get the same reply "He's not in, he's in a meeting, or with another client." After 9 months of trying I'm writing to you for help.

Baltimore City Jail and Lewisburg Prison were real hellholes—dirty and dehumanizing. When I was in Baltimore City Jail I was locked in a cell 23 hours a day and allowed to leave for a short time to eat and shower. It was dirty, noisy, and I was forced to witness sexual crimes, beatings and police corruption.

My family was living in Florida and sold everything to be by my side. (My wife) moved with the children to Baltimore. With no money and no place to stay she was forced to move to Texas and live with her aunt.

Transferred to federal prison in New York, I was told I had blood in my urine but I was never treated or tested as to why. . . . At Lewisburg an asbestos liquid (had dripped) from the ceiling onto my arm, causing a rash. I showed the rash to a physician's assistant and he did nothing about it. When the rash had spread across my chest to my other arm, I finally saw a doctor. After a week, my skin fell off across my chest, and the rash disappeared in two weeks.

I can't eat. I've lost thirty pounds from not eating for two weeks, worrying about not seeing my family. I don't even care to eat. My life has been spent caring for my family. I've worked 6 and 7 days a week to support 5 children and that has been my whole life. I feel all is lost and I may never see my family.

The next letter, dated September 2, 1989, was worse:

My son, after being beaten in error by two Broward County (Florida) sheriffs, was left in the care of doctors, the last I heard. My wife got a job at the 7-11 to support my two daughters (age 12 and 16) and took the night shift to make 20 cents more an hour.

Two months ago while I was in the hospital in El Reno, my wife told me that my 12 year old daughter was kidnapped by a black man at gunpoint when she was coming home from school. She was raped repeatedly, beaten and left in the road. She has not been right since that day—my wife can't afford to buy her clothes or get proper medical attention. My (other daughter) is sick and needs a (brain scan) when my wife can afford it.

(My wife) has discovered a large lump on her breast but can't afford to see a doctor. She is being evicted on the 8th because she can't afford the apartment. No one has helped us at all, and what was a loving family has been torn apart.

In his next letter, dated November 29, 1989, Liberto acknowledged that Motz had responded to him. He wrote:

There is not much left at this time of my family. My (eldest) daughter has left home and I don't know where she lives. My wife makes $600 a month and just can't make it with her bad health. My 13 year old needs medical attention and is not getting the help she needs. I don't think my wife is mentally capable of handling things anymore. She is just devastated. She works crazy hours and makes just enough to pay rent and eats very little. There is little or no hope left for us at this time.

We have been living in fear for two years of the Luskin family. From the start I was threatened by the Luskins with harm to my family. It doesn't matter anymore. My family has tried to make it but we just can't.

Then on Christmas Day, 1989, more about the Luskin threat:

My life has been hell worrying about whether the threats made by Joe Luskin to me would come true. My lawyer does nothing to help me. I was not allowed to give testimony to help me in the trial for fear for my family being killed. That fear has made my family live in the streets and be raped and starving. Yes, starving in America . . . I'm glad to give a statement if it can save my family.

Did the Luskins send a man to rape Joe Liberto's twelve-year-old daughter "as a warning" to Liberto?

In Liberto's 1990 motion for sentence reduction, filed by Mike Libowitz, he included a hospital report of the sexual assault, which occurred on April 8, 1989. In it, the doctor handwrote:

"Was walking with friends near 7-11 about 10 p.m. A man stopped and asked her about getting drugs— followed them, so they ran to the apartments. Talked to a man about the incident—thought the man was gone. He came back again—singled out (victim)—put a gun to neck and forced her into a car. Drove down I-20. Stopped car and penetrated (victim) with his penis."

This is where the Luskin connection to the rape strained my credibility—for two reasons. First, Liberto blamed the Luskins for the rape in his 1994 sentence reduction, but not when he filed in 1990, eight months after it happened. Of course, since Mike Libowitz had filed it, Liberto could say he was restricted from doing so. And, of course, Libowitz would dispute that.

Second, since the rape occurred in Arlington, Texas— a thousand miles from Miami, while Joe and Mildred were on the run offshore, and the Libertos were living like transients—it just didn't ring true.

And if that part was crazy, could anything else he had said about the Luskins be true? Liberto's letters sounded so desperate, he might have been willing to say anything. And in fact, in 1990, Judge Motz did give him a seven-year sentence reduction. Perhaps it was just out of pity.

I called Mrs. Cohen that night. She said Sonny had called her the day after I left, concerned that he had said too much about Jim Liberto and his drug business. I explained Jim Liberto's reaction, that he admitted to me financing Sonny's drug business, just that Liberto didn't handle Sonny's drugs himself.

She asked about my meeting with Darden.

"Well, Mrs. Cohen, there might still be life in Jimmy Manley's ashes, after all."

"But Jeri saw him in his coffin."

"Well, I don't know, let's ask her again."

I wanted to see if Sonny had told her what he had told me, that it was him in Marie Luskin's house that day. "Yes, but he was there just to rob her," she said.

Then I raised the bail-jumping story. That was true, too, Sonny was going to jump, and he would have gone somewhere in Europe if he could have gotten bail.

"But Luskin and Jim Liberto didn't follow through," she said.

Now that that was the third reference, I had no reason left to disbelieve it. I spouted out to Mrs. Cohen what it meant, that there really was a murder-for-hire. She seemed not to understand, so I repeated myself.

But apparently she did comprehend. Her response was, "So, does Darden think they're all guilty?"

Now I was on the defensive. I did not want to answer that, nor as it turned out, did I have to. At that moment, my sister called downstairs, telling me to get ready, we were leaving to shop for Thanksgiving dinner. I gratefully excused myself, and promised to call back later.

On the other hand, I realized later, I had missed the window to ask the critical question—So, which Luskin had arranged for the bail?

A day out of Ithaca, I thought again of my "trash file"—where I'd discarded everything that didn't fit into the theory that the assault was a robbery.

I thought of Patty Parks and James Raidy.

Driving between Florida and Baltimore, Cohen asked Parks—the Miss Maryland runner-up—her view of the death penalty, after they had listened to a radio talk show together. He suggested various What ifs?, including one where someone "was being paid to kill someone that the killer did not know."

Later, during a phone call from Baltimore City Jail, Cohen told Parks that he was being implicated in a murder attempt, "but the lady will not be able to identify him."

James Raidy was the prisoner with a second degree murder rap who snitched on Cohen's escape attempt. He told the FBI that Cohen told him he had gone to Florida to kill a woman and he had "went up alongside her head with a gun."

He supported Manley's testimony that two more murder attempts had followed. He said Cohen told him Manley could "sink him" at trial because he had told him that Marie Luskin was supposed to be at a particular shopping center.

Raidy reported that information in November 1987. It wasn't public knowledge until the trial, in January 1988. Nor had the newspapers to that point written anything that specific.

On the night before Thanksgiving, it snowed in Baltimore. Little flurries stuck to the ground and window screens like feathers from a torn pillow.

It's the Richard Nixon question, I thought. Nobody blamed Nixon for planning the Watergate break-in, just for covering it up.

My question was, What did Paul Luskin know, and when did he know it?

November 25

Two days before, I had made appointments to see Steve Allen this day and Russell White Monday. I had to prod White to see me, but Allen was pleased I was in town.

I had never spoken to Steve in person alone. Since it was the Friday after Thanksgiving, Steve was dressed informally, wearing an ironed blue shirt, blue jeans, and well-worn leather sailing shoes. His tortoiseshell eyeglasses and blond hair completed his preppy look, for someone in his early forties, but his soft voice couldn't hide traces of a Baltimore accent that I associate with the city's longshoremen. Why, why, do intelligent people in Baltimore sound like they used to work on the docks?

He sat me in his chair behind his antique wooden writing desk. We talked about how he got involved in the case. As an assistant U.S. attorney in 1982, Steve had prosecuted a heroin case against a Pakistani whom Alvin Entin and Shelly Schwartz represented. From mutual respect they became friendly, and in 1987, when Entin needed someone in Baltimore to nose around preindictment, he called Steve.

It was also unusual that Steve and Paul knew each other from law school at the University of Baltimore, although they weren't close.

Allen's assignment was to talk to Bernstein and research what he could about Cohen and Manley. Since the FBI had talked to Joe Liberto on September 18—four weeks before the indictment was announced, I had figured that the Luskins knew an investigation was out there. But the FBI wouldn't have leaked the names Cohen and Manley. I asked Allen how the Luskins would have known the names back then. He said he didn't remember.

Allen found the drugs and guns case against them both, but Manley's folder was sealed. "That usually means the witness is cooperating," he said. He called Manley's federal public defender, Brooke Murdock, who denied her client was cooperating, or that she had ever heard the name Paul Luskin. A few years later, Allen said, Murdock apologized to him—she certainly did know at the time that Manley was cooperating.

At Paul's bond hearing, Judge Motz ordered him detained without bond and placed in Baltimore City Jail to await trial. Allen argued that the jail was too dangerous for him—"he was a fat, little pudgy Jewish guy, with the Luskin name—he would be killed there." He remembered Motz rubbed his forehead for five minutes, clearly agonized, then reversed himself and placed Paul in a halfway house.

After the indictment, Paul's cousin Steve Miles played a "critical role" in the defense. Since Miles didn't know Allen, he wanted a local attorney he had confidence in.

Entin, however, wanted Allen in. Only after someone else turned Miles down did Allen get the assignment.

We talked about the government's theory of the case. Paul had made a number of trips from Pittsburgh to Baltimore in 1987, documented by Paul's car phone records. "They showed he could have come in to meet with Jim Liberto," he said. "We said they were meetings with friends. The closest thing the government had was that phone call in November 1986" when Jim Liberto's room at the Marco Polo called Paul's apartment, documented by his hotel bill.

"Do you believe it?" I asked. "Were they meetings to discuss a murder-for-hire?"

"I won't answer that without a waiver from Paul," he said.

That was something short of a flat denial.

My next question was why the government thought Joe Luskin was involved.

"It's a natural," he said. "Father-son, and Marie mentioned Joe Luskin. Marie was destroying a family and their business. It doesn't take a rocket scientist to figure he's involved if his son is involved."

Another assignment Entin gave Steve preindictment was to find out if the government was going to indict Joe Luskin. Bernstein told Allen they would if they could make a case, but they never could.

"I thought Joe Luskin might have been indicted back then. The government hoped that Joe Liberto would roll over as a witness. They always believed that if Joe Liberto flipped, he would implicate Joe Luskin."

That was just what Joe Liberto said, I thought.

"Some prosecutors would have indicted just on the supposition that he was involved, and let the jury decide. The worst that happens, they find him not guilty. I think Bernstein handled himself very responsibly in not pursuing the father."

However, if Joe Luskin had been indicted, "we had enough lawyers to hand out."

"Why were there so many lawyers?" I asked.

"I have no answer," he said.

"Was Russ White hired in the expectation he would

defend Joe Luskin?" I tried to confirm what Darden had told me.

"No. There was no connection." But ironically, the government could have won a conviction against Joe Luskin, he said. A newspaper reporter who had talked to the jury after the verdict told him they believed Joe Luskin was involved.

I described some of Joe Liberto's accusations against the Luskins. He stopped me before I got very far.

"I'm the one guy who doesn't feel sorry for Joe Liberto, one iota. If you believe that Jimmy Liberto hired Sonny Cohen to do it, then Joe Liberto is the linchpin. He's the connection to Jimmy. Plus, Joe is deeply involved in Jimmy's drug organization."

I think by now Steve had picked up that I no longer believed everything Paul said since I was probing the dark bowels of the case. I had felt in somewhat of a crisis that day and the days prior, and I think he realized I needed some perspective. It was then that he gave me the words that carried me through the day and many days after it:

"If you believe Paul Luskin is innocent, he's a victim. If you believe he's guilty, he's still a victim."

He explained: "I feel sorry for Paul, irrespective of whether he's innocent or guilty. The divorce case had run amok, and his whole world was falling apart, as well as others who were innocent who were dragged into it."

Allen was likewise bereft of sympathy for Marie. "Marie Luskin was a woman who clearly had an agenda." Obviously, he said, he didn't condone the idea of trying to kill her for the hell she had put him through, "but intellectually, you could understand why he might have done it. Objectively, you could say that his judgment was skewed. Paul is not a bad guy, he's not an evil guy. He's a terrible, tragic figure. It's a tragic set of circumstances, either way."

Allen said the "protagonist of the tragedy" was the divorce court judge, Constance Nutaro. Allen had watched the trial.

"I have never seen a judge in twenty years as a lawyer interject herself so much in a case. She made up her mind on day one, and became a member of Marie Luskin's trial team. She exercised no discretion or restraint."

"I want to ask you, but I can't ask you, is he innocent or guilty?" I said.

"You can ask, but I can't answer. Maybe twenty years after he's deceased. I have my opinion, but it's irrelevant."

I suggested the Richard Nixon question, What did Paul know and when did he know it? Steve smiled again, and without answering it, implied to me I was on target.

Now it was time to ask the question I had come for—What about your notes from the Steve Miles interview? Mike Wallace might have shoved the page in his face and demanded, Is this your writing? I knew it was.

But slash-and-burn journalism is not my style. I hadn't even brought the paper with me. What I did do was suggest that I had information gathered long ago that Steve Miles knew there was a murder-for-hire.

"I don't think Steve Miles would have had a clue about the murder-for-hire," he said. He didn't remember discussing the issue at all.

"Steve Miles did not like me. We had a minimal amount of contact. Steve wouldn't tell me the time of day, much less confide in me that." He even remembered a snub—Miles had left him off his Christmas card list, with trial approaching in just weeks.

I didn't press him any farther, and didn't feel bad about it. Either he really didn't remember, or just couldn't say. In any event, *60 Minutes* should remember not to hire me if I ever ask them for a job.

"I think about the case often," Allen said. "I've always regretted the result. I replay what I'd do differently, but I'm not sure it would have made a difference.

"Problem was, the case made sense." Then he repeated Alvin Entin's joke, the one I had always considered the best line from the case, that the jury believed "Even if he didn't do it, he should have."

He remembered something else the reporter who had interviewed the jurors had told him. They had focused in on when the cops broke down Joe Luskin's apartment door to arrest Paul for late support payments. When they found him, he was hiding under a blanket on a neighbor's balcony.

"A guy of Paul Luskin's physical stature, to jump balconies twenty-four floors up, is a pretty desperate guy" who might resort to anything, Allen said the jury felt. "I never thought about it, and the government didn't focus on it," but the jury did.

I'm sure the incident sounded worse than it was. Although hiding under a blanket sounded childish, I'm sure he was able to step from one balcony to the next, and that's probably why neither side made a big deal of it.

We talked about the chances of him getting a sentence reduction. Allen said he didn't see "a miracle over the horizon" that would get him a new trial, but a sentence reduction was not a prohibitive long shot. With a new sentence, he might be eligible for release in a few years.

"I think he will have paid his penalty—if you assume he's guilty—and still have some life left. Then Paul and Susan will go off somewhere."

As I walked on East Baltimore Street outside Allen's office, then up an alley to East Fayette Street, a cathedral bell rang that it was noontime, its sound reflecting off the walls of the city. The street was nearly empty on this day after Thanksgiving; I felt it was speaking to me.

The story wasn't simply about guilt and innocence. It was about falling in love.

Don't fall in love. What cynical advice from a lawman and an attorney. What kind of world would it be if nobody fell in love?

There was a lot at stake in this story: whether Paul Luskin was wrongly convicted and sentenced to a long prison term for something he did not do and whether that was a result of mistakes, arrogance or meanness by the government. The initial evidence indicated Luskin was right.

I shouldn't be embarrassed that I was taken in for so long, I thought—rather, I should be pleased that I had allowed myself to be open. And it wasn't all a waste of time—some of what I had found was going to help him get out sooner.

I was still in love after all. Even if I no longer believed everything Luskin said.

In Fort Lauderdale, *The Miami Herald* had bought billboards promoting one of their accomplishments: "Innocent man released from Broward jail . . . because the State Attorney read the *Herald.*"

My billboard would be similar. "Guilty man released from federal prison" because of me.

We all make our small, twisted contributions to the world we live in.

"Ask not for whom the bell tolls." The sound bespoke a cliché. "It tolls for thee."

November 28

I met Russell White at 9:00 A.M. at his office, which was the basement of his home in Towson, the seat of Baltimore County. It was only a few blocks from its downtown and county courthouse.

Since White had been hesitant to make an appointment with me, I figured I'd only last a half hour there, if that. He was in his fifties, about six feet tall, and had a conservative appearance. He wore gold-rimmed glasses and a white shirt with a monogram RJW, but his thinning hair was red, and that was a clue to me that he was something out of the ordinary. He warmed up to me a lot faster than I expected.

Considering that I had written the *Sun Magazine* story three years before, I apologized for taking so long to contact him. He wasn't even aware the story had been published, and he didn't feel slighted for being left out since Steve Allen and Alvin Entin had left him out during the trial and since.

"I sat through the whole goddamn trial. It was the most boring time of my life. I was not really taken into confidence. I was an outcast. I would have gladly bowed out of this damned thing. It was the biggest waste of money."

I asked how he got in. "Steve Miles hired me." Miles

had worked for him in the early 1970s, and they had stayed friends.

At trial, Paul was the ultimate authority, he said. It was Paul who decided White should cross-examine Manley. When the decision was made to keep Paul off the stand, White went to Entin and protested.

"Triple-hearsay was the only thing that tied him in. It seemed the right thing for Paul to testify. Anybody who's tried cases knows the jury expects to hear from the defendant."

"But Luskin and the other lawyers said they were threatened by Jim Liberto," I said.

"That's B.S. I had no knowledge of anybody threatening Paul. The theory was Paul would be a lousy witness. They thought Paul was not the best witness at the divorce trial. Had he testified—and made a good witness—he had a hell of a chance of acquittal.

"Damn few cases are won where the defendant doesn't testify. The jury must have thought the son of a bitch must be guilty. Jurors don't buy that B.S. about having the right not to testify. All he had to do was get on the stand and testify that James Manley was a liar, or that someone was mistaken.

"Why would they have threatened him?" On the stand, "There was nothing Luskin could have said about drugs. His testimony wouldn't have hurt them.

"I sat on my ass for five weeks while the great Entin and Steve Allen devised all their strategy. I can't help feeling that they completely missed the boat."

White said Manley was tough to cross-examine "because I think he was telling the truth, what Sonny Cohen had told him."

I then told White what Darden had said Manley told him, that Bernstein put the name Paul Luskin in his mouth.

"I don't believe it. Gregg Bernstein doesn't have a reputation for doing that sort of thing."

"Do you think there was a murder-for-hire?" I asked.

"There was a murder-for-hire. I don't have any doubt about it. I think the evidence was pretty clear."

I asked how he knew that, had anyone told him? No, he said, he just got that impression from listening to everything in court.

"Until you've been through a nasty divorce—well, some of those thoughts can go through your mind. You think about your estranged wife getting hit by a tractor-trailer crossing the wrong side of the road."

I joked that if it turned out there were phone calls beforehand between you and the tractor-trailer driver, then you're in big trouble.

"I represent guys all the time who say something in a bar, someone hears it and calls the police, they set him up and see if he follows through. I had one recently. He got one year."

"One year!" I said. "Luskin got thirty-five."

"That's Motz," he said. "He should have gotten five years. If Motz could have seen what a bitch this woman was . . ."

I asked if he thought Marie was shot instead of hit.

"I believe the bullet was fired. She was the luckiest person in the world." But when I reminded him Steve Allen had conceded that in closing argument, White said that was a mistake.

Then I asked the question I had come here for: Had he been hired to represent Joe Luskin?

No, he answered. When he was hired he expected to take over the defense team, but he could never take control.

I described some of Darden's theory that Joe Luskin was behind the murder-for-hire, not Paul. White crossed his arms defensively. Then I suggested the Richard Nixon question, What did Paul know, and when did he know it? He liked that, and brightened.

"That's a good defense. Blame it on the old man." I didn't get the impression that he bought it. On second thought, maybe it wouldn't have been such a good idea for trial, because it would have risked getting Joe Luskin indicted.

Later I slipped in the question about Steve Allen's handwritten note that Paul had paid $65,000 for the hit.

"It wouldn't be proper for me to say anything," he answered.

I also summarized Joe Liberto's pleading, that the Luskin family had threatened him and was responsible for the rape of his young daughter.

"Jesus Christ, I don't believe that." However, he said it was possible that the Luskins had paid for Joe Liberto's attorney, although he didn't know one way or another. "I know Mike Libowitz is a good friend of Steve Miles, but I'm dubious he would take instructions from Luskin, and not his client."

Later that morning, I got Mike Libowitz on the telephone briefly. He repeated what he had said in his sworn statement; the Luskins did not pay his fee to represent Joe Liberto. "I represented Joe—he was the only one I represented," he said.

I had long since promised Mrs. Cohen I would come by her house and meet her, and now, as darkness fell on the last night I would be in Baltimore, I finally got the chance. She lived on Winner Avenue, in Pimlico, no more than a few steps from one of Pimlico Race Track's entrances.

Her home was a row house with a creaky wooden front patio. Thirty years before, it had been a good address in Jewish Baltimore. The original Luskin's store was about a mile and a half away, and still remained. Even closer nearby, but long gone, were Barry Levinson's father's store and the Hilltop Diner—Barry's now-famous 1950s hangout.

Now, I safely assumed, Mrs. Cohen was one of the very last Jews in the neighborhood, as well as one of the very last whites. Later, she told me, as a single mother, she couldn't afford to move when everyone else did.

Mrs. Cohen was dressed up for my visit. She was in her seventies, with coiffed hair somewhere between blond and white, and she had no shortage of energy. We chatted about the neighborhood—she said her house was more than a hundred years old, to my surprise—and whether the owner of the race track was going to sell the land and develop it.

Now that I had told her there probably was a murder-for-hire, which meant I no longer believed Sonny, I didn't know how she would view me. I was reluctant to break the ice.

Finally, mercifully, she opened the real discussion by volunteering that Sonny had made a fortune selling drugs, and loved spending the money. He bought a lot of gifts for people, tipped well in restaurants, bought diamond rings and a baseball signed by Babe Ruth. He had a room full of clothes he bought at Hamburgers, which at least when I lived in Baltimore was considered one of the best clothiers in the city. He pissed away a lot of money on his girlfriend, she said, "but he had a good time."

"Sonny says, 'Mom, if you do the crime, you got to do the time,'" she said.

"It doesn't make sense, Mrs. Cohen, does it?" I asked, appealing to her Jewish mother instinct. Jewish mothers teach their children to delay gratification. Of course the children recognize the obvious flaw that the future never comes.

"No, it doesn't," she said.

Here I was, interviewing a sweet Jewish mom of an alleged murderer-for-hire. Mrs. Cohen's two daughters had turned out perfectly well, in fact, very well. One was an executive for a railroad. The other was a bank vice president. Sonny was in banking as well. He robbed them.

She tried to explain that although she knew her son was guilty of various crimes over the years, and now, at least an assault on Marie Luskin, she had trouble justifying that he was a dangerous man when he was so kind to her as a son.

"I can't believe my son would hit a woman—or want to kill her. He doesn't treat women that way. All I know is my son is in jail, and it hurts."

Like me, Mrs. Cohen liked playing detective. "But why was he in Florida? Why get drugs from Florida? He got them here from Jim Liberto. They were all part of a big drug ring."

"Do you think there was a murder-for-hire?" she asked me point-blank.

I was less off guard this time. "Should I?" I asked.

Mrs. Cohen gave me the impression she really didn't know for sure whether it was a murder-for-hire, or a robbery, as Sonny said. Besides that, she really wanted to know. Between the two of us, I think she felt, we could do better than either of us alone.

We talked about the Joe Luskin theory. When Darden came to see Sonny a year before, she said, "Darden wanted Sonny to say that Joe Luskin did the hiring, not Paul. But Sonny said, 'The poor man is dead!'"

"It was Paul. It wasn't Joe," she said.

Then she qualified that a bit. "I believe the story it was Paul who said to Joe Liberto, 'Do you know somebody who can do whatever?'"

Then realizing she had said too much, she backed off even farther.

"So it wasn't a robbery, it was a murder, then," I said.

No, she said, she didn't know.

There was no motivation for Sonny to admit he was a hired killer, she said. "When you're labeled a hit man, parole says 'we don't want you to get out on the street.'"

She had no kind words for Paul. His affair with his girlfriend made him "a bad guy. If I were her (Marie), I would have taken him for every nickel he had."

"Well, that's what happened," I said. Sleeping with your old flame while married to a wife who was ignoring you didn't seem to me like the most heinous act in the story, but I pick my arguments better than that, with someone's Jewish mother.

I brought up Manley's discussions with Darden. That was phony, she said. "I think Jimmy Manley was out to get money from the Luskins—to cash in on them."

That had crossed my mind long before, and Susan's, too.

I returned to the bail story. "Every day, they said, 'Yeah, we're coming up with the bond money.' Every day, I expected Sonny home," she said. But this time, when I asked her about Luskin being part of the bond equation, she said she didn't know if he was.

It was a perfect gray note on which to end my trip.

November 29
Miami

When I got home to Miami, there were messages on my answering machine from Bill Genego and Jim Liberto. I couldn't return Liberto's call, but I called Genego.

Jim Liberto had told Genego he had discussed his brother's sentence reduction with me. Exactly contrary to what I thought, Genego thought Joe Liberto's motion could help Paul.

While I was up north, Genego had come east to meet with Paul. It was their first meeting, delayed a week because of Paul's hospitalization. He said they discussed the pleading together.

"I said in some ways it makes a lot of sense." He asked Paul his opinion, and he responded, "I really don't know."

Genego said Paul recalled a conversation with his dad before the trial: His dad had offered "Do you think I should tell them that I did it?"

Paul's response was, "Did you?"

When his dad didn't answer, Paul said, "Well, I'm already under indictment, no point for both of us."

"So you think there was a murder-for-hire?" I asked.

He didn't answer that with a yes or no. "Let's say we're there—as the judge is, and Gregg Bernstein is. Paul had a really terrible relationship with Joe Liberto. It fits in with what the judge and Bernstein already believe."

Genego said he asked Paul, "'Do you think your father could do it?'

"He couldn't see his father going to Joe Liberto, asking for it, but if they were hanging out, maybe Joe Liberto asked his father, 'Would you like me to take care of the bitch?' He said his father in many ways was an unknown quantity.

"It's a believable story," Genego said.

I said if it was true, Paul could forget about a new trial, and should concentrate on a sentence reduction. Genego agreed. But Paul hadn't given him the authority in his upcoming filing to make the argument blaming his father.

I renewed the hit or shot discussion for its bearing on whether the assault was a murder attempt or a robbery. Genego said he had recently talked to Steve Allen, who told him his expert at trial had looked at Marie's wounds and decided that because of the way they went in, and down, "No way it could have been done by anything besides a shot."

"But they never found a bullet," I said.

Steve Allen had responded to that, too, Genego said. Cohen's lawyer had once mentioned to Allen that there might have been a misfire—"something fucked up with the bullet."

"So what happened to the rest of the bullet, then?"

"The rest of the bullet is in the gun. Cohen ran because he thought she was shot," Genego said.

By the end of the conversation, perhaps after listening to my dubious tone, Genego realized that Judge Motz wouldn't buy the my-dad-did-it-not-me theory. "There's just no way out," he said. Since Joe Liberto was already on the record, a better idea would be to challenge his credibility than to admit what he said, Genego decided.

November 30

I wasn't anxious to talk to either Paul or Susan, but they both called this day.

I didn't talk to Susan for long. She wanted to know had I heard the Manley tape. In the scheme of the last two weeks, it had lost most of its importance to me.

I told her the story about monitoring both sides of the cassette tape, but finding nothing.

"Darden has the credibility of a toad," she said.

"This is the ghost of James Manley!" said the voice on the phone when I picked it up.

"Are you sure this isn't the ghost of Paul Luskin?"

"Almost!" he said.

He sounded good, but beyond even the exhaustion of

recovery, he seemed a little resigned, a little bit of his punch was missing.

"I was down to three units of blood. Two and a half units is death," he said. I asked how many units were normal, and he said fourteen.

"The doctor at the hospital thought I had six hours to live. I had collapsed on the doctor's floor in prison, and he thought it wasn't important, it could wait for the next day."

At the emergency room of the hospital, in shackles, passing out, a nurse asked him, "Do you have insurance?" He was on the federal plan, he answered.

I wanted to ask Paul all the questions I had from the trip, but there was a right way and a wrong way to do it. Since Joe Liberto's filing was on the record, I thought I'd start there.

"I told Genego that Joe Liberto had called Steve Miles for an attorney reference. Libowitz had worked with Steve Miles at one time. My father had nothing to do with it.

"Steve Miles and Joe Liberto had worked together at Luskin's (in Baltimore, at the Pimlico store) as salesmen in the sixties. They had always been the best of friends. They were the same age. Steve Miles and Joe Liberto used to go out together to bars after the store closed."

"Did your father pay for Joe Liberto's attorney?"

"No. I remember my father asking Steve Miles, 'Where did Libowitz come from?' Steve Miles said Joe Liberto had called him when he needed an attorney. He didn't pay him much. Besides, the lead counsel for Joe Liberto was Howard Cardin (Jimmy Liberto's counsel). They piggybacked—they had the same defense."

We talked about Joe Liberto and Joe Luskin's relationship. They had known each other since about 1960, and Paul said Joe Liberto wanted to be like a son to Joe Luskin.

"He would do anything my father wanted. My father rehired him at Luskin's after I fired him. I fired him during Thanksgiving (1986). We didn't have an Expo sale that year.

"Then I went to the hospital for a week, and then to Pittsburgh." Months later, when Joe Luskin rehired Joe Liberto, it was "over my objection. I guess he needed somebody, and I was gone. Bob Kempler (a former general manager) was gone, and only Nikki Hart was there."

Paul remembered reading in Jack Luskin's deposition in the divorce case that Joe Liberto had asked to work for Jack if he bought the chain of stores in Tampa he was negotiating for.

"When I heard that, that Joe Liberto was meeting with Jack, I went up. I knew Joe Liberto was backstabbing the whole thing. We fired him just in time."

I found Jack Luskin's deposition, dated December 22, 1986. In it, Jack was reluctant to provide too many details to Marie's counsel Barry Franklin, for fear it would cost Joe Liberto his job—which Jack said he didn't know Joe Liberto had already lost.

Barry Franklin: "What discussions did you have with Joe Liberto?"

Jack Luskin: "Joe would call me on his own volition occasionally indicating that he heard that I am coming into Florida or he heard that I am going into Tampa, and he would be available. At that point, he would volunteer some information regarding what was going on in Florida from his perspective."

"What did he say to you specifically?"

"At one point, he indicated Paul was going through a rather trashy divorce and circumstances around it."

"You indicated you were afraid to say something for fear this man's job would be jeopardized. I am going to ask you to tell us what he confided to you about the business, if indeed he said something to you about the business."

"Business was suffering to a degree because of the inattention by Paul, because the thrust of his thinking was involvement in the divorce proceedings, that Joe (Luskin) was coming back to take a more active role in the business."

"What else did he say?"

"That is about it."

"There has got to be something more if you thought his job was going to be lost over questioning on the matter."

"I think the mere fact that Joe Liberto was even talking to me, from Paul Luskin's perspective, is sufficient reason to fire him."

"He's a real snake in the grass, a backstabber. Exactly what I said. My father's dead, and there's no records around. Why did he wait until now?" Paul asked.

"This is a big hoax on Joe Liberto's part. He figures he's got Motz's ear."

"But I don't understand," I said. "He has less than two years left anyway. He's almost out. Why go to this trouble?"

"He's going to try to get a reversal. That way he won't be an ex-felon when he's out."

ELEVEN

December 1994

December 1

Before I left town, I had made an appointment for this
date to see Rabbi Moshe Horn, who had helped Paul in
some conflicts with prison officials. Rabbi Horn, also a
lawyer, was a program director for Aleph Institute, a
prison ministry for Jewish inmates, whose national
headquarters happened to be nearby, in Miami Beach—
Surfside to be precise. Aleph was an arm of the ultrareli-
gious Lubavitch sect.

So when I met Rabbi Horn I wasn't shocked that he
had a full, curly red beard and wore a blue skullcap
attached with a hairpin, but I was mildly surprised that
he appeared about thirty-five.

During the interview, we were constantly interrupted
by collect calls from prisoners, most just wanting to
chat. In another call, he explained the meaning of a
Chanukah menorah to a food service director of a Dade
County jail. Horn said many of his accomplishments
were ensuring that Jewish prisoners had access to traditional meals at Jewish holidays, and Jewish religious
items, including prayer books.

He wasn't interested in prisoners' protestations of
innocence, again to my surprise. "Prison is a sign on the
wall that they have to change. As far as God is concerned, they've committed a crime," he said.

I took that to mean he believed that everyone in
prison was guilty. "If they're in jail, God put them i

283

for a reason," he said. Rehabilitation, as far as he was concerned, was embracing God in prison.

"People ask why they're in prison. If you take a true retrospective of their lives, you'd see there were signs on the wall telling them it was coming. It didn't have to end up the way it happened."

But, "That God put them in prison, shows that God cared about them, more than another person."

Since I was consulting a rabbi, I had my own conundrum to ask. The assault on Marie Luskin was a simple act, it took ten minutes, if that. But people like Cohen, the Libertos, and Manley—a bunch of street guys from Baltimore—had woven a tale of deceit mixed with truth that was taking me four years to unwind.

"What's wrong with me? Why can't I figure this out for certain?"

I had asked the right person. He had a Yiddish proverb, just for the occasion.

"A fool throws a stone into the garden, and ten wise men can't get it out," he said.

Although Genego's upcoming motion would center on errors the government had allegedly made by not providing discovery, and even though I had found most of it buried in Darden's files, I didn't know whether to say anything.

The real problem was, I didn't know at the moment if I should be helping Paul or not. If I told Genego, he'd be obligated not to argue almost the entire appeal. On the other hand, I had to wonder if the government would find the stuff on their own.

Sherlock Holmes, who was not the official police, did not feel bound to tell authorities everything he knew. In *The Adventure of the Devil's Foot,* he deduced how a murder had been committed, then summoned his suspect Sterndale to hear his calculations. Sterndale's hand forced, he admitted his crime but explained it was to revenge the victim's own murder of his sister, who was Sterndale's secret lover. Sterndale then put himself in Holmes's hands.

Holmes went silent while he sat in judgment. "I think

you must agree, Watson, that it is not a case in which we are called to interfere. Our investigation has been independent, and our action shall be so also. You would not denounce the man?"

"Certainly not," answered Watson.

December 2

In the afternoon, Susan called and asked me if I could come over and talk to her immediately. Something serious had happened, and she wouldn't tell me what.

I guessed it was a death in the family. I hoped it wasn't Paul. He had sounded resigned earlier in the week when I talked to him.

Twenty minutes later I was at Susan's office, but she had gone home earlier in the day. Now I drove to Hollywood, and found her alone, slouching on her sofa.

It wasn't Paul, wasn't a death, it was something involving one of her sons, something that solved itself within a week or so.

After we talked it out, we talked about Paul. Susan had sounded nervous just talking to me in a phone conversation after I had told Paul I knew about Joe Liberto's pleading. Did she wonder, Could I still be trusted to help? Maybe, I thought, she just knew that I knew, and neither she nor Paul was anxious to face it.

She asked me what I thought about Joe Luskin. I said Darden believed there was a murder-for-hire, that Joe Luskin was behind it, and he expected him to admit it on his deathbed.

I wasn't expecting a confirmation. "Paul let it out once that he thought his father would have admitted it on his deathbed, too," she said.

However, Susan still didn't think there was a murder-for-hire, but I was holding back some of my evidence. Still, she admitted it had crept into her mind that maybe Joe Luskin had sent someone, for some reason, to Marie.

We talked about my conversation with Rabbi Horn, that God puts people on trial, convicts them, and s them to prison.

She had heard the same thing in the Lubavit

group she attended. Another rabbi had lectured we should bless all of God's acts, including tragedy, because they are God's acts.

"I stood up and said I might be able to accept Paul's imprisonment as God's act, but I would always refuse to bless it. The rabbi said I just needed more faith."

We laughed. "Is Paul in prison for God's reasons, then?" I asked.

"He might be there to help someone else who's there. But that shouldn't stop him from trying to get out. He might be needed elsewhere."

"Rabbi Horn says everyone in prison is guilty of something," I said. "If that's true, if Paul isn't guilty of trying to kill Marie, then what is he guilty of?"

Susan thought about it. "He wasn't shomer Shabbos"—keeping the Sabbath. "He'll never be able to do that—not write on Shabbos, not turn on a light."

"But I don't do that, and I'm not in prison," I said.

I suggested Paul's root crime might be arrogance—although that didn't diminish either of us liking him.

"He is arrogant. He's less than he was—and less than the other Luskins, save his sister Nance, who isn't arrogant at all," she said. One of Susan's favorite topics was the Luskin family's arrogance toward her.

"But still," I said. "Go back to when he was married to Marie. Marie couldn't have been one hundred percent wrong in everything."

"That's what I've said all along," she said.

"Darden says it all goes back to the one-third ownership of the business he tried to keep from her."

"That was phony," she said. "Marie is smart, and was used to dealing with the Luskins. That was something the Luskins cooked up, not just Paul.

"I can see how my in-laws have treated me, and I'm sure Marie must never have been accepted by them. I know that Joe Luskin never accepted me as a daughter-in-law."

Susan said she could still feel the subtleties of not being a born Luskin. "When I get a birthday card from them, it's signed "Nance, Donna and Mildred. What happened to (their husbands) Richard and Henry?"

*   *   *

I told Susan about Mrs. Cohen's idea of justice for Paul because he had an affair. I added I obviously didn't agree, but had to admit that what had followed seemed like something out of classical literature.

"The punishment is too extreme," Susan said. "He shouldn't get a death sentence for it. He should get out soon."

Then she asked me if I was going to include in my story speculation that there might have been a murder-for-hire.

"Of course," I said.

"But you think he got too much of a sentence," she probed, trying to find out where I now stood. Yes, I said.

The phone rang, and it was her son. I had encouraged her to embrace him instead of be mad, because he needed her support now. She spoke to him while sitting on the kitchen counter, her bare feet touching the sink. I heard her say:

"Paul has done many things wrong, many dumb things. But I love him, and stay by him. That's what love is. Yes, this is a dumb thing you've done, and I hope you won't do many more dumb things like this.

"But we love you."

That evening, Paul called me. He said he had asked his mother if his father had paid for Joe Liberto's attorney.

"She laughed, and said, 'Why would he do that?' "

December 4

I have a longtime personal friend who had gone through a divorce in its way as bad as Paul Luskin's. He said two people had suggested to him they knew ways to kill his wife.

My friend raised his voice. "I always said No! If I was ever going to kill someone, I would do it with my own hands. Otherwise, I could be extorted forever." There was no murder attempt.

He had sympathy for Luskin. "People who haven't gone through a divorce just don't know. The person closest to you is the one who can hurt you the most."

*   *   *

December 5

At the post office I signed for a certified letter from the U.S. Marshal's Service regarding my FOIA of James Manley. It was dated November 18, and had been held for me while I was out of town.

"The United States Marshal's Service is responding to your request for information pertaining to a James Thomas Manley Sr.

"The Marshal's Service is unable to confirm or deny the existence of records and/or information on this individual." However, if information existed, they wrote, it would be exempt from disclosure because it "could reasonably be expected to disclose the identity of and information furnished by a confidential source . . ."

I had plainly stated in my letter to the marshals that Manley had been in Witness Security, but since I had his death certificate, that meant he no longer had a right to privacy.

That was the fastest response I had ever gotten to a FOIA request, and the first time anyone had sent me a certified letter refusing me. I wondered if someone from the government was going to knock on my door.

I decided I would answer it, "So he is alive!"

December 15

Alvin Entin invited me to his firm's holiday season party at his plush new offices across the street from the federal courthouse in Fort Lauderdale.

While the usual bunch of friends, clients, judges, and attorneys drank his liquor and ate off the catered tables, Alvin preferred to stay in his office, a little off the beaten track. When I walked in, he was talking to Cal Abrams, a forties and fifties era baseball player.

Alvin introduced me, knowing that Abrams was a little before my time. He asked if I knew who he was.

"Of course. You played for the Orioles."

"The Orioles!" Entin interrupted. I was right; he had played for the 1954 Orioles, their inaugural year in Baltimore. But the correct answer, as far as Alvin was concerned, was the Brooklyn Dodgers, the team of his youth. Abrams was a star hitter for them, and had played next to Jackie Robinson and Duke Snider.

When Abrams walked away, I told Alvin about Darden's Joe Luskin theory. Alvin didn't flinch. He said he and Steve Allen had wanted to use that as a defense, then prove that Joe Luskin had more motive to kill Marie than Paul. He reminded me Manley had first testified to the grand jury that Cohen had told him "a guy named Luskin" was behind the plan, but he wasn't specific as to which Luskin.

"What could he do? Turn in his dad at trial?" Alvin figured Paul didn't know in advance about Marie's flower delivery, but probably figured it out afterward. But that didn't mean he knew there would be additional murder attempts, or that he could have told his dad to stop.

"Joe Luskin blamed Paul for everything. He was angry at Marie, and scared of her. She wanted to go through their books and destroy the business—which, for Joe Luskin, was like destroying his life.

"We had two credible defenses we couldn't use. This, and the drug defense. We couldn't use that because we were threatened."

Then, like everyone else, Alvin had his own bomb to drop on me.

"There was a smoking gun the government didn't pick up on," he said. "We found it, but obviously, we weren't going to introduce it. There was a call Paul had made on his car phone to the Marco Polo."

Alvin wasn't sure of the date, but Steve Allen knew it. He said he would ask Steve for the details, and tell me later. Alvin and Steve had asked Paul at the time about it, and Alvin didn't remember getting a satisfactory answer. It had bothered them both for a long time.

I couldn't believe it.

So now, with Alvin saying there was a murder-for-hire, four of Paul's attorneys had basically agreed that it had occurred. Only Bill Genego—who had come lately to the case—hadn't really said so.

I brought up Steve Miles's comments, again without

referring to where I had gotten them. Like Steve Allen, Alvin dismissed whatever Steve Miles had to say.

"Steve Miles thought Paul was guilty from day one. Paul didn't pay anyone $65,000."

Nor did Alvin believe Joe Liberto's story that Joe Luskin had paid for his attorney. The proof was that Mike Libowitz was extremely uncooperative with Luskin's defense team.

"If Joe Luskin had paid for him, we would have gotten more cooperation. As it was, we couldn't get a straight answer from him."

"Are you surprised that Joe Luskin never admitted he was involved, even on his deathbed?" I asked.

"No. I'm not surprised. That wouldn't have been consistent with Joe Luskin."

By now we had been joined by one of Alvin's younger associates, who had been hired long after the Luskin case.

"What kind of a father would let his son take the rap?" she asked him.

"Joe Luskin would. Remember, he hadn't talked to his brother for twenty years."

"But how can you argue that 'My dead dad did it' but the son didn't know about it?" she protested.

That question was left unanswered.

December 16

Paul called. I told him a lot was pointing to his father as having solicited the murder-for-hire, and I asked him if he knew anything.

"Nothing," he said. "Darden asked me if it was my father. I answered that my father was bright enough to know that if anything happened to Marie, it would have come back to me. And it did.

"It's just ridiculous. I pointed that out to Darden. I said, 'Don't be stupid. If my father did it, then my father had me set up.'"

I felt drained, sapped. I had to come to grips with what had happened. Some of my less kind friends berated me—some not very subtly—for having my eyes closed for so long.

I reread the piles of papers I had copied from Darden's office. It was one thing to say there was a murder-for-hire, and Joe Luskin was behind it, but what about Paul? Whenever I got to the interview with Steve Miles, I felt like I had pulled the Death card in tarot. "Plot to kill. Price tag $65,000 to be paid by Paul."

I couldn't get around it. This was his own cousin saying this. I felt burned.

I thought back to Cohen. Yes, he's a con man. But con men are good at getting you to believe. If you can tell on the surface that someone's a con, he's not very good.

So how do you tell for sure? The answer is, probably, just the way I've done it. I get people to talk, let them keep going, all the while I am taking notes. As my investigation gets deeper, the statements of con men inevitably get contradicted. Then the question is, Who is lying?

Kelly Woodroof, the detective in *Until Proven Innocent,* calls this the "shooting the breeze" method. He agrees—that's how you do it.

Some lies are easy to detect. Others take a lifetime to figure out. Three and a half years is right in the happy medium. That's about how long it took Woodroof and the state of Florida to realize their lead suspect wasn't lying.

How the hell do juries figure this all out? I thought.

Around this time, South Carolina mother Susan Smith went on national TV with an emotional plea that her children had been abducted. Everyone watching believed her. Then the country was shocked when she was arrested and charged with drowning them. We believed because we had no context to disbelieve her.

What makes a lie so difficult to detect is the way it's dropped in the midst of otherwise truthful statements. Even people labeled "liars" cannot lie about everything. That's what Holmes was referring to when he said to Watson, "The game is afoot!"

My musician friend Yarko told me I had found the zen of the story.

I think the zen is that a deep story "turns" if you ride it long enough. A story is a powerful thing. The most common error is trying to make it turn the direction you want.

Joe McGinniss's book, *Fatal Vision,* turned. Unfortunately, he had signed a contract with his subject to write his story and split the revenues.

Jeffrey McDonald said he was falsely convicted for the murder of his wife and children. McGinniss, somewhere during his research, stopped believing him. Why and when McGinniss changed his mind was the subtext of his story.

But McGinniss had a problem—the contract. By being true to himself, he risked a legal conflict with his subject.

I have no such agreement with Paul Luskin, and it was about this time when I realized how fortunate that was.

December 24

Susan, who I had perceived was avoiding me, called at noon. We didn't speak long; I could tell she was nervous. Steve Allen was in town visiting Alvin. Would I call Alvin to see if they needed my help?

I did. He was on the golf course with Steve, and he returned the call late in the afternoon. He told me they had spent most of their conversation on the Luskin case.

The news was—which Alvin swore me not to tell Paul—Gregg Bernstein had told Steve that he would no longer oppose Paul getting a sentence reduction.

Alvin said he had seen the most recent draft of Genego's motion, which I hadn't. Alvin thought it was strong.

"If the government had conceded they had a current investigation that the codefendants were drug dealers and dealing in guns, we would have gotten our severance. In a severed trial, with a drug defense, we had a reasonable explanation for what happened, and you put

on anything you want without any fear from the codefendants. Paul wins in a walk.

"A lot of these cards are falling into place. If the
government agrees to undo the trial, they'd probably
work out a plea that Paul would have to swallow. You
don't risk going to trial, losing, and going back to prison.
You plea to something you didn't do just to get out of
jail, go home, and go on with your life.

"We have an innocent man sitting in jail, and it's
taken seven years to find this all out. He's been rail-
roaded by the system—first in the divorce case, then the
criminal case."

On Alvin's use of the word "innocent," I invoked Joe
Luskin's name. Alvin asked me had I asked Paul what he
thought. I said he denied his father had anything to do
with it.

"He still won't blame his dad," said Alvin. Then he
added, "I believe more and more that a Luskin was
involved in a murder-for-hire."

"When did you start thinking that?" I asked, since
that wasn't the impression he had given me for three
years. One of the reasons I thought it for so long was
because Alvin had been so convincing and sincere.

"We thought it a little bit during the trial. Paul called
us off, and we left it alone. But the more you think about
it—the close ties between Joe Luskin and Joe Liberto—
it makes sense that there was a murder-for-hire. It fits."

The problem with the theory that there was no
murder-for-hire, he said, is "you have to explain what
Sonny Cohen is doing there at Marie's house. Was it a
side trip to rob the broad and not take anything?"

I said I had long disbelieved Cohen's version of how
he saw Marie's license tag while sipping coffee in the 7-
Eleven parking lot.

"That's why I think there was a murder-for-hire," he
said. "It's probable he was there to kill the lady."

But the motive pointed more to Joe Luskin than to
Paul. "Paul was already beyond it at that point. He was
living in Pittsburgh, he was fired from the business, and
Marie wasn't a factor in his daily life.

"Who was the one at risk? Joe and Mildred. It was

their underwear she was going for. Joe was a lot colder, tougher than Paul."

"But Joe had to realize that if Marie was killed, the first place the cops would look would be to the son, not the father-in-law," I protested.

"That's true. But Joe figures, Paul's in Pittsburgh, let 'em look. Besides, if it was perfect, they wouldn't have gotten caught, they wouldn't have found any phone records.

"If it had worked the first time, Cohen wouldn't have opened his mouth. In fact, he never opened his mouth. The problem was, Cohen hired Manley for the second attempt. Manley opened his mouth. He was a bit of a wuss."

What about Marie's wound, I asked. What about the solder in the barrette that explained the metal fragments if she was hit, not shot? When I had first proposed it, Alvin said I might be right.

"Ripping or tearing of the skin would have been consistent with hitting, or a blackjack. Our expert saw a lack of ripping or tearing. He was telling us, it was a shot. So testing the fragment didn't matter."

I'd held for a long time that if Marie was hit, it was a robbery. If she was shot, it was a murder-for-hire.

Now Alvin Entin was telling me she was shot.

"I think it was a murder-for-hire," he said. "Just another Luskin."

I was hoping Alvin had asked Steve Allen on the golf course about Paul's call to the Marco Polo. He said he hadn't, but he did recall a few more details.

"It was a critical date situation"—before Marie was assaulted, sometime around Jimmy Liberto's visit to the Marco Polo in January 1987, an early-morning call. "I don't remember it exactly, but I think Steve Allen does. It really bothered us at the time."

Still, he said, if they had to, they could have alibied it at trial. They could have proposed that Joe Liberto had left a message for Paul to call him at his brother's hotel room. But they were lucky. "The government absolutely missed it. It didn't show up on Bernstein's phone list, and we certainly didn't put it on ours."

"When did you begin to think there was a murder-for-hire?" I asked once again.

"I very recently thought so. First, at trial, but then we dropped it. Now, with the stuff coming from Genego, I thought about the relationship between Joe Liberto, Joe Luskin, and Paul. I began to focus on it—I hadn't before.

"Sometimes, you can't see the forest for the trees. And neither you nor I are Sherlock Holmes."

TWELVE

January 1995

A phone call:
  "So, Art, do you think I did it?"
  "I don't know, Paul, did you?"
  "Well, I don't know."
  "Well, how am I supposed to know?" my voice rising in mock anger. "You should know better than me. Maybe when you get out we'll have a séance and bring your father back and ask him some questions."

I wasn't sure I was going to hear from Joe Liberto again, but he called, cheerful, this evening. He knew I had been to see his brother, which meant he also knew I was aware of his sentence reduction motion. I asked him first whether Judge Motz had ruled on it, because the last entry on the case docket was sealed.

Motz had denied it without granting a hearing, he said, just as he had denied all of Luskin's motions without hearings. But, he had appealed the denial to force Motz to hold an evidentiary hearing, and he expected a response in about a week.

"So did Joe Luskin really pay for your attorney?"

Yes, he told me. Mike Libowitz was high-priced, and he couldn't have afforded him otherwise. The proof was in the legal briefs and court transcripts that Motz had sealed during his 1990 sentence reduction.

"Do you have a copy of them?" I asked.

"No. I need an evidentiary hearing to get the evidence out. If I can't get it unsealed, I can't win."

"Joe, it sounds like, if Joe Luskin paid for your attorney, then there really was a murder-for-hire."

"No. There was no murder-for-hire. That's the point."

"What's the point?"

"Ah, the plot thickens."

"So what was it?"

"There never was a murder-for-hire. There was something else. Joe Luskin had something to hide. The Luskin family had something to hide." He implied that it had to do with movements of cash.

Liberto referred to the motion Steve Allen had filed after the trial ended, claiming the Libertos had threatened Paul during the trial. Paul said that was the reason he didn't testify in his own behalf.

"It was something that would come out. Only Paul and Joe (Luskin) know—and me. If I win, you'll find out."

He wouldn't answer any of my further questions, including the obvious one whether it involved drug money.

Liberto said I had found the evidence that broke the case. "It was the only valuable thing you sent me."

"I don't remember what I sent you."

"It was the thing about Manley being a confidential informant for the ATF. The government suppressed evidence pretrial."

A year before I had obtained a one-page document in my FOIA request with Paul's signature to the Bureau of Alcohol, Tobacco, and Firearms. It referred to an unnamed "ATFCI" who was obviously Manley. I had always been under the impression that Manley had become an FBI confidential informant, so for ATF to call him a CI was no big deal.

"Wrong," Liberto said. "Manley was working for the ATF. He was an agent for ATF. When Manley got in trouble, he got hold of the ATF, and they got hold of the FBI. At trial, the FBI didn't say so—they lied at trial.

"It's impossible that Marie Luskin was shot in the head. She was supposedly shot from no more than six inches away, but there were no powder burns. From that distance, her hair would have to have been burnt. There was no burnt hair. Don't you think you would smell a burn? Did she smell the smoke? The powder? Any doctor can tell if there's a powder smell. It stays in the hair.

"The only way would be if it was a clean bullet. Was the bullet made of ice? Did it disappear?"

"What about a misfire?" I asked. "That's what Steve Allen thinks."

"No. Do you remember about two years ago, a movie star was killed by gunfire, even though there was a blank in the gun?" Even blanks are dirty, he told me.

"All Luskin's attorneys had to do was buy a wig and a dummy and fire a low-caliber pistol at it—the way a crime lab would. A higher-caliber gun would have left even more burn and smoke. It would have proved their case. Go out and do it.

"There was no frigging smoking gun. They never found the gun, there was no bullet, no powder burns. She wasn't shot. It's a bullshit case.

"If Manley's working for the ATF, and he knew there was a murder-for-hire, do you think ATF was going to let Manley make two attempts on her life? If ATF was a party to it, it was a sham—or it wasn't a murder-for-hire."

"If the government knew about it, then why didn't they stop it?" I asked.

"Isn't that interesting? Because it wasn't a murder-for-hire. It was a gun violation."

The ATF was abreast of the whole case, he said. "They let Manley go along on a gun deal. All they had was Cohen and Manley doing burglaries."

What must have happened, he figured, was Manley

went to Bernstein and said it was a murder-for-hire. When Bernstein called ATF, they told him it was a gun violation case, or a robbery. But Bernstein wanted it to be a Luskin murder-for-hire case. That was a lot bigger than just Cohen and Manley doing burglaries.

Bernstein's motive was vendetta, he said. Just before the U.S. Attorney's Office hired him, he did legal work at a firm that represented the Baltimore Luskins and "he was canned for incompetence," Liberto said.

"I did business with him years ago. I have receipts from it. I know what kind of person he is."

"Then why didn't he indict Joe Luskin? He was a bigger Luskin than Paul," I asked.

"They wanted to go for Jack Luskin. That came out at my Rule 35 (sentence reduction hearing) in 1990. Bernstein was just after the Luskins. It was not a murder-for-hire."

Meanwhile, they all could have won at trial had Paul taken a different attitude toward his codefendants, he insisted. "Paul didn't want to disprove the murder-for-hire. His lawyers wanted to prove a drug case. He was trying for a severance—even through the trial. In a severance there was no case.

"It was Anybody But Me. That's Paul Luskin. He didn't care if the rest of us went to jail. He created the antagonistic defense.

"I'm telling you, the victim in this story is not Marie Luskin. It's not Paul Luskin. It's Joe Liberto. Without me, they had no case. There was no evidence linking me, no phone calls, nothing. They had me calling my brother, but I had a wife and kids in the house, and they used to call him, too.

"Here's a poor guy who was straight all his life, no record, no traffic violations—and his boss put him in a cage. Whatever Paul Luskin is in prison for, all I can say is Good Luck. He made me look like I did something wrong when I didn't. He took me from my family."

"Yes, being an ATFCI is different than being an FBI CI," said my friend Dennis Kainen, a federal criminal defense attorney in Miami. It meant very specifically that he was a CI for ATF, not a CI for the FBI, which he might have been as well. He added that agencies are under obligation to make sure their informants don't commit crimes.

At trial, Manley testified there was an intent to murder both occasions he was with Cohen in Florida, but in reality, nothing happened.

Again, if Manley was working for the ATF at the time, would they have let him on a real murder-for-hire—twice?

Here was the kicker—two days before Joe Liberto's call, I had gotten notice from ATF that my FOIA was ready, they just needed a check for copying expenses. While visiting Cohen and Jim Liberto, I had gotten them to sign consents so I could get their FOIA from all the federal agencies, as well as Manley's. I had asked Joe Liberto by mail, but he didn't respond.

Perhaps in two weeks, I was to get 196 pages of FOIA. If Manley wasn't dead, his death certificate had fooled them.

It had fooled me too, by the way, if he wasn't dead.

I reread the one FOIA page I had from ATF, dated September 24, 1987, the same day Manley testified to the grand jury. Part of it had been whited out, and I filled in some obvious spots, using brackets:

"This will act as a transmittal for the attached Criminal Case Report regarding Milton Cohen and James Manley for Violation of Federal Firearms and Narcotics Laws.

"A. The F.B.I. Baltimore, Maryland is attempting to make a contract for hire murder conspiracy, on information provided by ATF Confidential Informant (ATFCI). Information by a ATFCI reveal that Paul Luskin asked [Joe Liberto] (brother of [Jim Liberto]) to ask his brother [Jim] did he know anyone that could kill his wife. The price was $50,000.

"Milton Cohen and James Manley were hired by [Jim Liberto] to kill Ms. Luskin. Several attempts were made with negative results. Ms. Luskin was made aware of the threat, as well as the Hollywood Police Department. On March 9, 1987, Ms. Luskin was attacked at her residence in Florida, and hit in the head with a firearm and left for dead by Milton Cohen. Cohen thought he had killed her.

"An additional case report will be written when this investigation is completed on the conspiracy to sell firearms on [Jim Liberto]. This investigation is jointly being worked on by ATF & FBI.

"C. This investigation was discussed with AUSA Gregg Bernstein prior to submission of a criminal case report, August 20, 1987. In addition, AUSA Bernstein is proceeding on the contract murder with the assistance of the 1st assistant, Gary Jordan."

Two questions now came to me: What was the "additional case report" on the "conspiracy to sell firearms"?

And what was the criminal case report dated August 20, 1987—two weeks before Manley came forward to Bernstein with information about the murder-for-hire?

A little later I tried to put two and two together. According to Steve Allen's notes, "Goldstein," another Luskin's employee, said Joe Liberto showed him a large amount of cash in a briefcase in December 1986. If it wasn't murder-for-hire money, it must have been drug money. But whose? If Joe Liberto was a conduit for any Luskin drug money—and the FBI at trial specifically denied having any knowledge Paul was involved in drugs—that might be motivation enough for the Luskins to want to make sure he wouldn't take any deal from a federal prosecutor. And Joe Liberto was offered a deal, testimony for a five-year sentence.

From the divorce I knew the Luskins were cash wealthy, but it had never been suggested it came from anywhere besides the business.

Alvin Entin's mention of Paul's call to the Marco Polo—implying Jim Liberto, that the government missed—might fit in this explanation, too. Jim Liberto admitted to me in Allenwood that he was involved in the

financial end of the drug business, laundering money
through his restaurant.

He also said to me he had threatened Paul if he was
going to testify. His exact words were, "What are you
trying to do, hang yourself, *Boss?*"

Was Paul planning to testify he knew his codefendants
were involved in a drug ring?

For that matter, it could also explain Cohen's story
that both Luskin and Liberto were supposed to bond
him out after his arrest on Amtrak in July 1987.

About the only thing Joe Liberto's theory didn't
explain was the assault on Marie and how Cohen found
her. Maybe it was a robbery for the $100,000, and Joe
Liberto provided the address. Only if she was shot did it
add up to a murder attempt.

There was something else that had bugged me that
suddenly dropped into place. Six months after Paul's
sentencing in 1988, he summoned the FBI from prison
in Marianna, Florida, and began telling them how
consumer electronics distribution companies were being
used to transport narcotics, concealing them in boxes of
legitimate units; that Florida electronics dealers were
importing drugs through Panama; and how drug money
was being laundered through them. There were high-
level political connections, too.

Paul had told me some of this, and I had obtained
papers verifying it through my FOIA to the U.S. Attorney's Office.

Luskin had met with Bernstein in Baltimore in December 1988 in an attempt to provide "substantial
assistance" for another case that would get him a sentence reduction and set him free. Ultimately it didn't
work. Paul said he wanted to talk directly with attorneys
from the main Justice Department in Washington, and
Bernstein wanted to keep the case. Talks broke down,
Paul was sent back to prison, and nothing happened.

One of the problems Paul had, which Bernstein addressed in a letter to Ben Darden on January 9, 1989,
was that he felt Bernstein had a conflict of interest.

"It is your client's belief that, because I worked on
certain matters for Luskin's, Inc. (the Baltimore
Luskins) during my prior employment, there is a conflict

in my continuing to coordinate the proffer." Bernstein then denied it was a problem.

It was true, then, that Bernstein had worked for Jack Luskin just before prosecuting Paul Luskin.

Then another zinger: "Thus far, your client has provided us with no information which indicates any alleged criminal activity by his uncle (Jack Luskin) or his uncle's business. If such allegations are made, we will conduct the appropriate investigation to ascertain their substance."

Was part of Paul's plan to get a sentence reduction for himself an attempt to rat on Uncle Jack?

It was during those meetings in Baltimore, Paul told me, that FBI agent Pat Connolly said he was in prison only because he had "lousy lawyers."

January 13
CARL HAEMMERLE
FIREARMS EXAMINER

I took Joe Liberto's suggestion about looking into the powder burns question. I called the crime lab of the Broward County Sheriff's Office, and wound up speaking to Carl Haemmerle, a firearms examiner.

The problem was I had to speak in hypotheticals. There was no gun in evidence traced to the assault, so I could only guess at the caliber. There was no bullet, of course. I went with Joe Liberto's suggestion that the gun was a .22, and it was fired (if it was) six inches from Marie's head.

Marie had long, thick blond hair. Considering these sketchy details, I asked "Wouldn't a powder burn on her hair be obvious if she was shot?"

"No, it wouldn't be obvious if it was from a .22," Haemmerle said. "Yes, if it was from a larger caliber."

I explained that the police came within about ten minutes of the crime. "Would they have been able to smell smoke?"

"Theoretically, there could be an odor of gunpowder. But five to ten minutes later, if there was one shot with a .22, they'd be unlikely to smell it, unless they were supersensitive."

But the important question, he said, was how direct the hit was. Was her head moving, did the shot glance off her—all these things made a difference when it came to powder burns.

"If it was a straight-on shot, there'd be a lot of powder. If she was hit on an angle, gunpowder would blow right past the head. It would depend on how much the shot glanced."

"How about the noise of a shot, in a small enclosed room? Wouldn't it be loud? Wouldn't your ears be ringing?"

"A .22 shot makes very little noise. If I popped a big balloon, your ears would ring about the same."

"What about the gun emitting a fragment in a misfire?"

Not in the real world, he said.

I moved on to the solder question. Could solder and a bullet fragment get confused in the crime lab?

That was possible, he told me. Both have lead.

"This case should have been resolved by the crime scene evidence." I sighed. "Even though you can't trust the characters in the story, I figured the evidence would tell me the truth."

"It's true, the evidence doesn't lie," he said. "But sometimes it's just not as clear as you hope it to be."

"Still, the crime scene team didn't find a bullet in that room," I said. "Of course, it's possible they could have missed it."

"The angle was downward?" he asked. "A bullet can easily slide under the carpet, and you can't see the bullet hole. Up north, they have basements in houses. You'd go into the basement, shine a light up, find a hole, and take a rod to measure the angle. Especially a .22, it could very easily be missed. Eight years later? It could still be there today."

I thought, Joe Liberto has provided me with a brand-new—vague—theory that might explain everything, and isn't a murder-for-hire. Meanwhile the crime scene is inconclusive to whether a shot was fired or not.

Also, meanwhile, all the Luskin lawyers are pushing a murder-for-hire explanation now.

SCORECARD

It was time to take a tally. I summarized what each of the major characters were now saying. Let's talk contradictions:

JOE LIBERTO: There was no murder-for-hire, but there was something else—and it sounded drug-related—going on in the Luskins' business, something that with Joe Luskin's death, only he and Paul know of. Joe Luskin hired an attorney for him, so he wouldn't take a plea agreement with the feds and spill the beans on the "something else." Paul didn't care whether his codefendants went to prison on drug charges, as long as he didn't. The Luskins threatened his family, and in fact arranged for his young daughter to be raped.

PAUL LUSKIN: There was no murder-for-hire. Joe Liberto is a backstabber, and volunteered business information about Luskin's of Florida to Jack Luskin when he tried to get a job with him. Denied his father hired a lawyer for Joe Liberto, and the "Luskin family threats" and rape of his daughter by them is patently ridiculous. In 1988, Paul volunteered a long outline of how the electronics business was infiltrated by drugs, but because of a disagreement with Bernstein, never offered many details.

JIMMY LIBERTO: There was no murder-for-hire. He was in the drug business, a small part of a big ring. He admitted threatening Paul at trial that if he introduced more evidence of their drug ring, Jimmy and Joe would claim Paul was their boss in it.

SONNY COHEN: Denied he shot Marie Luskin, denied it was a murder-for-hire. He was in Florida to pick up a couple ounces of coke to sell in Baltimore, and while there, he (and later Manley) planned to stalk Marie Luskin so he could rob her house. He learned where

Marie lived by spotting her car while hanging out at an
Emerald Hills 7-Eleven. But he dropped that both
Luskin and Jim Liberto were supposed to bail him out of
jail—six weeks before Manley went to the feds and told
them of a murder-for-hire.

JAMES MANLEY: I've got a 1992 death certificate on him
that says he was cremated, and a relative who says she
saw him in his coffin, but nobody else besides Cohen
believes he's dead. Darden says he signed for a car
payment after he was supposed to be dead. He told
Darden there was a murder-for-hire, but Gregg Bernstein told him to include Paul's name—which he didn't
know on his own.

BEN DARDEN: There was a murder-for-hire, and Paul
Luskin had nothing to do with it. Joe Liberto, with
his Mafia connections through his brother, suggested
to Joe Luskin that they could get rid of Marie, who
was killing the business. Joe Luskin, perhaps suffering
from the initial stages of Alzheimer's disease, gave
the go-ahead. Paul and Joe Liberto hated each other, but
Joe Liberto and Joe Luskin were close. Joe Luskin
expected to be indicted, and hired Russell White for
himself.

RUSSELL WHITE: He was out of the loop, but from watching
the trial, he figured there was a murder-for-hire and that
Manley was telling the truth on the stand. He denied
being hired to defend Joe Luskin.

STEVE ALLEN: Implied there was a murder-for-hire. Said
the forensics expert he hired told him Marie was probably shot.

ALVIN ENTIN: At trial, he wanted to blame Joe Luskin, but
Paul stopped him. Disbelieved Joe Liberto's story that
Joe Luskin paid for his attorney—if it was true, then
Entin would have gotten a lot more cooperation from
Joe Liberto's counsel. Thought it was credible that Joe
Luskin might have cooked up the plot with Joe Liberto,
but not credible that he never told Paul, or that Paul
wouldn't have figured it out after the flower delivery.

Added that the government had missed an unexplained call between Paul and the Marco Polo.

January 18
FOIA FROM THE BUREAU OF ALCOHOL, TOBACCO, AND FIREARMS

My package in the mail from the ATF arrived, and it contained big news—the first clear evidence that the government had held back relevant material from the defense. Conceivably, that in itself could overturn the verdict.

The government was obliged to share with the defense reports of all of its interviews with James Manley. The government never mentioned that Manley had talked to ATF, but in fact he had talked with them *before* he ever talked to the FBI or Bernstein.

When I showed the 196-page package later to Alvin Entin, he told me he had never seen any of it.

What did the government not want the defense to know? Since the FOIA package provided only summary reports, not full interviews with Manley, I could only speculate.

The ATF investigates firearms violations. They entered the case July 30, 1987, the same day Cohen and Manley—both convicted criminals legally prohibited from owning guns—were arrested at the train station carrying heavy firepower.

On August 20, a grand jury listened to testimony by ATF Special Agent Roy Cheeks and others, then indicted Manley and Cohen on seven counts of drug and gun charges. Later that day, ATF "arrested" them both, although they were already in Baltimore City Jail.

Apparently, that was the same day Manley first spoke to ATF. He didn't mention the murder-for-hire that day; he did hint he knew the origin of the guns.

(FOIA officers blank out spaces for privacy reasons; I've placed those blanks in brackets, and like a Dead Sea Scroll researcher, filled in as many as I could be certain of, since the names that fit appear elsewhere in the public record.)

"James Manley, who possessed these firearms and is being charged by ATF, was interviewed by Baltimore City (Police) and the undersigned [(ATF Special Agent, name blanked out)] and gave an indication he may tell [who acquired] the firearm that was purchased from the gun store in Baltimore by [Ms. Pat Widerman (Frank Liberto's wife)]. Manley did state that 'the people' that gave him the firearm are also paying for his attorney."

There was no indication anywhere in the package that Manley had been working on the ATF's payroll while on the street with Cohen, as Joe Liberto believed.

Some chronology is in order here. The government told the defense that Manley had first proffered information about the murder-for-hire through his attorney to Gregg Bernstein on September 4, 1987, and that the FBI didn't first interview him until September 16, the date he signed his plea agreement.

But in the FOIA package it said Manley spoke directly to ATF a second time on September 9—and this time he did talk about the murder-for-hire.

An ATF interoffice teletype dated September 9 read:

"Manley flipped on Cohen and several other individuals and has stated to ATF Baltimore that both Cohen and Manley went to Florida for a contract killing on a woman living in Ft. Lauderdale. This woman has been located by ATF Baltimore and Ft. Lauderdale and needs to be interviewed by ATF and the FBI.

"It is requested that an ATF special agent in Ft. Lauderdale assist Baltimore Md. Special Agent Cheeks in the investigation of this case. Special Agent [ ] (ATF Ft. Lauderdale) was contacted previously in this investigation.

"Special Agent [Cheeks] will arrive in Ft. Lauderdale, Fla on 10 Sep 87 at 11:35 a.m., Piedmont Airlines, Flight 591. SA [Cheeks] has already made hotel reservations."

Combing my files, I found another reference to this September 9 meeting, but it left out the news that Manley had "flipped" on the murder-for-hire. It only discussed the ongoing firearms violations investigation.

Two weeks later, the FBI and ATF had combined to write an affidavit asking a federal magistrate for a warrant to search for guns Manley said Cohen had hidden. ATF Special Agent Arthur Gordon and FBI Agent Pat Connolly wrote that Manley had been interviewed by "law enforcement officials" on September 9 and "has provided your affiants, and other agents involved in the investigation" with the information. The warrant on Cohen's garage was executed, but agents didn't find what they were looking for.

The agents did drop a hint that Manley had mentioned the murder-for-hire, but they couldn't divulge it just then:

"In addition, Manley has provided information regarding other ongoing criminal activity. To the extent possible without compromising the confidentiality of an ongoing investigation, the information has been corroborated by independent means."

When Connolly testified at trial, he didn't mention that either he or other agents had interviewed Manley about the murder-for-hire on September 9.

Maybe it wasn't what Manley said about the murder-for-hire on September 9, but what he didn't say.

An ATF memo dated September 15, 1987, may provide the answer.

Manley had told ATF that Jim Liberto was the source of the guns. Since Liberto was a convicted felon, ATF was investigating a possible illegal sale of weapons. Buried in the memo it also reads:

Recent developments in this case reveal that Cohen and Manley were hired by persons unknown at this time to murder a woman in Florida. Manley is now cooperating with ATF and the U.S. Attorney's Office.

Persons unknown on September 15. Was Manley holding back, or is it possible Manley didn't know—or wasn't sure?

(Once again I consulted my criminal defense attorney friend Dennis Kainen, a former assistant federal public defender: When defendants who try to get a deal first proffer an outline of what they know, do they usually hold back something important—just in case the deal doesn't happen?

Not in a case like this, he said. Even if the government doesn't do the deal, they can't use the proffer against him—unless he takes the stand at his own trial and contradicts what he said.)

So what did Manley tell the government before he signed his plea agreement on September 16? By piecing things together, I got an idea.

Pat Connolly testified at trial that Bernstein called him on September 4 to say that Manley's attorney, Assistant Federal Public Defender Brooke Murdock, had contacted him off-the-record with a taste of what her client knew about a contract murder.

On the fifth, Connolly checked out Manley's tip about the Dollar Rent-A-Car in Fort Lauderdale that Jim Liberto had prepaid for Cohen. On the eighth, Connolly teletyped FBI in Miami requesting assistance locating Marie Luskin. The next day, Miami FBI replied they had found her. Connolly flew south on September 10, and Marie confirmed Manley's story about the nasty divorce and that she had been attacked in her home in March.

From Marie, Connolly got Susan's name, and when the FBI tailed her the next morning, she led them to Fort Lauderdale airport, where she flew to Baltimore and into Paul's waiting arms. The FBI thought maybe Paul had been in Baltimore to see Jim Liberto. Susan told me they had spent the weekend in Washington doing touristy things although they did go to Baltimore to visit her parents. Susan didn't like Paul to drive fast, so after he dropped her off two days later, he must have resumed his normal driving speed. To the FBI it looked like Paul realized he was being followed and was trying to lose them.

Clearly impressed, Connolly apparently recommended to Bernstein they do Manley's deal, and it was signed on Wednesday, September 16.

But not only did Manley not immediately tell the names of those "persons unknown" who hired Cohen, it turned out that he wasn't even clear on the name Marie Luskin.

Connolly teletyped FBI Miami:

"We had certain information about the victim, certain information about where the victim lived, but we didn't have a positive identification of who the victim was," he testified at trial.

"Did you subsequently receive information from Miami?," asked co-prosecutor Wick Sollers.

"Yes, sir, the very next day, I believe on the ninth, we received information." Then Connolly flew to Florida.

But in cross-examination by Cohen's attorney Paul Weiss, Connolly added an interesting twist.

"So evidently, what I think we can glean from your answer is that when Mr. Bernstein called you and told you that Mr. Manley had given all this information, part of that information was not even the woman's name?"

"He—well, he'd—he'd actually indicated to me that it was a *Marcie* Luskin and then he said, 'I'm not sure about my writing,' so when I sent down the teletype I put Marcie and then a phonetic behind Marcie Luskin."

What did it all mean?

"Marcie Luskin" was close to the real name. It implied Manley had tapped into some sort of intimate knowledge of the Luskins. Although Luskin was a public name, Marie's name was not well-known outside of Hollywood society.

The real question was—If Manley hadn't mentioned Paul Luskin's name by September 15, out of whose mouth did it come on September 16? His, or the government's?

Pat Connolly had met with Marie on September 10. He most certainly heard Paul's name that day.

The issue was never brought up at trial. Had the defense had these ATF reports, they certainly would have asked those questions to Connolly and ATF Agent Roy Cheeks, who also testified, albeit briefly and strictly about ATF's firearms investigation. ATF Agent Arthur Gordon, who did not testify, would have also been a relevant witness.

On September 24, in his grand jury testimony, Manley was quite definite who had commissioned the murder attempt.

Paul Luskin, he said.

Brain surgery. A contract murder attempt on a wife during a nasty divorce. The husband, right?

What about the father-in-law?

In Marie's FBI 302, she talked about motive. It wasn't an open-and-shut case.

"Only her husband, Paul Luskin (and possibly her father-in-law, Joseph Luskin) has a motive to harm her. . . . Following a 1986 divorce hearing, Joseph Luskin told Marie that she'd be sorry, and she'd never get any money because of what she had done. Marie Luskin believes that Joseph Luskin is extremely angry with her. She believes that he (Joseph Luskin) perceives her as ruining their lives and business."

I reviewed Manley's grand jury testimony.

Bernstein asked him if he knew Joseph Liberto. Manley said no, but he knew who he was.

"Who is he?"

"Jimmy's brother."

"Do you know where he lives?"

"Yes, sir, he lives in Florida."

"And do you know where he works?"

"Yeah, he works for a guy named Luskin."

"How about an individual named Paul Luskin? Do you know him?"

"No, I've never met him."

"Do you know who he is?"

"It was my understanding through Sonny that he owns the Luskin's stores up and down the East Coast."

Neither Joe nor Paul owned Luskin's stores "up and down the East Coast," but that more closely described Joe Luskin than Paul.

Later, Manley dropped another clue. Talking about Joe Liberto, he said: "Yeah, Joe had worked for Mr. Luskin for, like, twenty years."

That "guy named Luskin" was Joe Luskin. Not Paul Luskin. Way back, when Joe Liberto was seventeen and he first started working for Mr. Luskin, his boss wasn't Paul. Paul was eleven.

Then toward the end of his statement, Manley said something very intriguing. Responding to an unrelated question, he volunteered, "I didn't know Paul Luskin's name."

When did Manley learn Paul Luskin's name? Russell White noticed the reference, too, and asked Manley about it at trial, in cross:

"When you first spoke with Mr. Cohen and so forth and he mentioned the name Luskin, you said, isn't that the first time that you heard the name Paul Luskin after you were arrested?"

"No, sir."

"Pardon?"

"He told me on the way to Florida about Paul Luskin."

"Didn't he just use the name Luskin?"

"No, sir, he did use Paul."

But it was Joe Liberto's attorney, Mike Libowitz, who asked all the right questions:

"Mr. Manley, when was the first time, as best you can recall, that you told these events to a law enforcement official?"

"Talking about this case, you mean?"

"Yes, sir," said Libowitz.

"About five or six weeks after I was in Baltimore City Jail."

"And who was it that you first told? I'm talking about law enforcement officers."

"Well, I told my attorney. The first one I ever spoke to was Mr. Bernstein."

Manley said that about a week after he was arrested, Baltimore City Detective Dorsey McVicker and ATF Agent Roy Cheeks came to speak with him for about five minutes.

"Did you tell Agent Cheeks and Detective McVicker about these incidents?"

"No, sir."

"When was the next time you spoke to a law enforcement officer? I want to find out when the first time was you told this story."

"I told you that," said Manley.

"Well, was it to Mr. Bernstein, that's the first time you ever told this story?"

"That's it," he said.

"Between those two times, the visit by the detective and your meeting with Mr. Bernstein, you had not spoken to a detective or a federal agent. Is that correct?"

"No, sir. Well, I might have. Not about testifying, no. If they talked to us, we would holler and scream and that was it."

"I'm sorry, sir?" said Libowitz.

"I never talked to no one until I talked to Mr. Bernstein about this case."

"And who was with Mr. Bernstein at that time?"

"My attorney."

Manley's plea agreement was dated September 16, but he said he and his attorney, Brooke Murdock, spoke with Bernstein—just the three of them—perhaps even a couple of days before the agreement was signed.

"After you spoke with Mr. Bernstein, that meeting with you, your attorney, and Mr. Bernstein, did you have occasion to speak to any federal agents—Agent Connolly, Agent Hill, or any of the agents involved?" Libowitz asked.

"I never spoke to no more agents until after I signed that agreement."

* * *

When Bernstein had a chance to clear that up on redirect examination, the silence was deafening.

By presenting that testimony, and allowing it to stand—and now comparing it to the ATF file that came in FOIA, in my opinion Gregg Bernstein presented perjured testimony.

Just what Ben Darden said Manley had told him—that the government had told him what to say. Darden also said they fed him the name Paul Luskin, and that it was really Joe Luskin's murder-for-hire plot.

In FOIA provided to me by the U.S. Attorney's Office in 1994, I found a letter written by Gregg Bernstein to the associate director of ATF, dated December 15, 1989. It commended the work of an ATF agent whose name was blanked out, but I think the name "Roy Cheeks" fits.

> . . . through the excellent investigative work of special agent [Roy Cheeks?] of your Bureau, [Manley cooperated?] with the Government and informed us he had traveled to Florida with [Cohen] to perform a murder contract on the wife of defendant Paul Luskin . . .
>
> The verdicts of guilty against all the defendants are the highest testament to Agent [Cheeks's] work in this case. In short, his skill in initiating contact with the cooperator, and his subsequent and tireless efforts in tracking down the bits and pieces of circumstantial evidence, proved to be the deciding factor in our ultimate success . . .

Here it is, Bernstein admits it was an ATF agent who initiated contact with Manley. That was not disclosed to the defense.

Why did Bernstein do it?

The government acted responsibly by quickly convening a grand jury. Manley said the contract was still out on Marie, even though he and Cohen were in jail. He said Jim Liberto was going to get someone else to do it. But had the government thought about it a little longer, they might have indicted both Paul and Joe Luskin.

I think, instead, they fudged and told Manley the Luskin in question was Paul. It was a small fudge, something that might have remained buried forever.

Except for unfortunate occurrences: Manley died, I managed somehow to get his death certificate, and then immediately filed a FOIA demand for his ATF file.

Darden could have blown the whole argument, though. In 1991, Sonny Cohen told him that when he and Manley were in Baltimore City Jail together after their arrests, they dreamed up a scheme to get them both out.

"We had to give them something worth a lot more, so the first thing we thought of . . . we were hired by Paul Luskin to go down there and scare his wife out of divorcing him, went in, hit her, told her don't file no more divorce, back off the divorce thing, and that we were paid $50,000 for it by Paul Luskin.

"So then we come to how did Paul Luskin know us. Well, I knew that Joe worked for Paul Luskin and Jimmy was his brother. And then we thought about it, it's just an assault charge. It is nothing, they are not going to give us deals or no breaks for just somebody paying to beat up their wife.

"So then Jimmy said, well let's make up a story that he hired you to kill her. So we discussed it, same scenario. Joe said, I will give you my brother and see if he knows anybody up in Baltimore. Jimmy Liberto approached me about it and I said yeah. And that's how we came up with the whole story."

But if there was a murder-for-hire, Cohen's story is a lie.

"Cohen is not worthy of belief," said Alvin Entin when I confronted him. "I never put any credibility, if you recall, in Cohen's statements. It's a crock of shit. Cohen's statement is unimportant."

Actually, I didn't recall him saying that before. That's what Maury Epner—the current assistant U.S. attorney—said.

Wouldn't it be ironic if the government now argued

that Cohen's statement is credible, and Luskin—who brought it—argued it isn't?

There was still another issue in the FOIA. When Luskin was desperately trying to establish a defense that his codefendants had made their trips and phone calls to Florida because they were involved in the narcotics business—a theory spiritedly denied at trial by Bernstein—he would have been pleased to read the following from the ATF's investigation, dated September 4, 1987:

> A criminal check on [Frank Liberto] and James Joseph Liberto revealed that both are suspected by DEA of drug smuggling. [Frank] was arrested and convicted in Washington, D.C. [ ] with four kilos of cocaine worth $1,500,000 in February of 1987. [Frank's] bail was $300,000, which his brother James put up the money. [Frank] started a six year prison term for possession of the four kilos on July 31, 1987.

(My note: some of those specifics are slightly wrong.)

> Intelligence information from the local and state police departments reveal that Jim Liberto has managed several bars in Baltimore City and Baltimore County. It is believed that Jim is a front for unknown persons who own and operate a pin ball/poker machine business. These machines are very lucrative and it would pay an owner/operator of these machines to finance a tavern/bar to make the machines available.
>
> Baltimore City Police Department has an active criminal investigation on [ ] Jim Liberto.

And on a teletype message dated October 16, 1987, listing all the defendants' prior criminal records and reputation:

> James Liberto, prior 1975 conviction for grand larceny, believed to be involved in narcotics trafficking.

"That proves the drug defense," said Alvin Entin. "It means Bernstein lied to the judge. Forget me. He told the judge at sidebar, 'If we had any information that the codefendants were being investigated for drugs, we'd let you know. There isn't any information in the government's possession.'"

Bernstein had since conceded that Jimmy Liberto was in the drug business, but not that the government had known about it as early as the ATF documents reveal. Responding on August 21, 1990, to one of Luskin's appellate briefs, he wrote:

> "The defendant contends that the Government did not disclose that, at the time of the investigation and prosecution of the defendant, it was also investigating a co-defendant, James Liberto, for alleged drug activity. As the Government advised the court and the defendant during the motions hearings (in December 1987), there was no such investigation pending concerning Mr. Liberto, nor did the Government have any information in its possession regarding Liberto's purported drug trafficking.
>
> "While it is true that the Government later discovered such information, and pursued an investigation of Mr. Liberto after the defendant's conviction and sentence, much, if not all, of this evidence was discovered during the preparation for (Luskin's) trial at the time (Luskin's) counsel also was discovering this evidence. Any information the Government found during this trial preparation, which consisted of witness's statements, travel records, and telephone toll records, was turned over to the defendant upon receipt."

In the same 1990 brief, Bernstein denied that Frank Liberto had any drug connection to Jimmy Liberto—a position contradicted by the never-provided ATF reports.

"The Government is somewhat perplexed with regard to the defendant's allegation concerning the arrest and prosecution of James Liberto's brother, Frank Liberto, in the District of Columbia for drug-related offenses. . . . The Government has no information linking Frank Liberto to any alleged drug activity by James Liberto."

January 25
PAUL LUSKIN

I sent full copies of the FOIA package to Paul and Bill Genego, and Paul called back, excited. He had read it completely differently than I had. ATF had prepared a full case report of exhibits and witnesses to assist in the prosecution of Cohen and Manley for drug and gun violations—the first indictment. Had the Luskin defense had it, they could have argued the government's own case that there was a drug conspiracy among the codefendants—at least Cohen and Manley.

When Paul compared the charges against Cohen and Manley in the first indictment compared to Cohen's charges in the second, it was strange, he thought, that they were identical—except that the government had dropped his drug charge and added a murder-for-hire charge.

"In order for the same counts to be applied in the Luskin case, the Government had to deny the basis of the facts in the ATF report and create a new set of facts for the same counts in the Luskin indictment," he wrote Genego and copied to me.

How could the government omit to tell the Luskin grand jury about the original set of drug facts, then deny that there was a drug alternative theory to the counts in the Luskin indictment?

Manley's arrangement was suspect, too. Six of his seven counts in the original indictment—charging him with firearms and drug violations—were dropped. He pleaded guilty to one count, carrying an illegal silencer. But that count, Paul pointed out, was from the first indictment, whose facts didn't explain a murder-for-hire. They explained a drug conspiracy.

"I'm just getting the enormity of the concept," he said.

"GOLDSTEIN"

In search of an oracle to consult—a Deep Throat—I found Goldstein, a former Luskin's employee whom Steve Allen had interviewed. For his personal reasons I have fictionalized his name.

Without compromising his identity, Goldstein well knew Paul, Joe Liberto, and Joe Luskin, and the relationship between each. Unlike almost everyone else I had interviewed, Goldstein was an independent observer. He had no apparent reason to mislead me. In fact, he had many more reasons not to talk to me—he no longer wished to be publicly associated with the Luskins—but he said he also wanted the truth to come out. And there was something he had known for a long time that he hadn't told anyone outside of his immediate circle.

When I approached him on the telephone, Goldstein knew who I was, even knew that the prison had taken Paul to the hospital in November for a cut inside his throat. He had saved his copy of my *Tropic* magazine story in his bureau at home.

"Luskin's was profitable hand over foot," he said. "We were making a profit every minute. Our overhead was so low, it was incredible. We made no deliveries, took no returns, did no service, had no insurance, and only advertised in newspapers. The showrooms were simple; the shelves were made of wood."

And they had a loyal following. "There were people who wouldn't buy anywhere else. We were 'The Cheapest Guys in Sight and Sound.' Even when we were in the newspaper for him trying to murder his wife, we were crowded.

"He fucking blew it, the schmuck," referring to Paul. "All they had to do was settle with her" and Luskin's would still be in business today.

I asked his opinion of Paul as a businessman.

"He was a scumbag. 'Baby Huey'—that's who he was,

the fat cartoon character duck. He thought he could get away with anything. He thought he was indestructible. His father never spanked him."

"Was he a good buyer?"

"No. He made me sick sometimes, the stuff he'd buy. I remember once we had only three models of VCRs to sell—that's all he could get."

"Did you sell them?"

"Yeah. Whatever he bought, we would sell eventually. We had tremendous salespeople."

Luskin's bare bones overhead—which kept the prices down—upset the local marketplace and enraged the manufacturers, especially Sony, he said.

"The other dealers are all squawking. They could buy something direct from Sony for, let's say, $100, but could go into Luskin's and buy it for $110. Paul was shortsighted, he didn't understand that you had to do things for the Sony name, you couldn't undercut their price. There were wars over it. Sony wanted to put him out of business. Eventually we lost the Sony line, so we bought Sony through a mom and pop stereo store in town."

Goldstein conceded that Paul was creative and very intelligent—and funny.

"Do you know about the Fakawe Indians? For newspaper ads, Paul had a book of dates. You're running a sale every week, but every week isn't Washington's Birthday or Memorial Day.

"The book had a mention of a celebratory date for the Fakawe Indians, which is a real tribe. So on the ad that week, Paul runs a picture of an Indian with his hand over his forehead, like he's looking forward. And it reads, 'We're the Fakawe.'

"Do you get it? We advertised in *The Miami Herald* and the Fort Lauderdale *Sun-Sentinel,* and one paper wouldn't run it, I forget which one. Paul called them up and said that the other paper was running it, so you have to run it. Then he called the second paper and said the same thing.

"It ran. Afterward we got angry letters from Indian groups."

* * *

I told Goldstein I still had a Luskin's receipt from a stereo receiver and speakers purchase I had made at their 1984 Expo sale.

"You can tell the commission right on the sales slip. On the right side there are numbers. We had seven prices for each item. There was the tag price—which was '6,' then 5, 4, 3, 2, 1, and one-half. You multiplied the number times .85, then add the second number on the right, and that was the commission. One-half is the price you got when you were ready to walk out."

I didn't have the receipt in front of me, so I didn't know how I did that day—although I remembered buying because the salesman told me I was getting a great price.

"So I'm going to show you a receipt with a '5'—and you're going to think I'm a schmuck too?"

"Right." He laughed.

No, I passed the schmuck test—at least as an electronics shopper. The salesman had told me the truth, Goldstein showed me when we met in person. The speakers were a one-half commission plus five dollars, and the receiver was a straight one-half commission.

"Who ran Luskin's?" I asked. "Was it Paul, or was it Joe Luskin?"

"Joe Luskin was in control of Luskin's, nobody else. Whatever his dad said, Paul would do it. He was the driving force behind it, yeah."

Joe Luskin had hired Goldstein, and they respected each other. But that didn't keep Goldstein from realizing Joe Luskin's flaws of integrity.

"Joe Luskin was a selfish motherfucker. He was a prick. He was only in it for himself."

The best example of that was when Joe closed one of his stores on Christmas Eve, and transferred his salespeople, and soon after laid them off. He did it to avoid the landlord, and didn't tell anyone it was going to happen until the same day. "That showed his character and how he operated. He was cold and calculating."

The staff knew that Luskin's would try to cheat them out of commissions if they didn't keep a record. "You'd turn in your commission slips, and each person would have a cubbyhole. We suspected that Paul would go into the cubbyholes and take a few slips out, so they wouldn't have to pay them all. That happened to me my first week as a salesman, but I kept records of all my slips. When they knew not to fuck with you, they wouldn't do it."

The last time Goldstein saw Joe Luskin, it was the bitter end. "He came to the store, walked in the front door and said, 'This is it. Good luck,' and he walked out. I gave the guy all those years, and all he said was 'Good luck.'"

Goldstein had never experienced a family like the Luskins. Joe and Jack, brothers, had fought over money in the sixties, and never made up. There was even some doubt whether Jack would attend Joe's funeral, although he did.

I asked about Joe's relationship with Paul.

Joe always had the upper hand, he said. He saw Joe put Paul in his place, even demean him in front of Susan.

"Sometimes Paul would be strong in public with his dad. He'd put his foot down, and you'd know that later on he was going to get it from his dad.

"Conversations always ended up with Paul whining. 'But Dad . . . eh, eh, but, but . . .'"

The combination of Paul, who was a young and creative idea man, and Joe, who was brilliant and was told he should have taught business to college students, could have been successful, he told me. But they couldn't work together.

"Why?"

"Because Paul was Baby Huey! And who could work with Baby Huey? He had to get everything he wanted!"

An example of that was when Joe Luskin stepped aside and let Paul be CEO, around 1984. Paul already had made his first million, and wanted to turn the business into an empire of stores. If he didn't get his way, he threatened to leave the business and go out on his own as an attorney. Meanwhile Joe was content to keep the chain at just the few stores he had. Oddly, it was the same argument that had caused the rift between Joe and Jack.

But even though Joe let Paul run the place, Joe still came to his office every day, and lurked in the background.

Goldstein figured Joe blamed Paul for bringing the family down because he married Marie. Joe never liked Marie, and after a while it became obvious she was going to get part of the company.

Then Goldstein parted with what he had kept to himself for the previous eight years. He slipped into the conversation that he knew there was a murder-for-hire.

I stopped him immediately. "How do you know that? What do you know that lets you say that?"

He paused. "One day I went into Joe's office—you rarely went in there, he didn't like visitors in the administrative offices at all. He was telling me that a judge had just ordered Paul to pay Marie $8,000-a-month support. He was upset that it was so much, it wasn't fair, and I joked with him, 'Well, why don't you get Guido from Chicago?'

"I'll never forget this the rest of my life. He perked up when I said that, and he looked at me coldly. I got a sick feeling. He said, 'Goldstein, what do you know?'"

The date corresponded to March 1986. Goldstein said Joe was inquiring if he was serious, if he had any connections to any real out-of-town Guidos who could do something. Goldstein said he didn't respond, and instead he immediately turned his back and left the office.

A year and a half later, when he heard the news Paul had been indicted for murder-for-hire, he instantly returned to that moment.

He struggled with himself on whether to tell what he knew to the government. In the end he didn't, but still felt tentative about not doing so.

"Do you think Joe Luskin remembered that conversation?"

"Joe Luskin didn't forget anything," he said.

There was a funny moment, too, when the store learned about the charges. "When we heard it was a Jewish hit guy from Baltimore, we laughed so loud. Couldn't they spell 'Corleone'?"

* * *

We talked about Joe Liberto. "Paul and Joe Liberto hate each other. Joe Liberto was Joe Luskin's guy. Joe Liberto wouldn't listen to Paul, only to Joe Luskin. If it was up to Paul, he would have fired Joe Liberto, but he couldn't, and it killed him."

In fact, he said, when Joe Luskin let Paul run the place, he had Joe Liberto *spy* on Paul. Paul figured it out quickly when things got back to him.

Goldstein didn't like Joe Liberto. He said he was incompetent, lazy, unimaginative, and the stores he was in charge of were badly organized. Paul thought the same thing.

"Did Joe Luskin think he was incompetent?" I asked.

"No. Joe Luskin looked more for obedience than competency. Joe Luskin would tell him what to do, and Joe Liberto would do anything he'd tell him.

"You know what Danny DeVito looks like? That was Joe Liberto, only taller, and fatter." They called him "Lumpy." "He'd tell people he was on a diet, and then you'd see him at the gas station at the end of the block, stuffing food in his mouth. Stuffing it in. I mean, it was disgusting."

I showed Goldstein the list of Western Union receipts, money wired from Baltimore to Florida, most of which were sent by Jimmy Liberto and picked up by Joe Liberto. All the transactions were less than $10,000, and most were a thousand or two, although they added up over two years to more than $375,000.

The list didn't surprise Goldstein. He had suspected that Joe Liberto was doing something with drug trafficking.

"Is there any chance that the Luskins were involved with this?" I asked him.

"No, this is penny-ante shit. The Luskins didn't need to get money from Joe Liberto. The Luskins were definitely not involved with this."

I told Goldstein that Joe Liberto had suggested to me there was "something else" between him and the Luskins—not a murder-for-hire, but something besides.

"Joe Liberto's full of shit," he said.

Goldstein echoed what Jackson had told me about Joe

Liberto. "He was a Mafia-wanna-be. He told everybody about his brother and his restaurant."

By now it was getting obvious that Paul Luskin didn't initiate a murder-for-hire by soliciting Joe Liberto. Suddenly a new premise occurred to me.

"Is it possible," I asked, "that Joe Luskin arranged with Joe Liberto for the murder, but Paul didn't know?" I told him the story Paul had told me—at the beginning of trial he asked "Dad, did we do something that maybe I should know about?" and Joe answered No; and also that some of the lawyers expected Joe on his deathbed to exonerate Paul by admitting he was behind the murder, but he didn't.

I could tell in Goldstein's expression I had struck a chord. "That sounds like Joe. Joe knew Paul was an asshole and would blab it if he told him. Paul was Baby Huey—I can't emphasize that enough."

"How would you describe Joe Luskin? Tight-lipped?"

"Tight-lipped, absolutely. He didn't give anything away."

I asked again. "Did Joe Luskin have a relationship with his son where he might have kept something away from him?"

"Yes. Absolutely," he said.

So maybe it was believable that the father didn't tell the son, and not only did Paul not participate in the murder attempt, but for all his protests that he really didn't know anything about it, maybe he was and still is telling the truth.

As illogical as that sounded.

Incredible. Goldstein was suggesting that the father conspired to solicit his daughter-in-law's murder, for which the son took the rap, then took the secret to his death. Meanwhile, the son—who may not know anything—continues to defend his father.

"Paul was the sacrificial lamb," Goldstein said.

Paul was closer with his mother than his father, he said. "How about Mildred? How could she have not known, then?" I asked.

"No. No way Mildred knew. Joe was conniving and cunning. He would not have told her anything like that."

Goldstein called it Karma that Joe Luskin died of cancer. "He had a guilty conscience. A lot of people suffered because of them. Everyone says they got what they deserved.

"But I can't figure—why did he hate his son so much?"

I asked Goldstein to speculate which scenario was more likely: if there was a murder-for-hire solicitation, would Joe Liberto have suggested it to Joe Luskin, or would Joe Luskin have asked Joe Liberto?

"I can see Joe Luskin initiating a conversation about his woes, and led Liberto into it. He might have outlined, 'Here's our problem,' and 'What can we do about it?' Joe Luskin would have led the conversation the whole way.

"There's no way Joe Liberto would go, 'How about we knock her off?' He'd be fearful and embarrassed.

"That's just my speculation. But they were tight. They thought alike. They were definitely in cahoots."

I told Goldstein about the time discrepancy between the date Joe Liberto was interviewed by the FBI and told about the murder-for-hire investigation, and two weeks later, when Paul, Susan, and Alvin Entin said they first learned about the charges. I asked him if it made any sense that Joe Liberto would have kept information about his interview away from Joe Luskin.

Goldstein took a full minute to think about it. "If they were in it together, he would have told him right away. He needed help from Mr. L. They would have hired an attorney to investigate the charges."

(I posed the same question to Paul, when he called later that same night. He came to a different conclusion.

"I talked to my dad every day. If Joe Liberto had told him, I think my dad would have told his son, 'Oh, by the way, the FBI saw Joe Liberto.'"

That Joe Liberto said he went immediately to Joe Luskin and told him, Paul said, "I would say Joe Liberto was absolutely a liar.")

* * *

As for Jackson's comment to defense attorneys that Liberto would have gotten part of the business had the hit gone down, Goldstein thought that also rang true.

"But he never could have gotten away with it. They would still have had to treat him like an asshole in public, or we would have known. Besides, Joe Liberto probably couldn't have kept it to himself.

"Joe Luskin had such a heavy motive. It's amazing that the government missed it. I liked them—but I always knew there was a dark side to them.

"What a story—if Joe Luskin was the perpetrator, and Joe Liberto was connected to the guys who couldn't shoot straight."

Goldstein's uncomplimentary references to Paul Luskin as Baby Huey made me think of a similar character in American literature, George Minafer in Booth Tarkington's *The Magnificent Ambersons*. That was a story about a Victorian-era family who thought their money, prestige, and high position would last forever. But their pride, and a rapidly changing world, brought them down in startlingly short order. Georgie Minafer grew up the scion to a fortune, never admonished for any of the indignities he did as a child to the lesser townsfolk—just like Goldstein thought that Paul Luskin had never been spanked by his father.

Georgie Minafer's small town suffered him, and wished someday for his "comeuppance." Ironically, when it came, none of the injured parties had remained to appreciate it.

Although Orson Welles's movie adaptation ended there, the book continued with Georgie's resurrection as a human being. To make enough money to support himself and his elderly aunt in a mere boardinghouse, he took a job doing hazardous manual labor. In adulthood he learned the lessons of humility and character he had missed in childhood. In the final scene, his body wrecked in an accident, he reunited with and apologized to the two characters whose lives he had done his best to ruin.

Then there were the Magnificent Luskins I remembered when I was growing up in Baltimore.

* * *

I thought now of two things I had picked up in Darden's files that were relevant. One was an FBI 302 of Olga Floridalma Valdes, Marie's maid, interviewed on January 12, 1988—a few days after the trial began.

Most of the interview concerned Paul's actions on the day he was served divorce papers, when he trashed the house. They also asked about the smaller incidences of violence to the house—air let out of tires, the doorbell ripped out, flower beds run through by cars, which Marie thought Paul did, but could never prove.

But "Flori" was in fact a witness to one of those acts. She remembered it was in either August 1986, or February 1987—when her mother came to visit from Honduras—that she saw a car drive intentionally across the yard, tearing it up. Flori's mother and brother saw it too, she said.

The driver was not Paul Luskin.

It was Joe Luskin.

Also, I found a four-page statement written by Joe Luskin describing the night of January 30, 1987, when police broke down the door of his apartment and arrested Paul for failure to pay child support. Joe dated the letter a week later.

". . . The door was broken in with a sledge hammer. Broken glass flew everywhere. Three armed people broke in with drawn guns. An unidentified female person pointed a revolver at me and stated, 'All right—hold it right there. Get out of the apartment.' Then turning to my wife Mildred, at gun point, ordered her out of the apartment.

"I stated, 'I live here! I want you out of this apartment. You get out or show me some legal reason why you should be here.' Two plain clothes people, with guns, pushed me aside and with drawn guns proceeded to search the apartment, doing a thorough job, going through all the rooms, bathrooms, showerstalls, under all beds, et cetera.

"Apparently, but never advising me, they were looking for my son Paul, who is presently involved in a marital matter . . .

"The 'police' now went to the balcony of apartment 24 J, which is contiguous to my apartment but separated by a wall. They apprehended Paul on the balcony of that apartment by ordering him at gun point to climb around the wall on the ledge of the railing, jeopardizing his life. He could have easily slipped and fallen 24 stories down to his death.

"Paul was handcuffed and taken out of our apartment . . .

"While we were waiting for the elevator, I demanded to know on what authority they broke into my apartment. . . . These police officers would not show me any warrants or break-in orders. The police officers said they did not need any.

"Approximately five minutes later my attorney, David Levine, arrived. When I told him what had transpired, he could hardly believe this incident could occur in this day and age in the United States."

Two weeks later, February 13, Joe Luskin rehired Joe Liberto. It was the day before St. Valentine's Day. According to attorneys' notes of an interview with Jackson, "Joe Luskin asked (Joe Liberto) to come back to eliminate Marie—contact brother and we are going to kill her. Gets piece of business in return."

Three weeks later, March 9, Marie was assaulted.

Paul Luskin wrote this in a letter to Ben Darden in June 1988:

Joe Liberto hated me for demoting him in 1982 and replacing him with Bob Kempler, who was made VP with Nikki Hart. When Kempler gave notice of resignation in November 1986, Liberto demanded to my father to be made VP in his place. Father refused and Liberto then gave notice. Liberto was demoted by me and sent to (the) Orlando (store) in 1984 and he never forgave me for not only Bob Kempler, but making Larry Levine General Manager in his stead. My relationship with Liberto turned into disgust when Uncle Jack Luskin, in his December 22, 1986 deposition, revealed that Liberto had been applying for a job in Baltimore with him and that Liberto was giving him Luskin Fla. company

*information. To conceive that I would now turn to
Liberto for anything is ridiculous.*

To me, the case that it was Joe Luskin, not Paul, who
solicited Joe Liberto for a murder-for-hire was overwhelming. There were only two things remaining that
pointed to Paul, and I didn't know how much weight to
give them:

- Steve Miles's interview with Steve Allen
- Alvin Entin's mention of a car phone call Paul
  made to the Marco Polo

Again, Steve Miles's interview two weeks after the
indictment read: "Joe (Liberto) can tie up whole case.
Hired by Paul. Price tag $65,000 to be paid by Paul.

"Plot struck before he was fired. He pointed out the
house.

"Plot to kill.

"Originally Joe involved. Make him a part of the
business.

"Joe originally going to get bad guy. Jimmy said let me
do it. Jimmy gets Sonny Cohen."

"Hired by Paul, to be paid by Paul." Was this the
attempt to make Paul the "sacrificial lamb" for Joe
Luskin? And was Joe Liberto the source of Steve Miles's
information?

I don't believe I'll ever be conclusive on this point,
unless Paul Luskin tells me someday he did it.
That's if he did it.

At Bonnie View Country Club in Baltimore, where
both Joe and Jack Luskin, as well as my parents were
members in the 1960s, the sympathy was with Joe when
the brothers Luskin broke up.

"Everyone, we all felt sorry for Joe," said my mother.
"Joe was like a *nemechal*. You know what a *nemechal*
means?"

Obviously it was a Yiddish word, (the "ch" sound gets

pronounced like "Chanukah," not like "chop") but I had never heard it spoken before. "A *nemechal* is the quiet guy who gets stepped on. Jack was stepping on Joe, his older brother, and nobody liked it."

I didn't have to point out the irony in what she was saying, she beat me to it. "It's funny that the *nemechal* turned into a monster."

Joe Luskin had seen one Luskin take his business away from him. Damned if he was going to watch another Luskin do it again.

Perhaps the anger he had for Marie was latent anger for his brother.

THIRTEEN

February 1995

When I first told Susan, in passing, that I wanted to talk about Paul's relationship with his father, she answered that that would take up an evening's worth of conversation. A week later, we did it.

"Just after Joe died, Paul said to me, 'I didn't even get to hear if there was a deathbed confession,'" she said.

"That's pretty funny," I remarked.

"He wasn't laughing. He was as agonized over that as not being able to go to the funeral. If he was there, he would have asked him."

In fact, Paul never saw his father again after the day he was sentenced. Joe never went to see him in prison—he and Mildred were on the run, out of the country, from Marie. And when he called, Paul couldn't talk openly because prison lines are monitored. However, after Joe died, Mildred began to visit him.

"That's why I asked you before, what kind of father-son relationship could they have had, that Joe might have kept Paul from his confidence? What kind of father was he?"

"I'll answer that easily. Nobody keeps Paul in their confidence if they want to keep a secret. You know as well as I, Paul's a blabbermouth. If it was really confidential, Paul would have been the last person on earth Joe would have told. Mildred would be the second to last

333

he would have told—she thinks the sun rises and sets with Paul.

"This is so incomprehensible to anyone who doesn't know the family."

Then Susan dropped something else interesting. After the family found out about the murder-for-hire investigation, "I can tell you, they were all extremely terrified that Joe was going to be indicted."

I asked her for details of what they said, but Susan had none. "They wouldn't talk around me, because I wasn't one of them."

Later in the evening, we met for pizza dinner with her youngest son Benjamin, who did his best to ignore us while we talked about Paul.

"I remember one night, I went to Paul's apartment in Turnberry and waited for him to come home. When he did, he was ballistic at his father. For a full hour, he couldn't talk, he was almost hyperventilating. I rubbed his back so he would calm down." He wouldn't talk about what they had argued about. "That would happen often," she said.

She remembered a typical Joe Luskin response to Paul. From prison, Paul kept asking where his personal effects were, such as his Krugerrand cuff links and Rolex watch. Joe would only tell him, " 'It's all under control, Paul, don't worry about it.' To this day Paul doesn't know where that stuff is," she said.

I asked if Susan had seen the two of them together twenty-five years before in Baltimore, when she dated Paul. She hadn't. Joe Luskin was around his house so little, she never even met him.

"The only way Paul would get to see Joe was to work at Luskin's. So he did, when he was eleven.

"Joe wouldn't let anybody get close to him. He'd put a magnetic shield down in front of him"—Susan waved her hand over her face to symbolize.

"He was only affectionate with Mildred. Nance told me he'd terrorize her and Donna, yelling and screaming."

* * *

Susan only saw Joe Luskin angry, but she sympathized. "When the divorce started, he was angry at Paul, angry at Marie, angry at the lawyers. Who wants to work hard all your life and see all your money go to some bitch daughter-in-law—and leave your child destitute? Paul could make it back—but Joe's life's work was over."

I speculated that although the evidence was mounting against Joe Luskin as the solicitor of the murder attempt, how could the prosecution have guessed that the father-in-law, not the husband, was responsible?

"Yeah? What about the in-laws case you wrote about?" she asked me.

I drew a blank for a second. Oh, no, she was right. I had written about a case in Broward County of a very crazy Jewish mother-in-law who didn't think her son-in-law was good enough for her daughter, and was caught on tape hiring her carpet cleaner to murder him. It turned out the son-in-law was an exceptionally nice guy, very successful in business, and the daughter was very happy with him and their sons they had together.

The carpet cleaner went to the police, and they let the mother-in-law continue to believe she was buying a murder. They arranged a code to indicate the hit had gone down: "The carpet is clean." Once she was convinced the job was done, she counted out hundred-dollar bills while police aimed a hidden video camera on her and miked the police lieutenant who played the hit man.

Apparently, Luskin was merely Story Two in my impromptu "In-laws Who Kill" series.

(Just as Paul was Story One in the series of "Luskin/Lusskin Hollywood, Florida Attorneys Convicted of Murder-for-hire on their significant others." On January 20, 1995, David Lusskin—also a Hollywood attorney—was found guilty of trying to arrange the murder of his former girlfriend. Oddly, I had actually met David Lusskin fifteen years before. And Paul told me the Luskins and the Lusskins were in fact distantly related.)

Back at Susan's house, Paul called. After he and Susan talked, I got on the phone.

"Paul, we were out eating pizza."

"Pizza? I'd like to go out for pizza."

"Well, maybe soon, Paul. Or—maybe you'll be able to send in for it."

He laughed. "Great," he said.

"If Paul had done it," Susan said, "he would have told me—and sworn me to secrecy. But he didn't."

February 5

Susan had suggested I call Alan Epstein to ask about Paul's relationship with his father. Alan met Paul at the University of Miami and stayed friends. He worked at Luskin's in 1971 while he waited for his Florida Bar exam results, and in later years, often dropped by the main store.

I didn't tell Alan what I was driving at. He felt bad for saying uncomplimentary things about Joe Luskin, but wanted to give me his true impressions.

"They fought a lot. Screaming fights, yelling. If you're trying to figure out, did Paul's dad fire him (in 1986), I'd say, yes, it's entirely possible. Even back then (in 1971) there was a time when he quit or he was fired. He would tell me, he didn't want to go back.

"Joe Luskin was a very difficult man. There was a time when I wanted to throw him through a plate glass window. Of course, I didn't really want to do that to the father of a friend of mine."

"Do you remember any of the arguments?" I asked.

"No. They were always over nothing important. It was always something small that would set him off. He was a terror, a controlled rage. He was also very generous to me, he had me over for dinner, hired me when I needed a job. But in business, he was no fun. It doesn't change the fact that this guy was very volatile.

"I tried to stay away from him. You never knew what would set him off. I never knew what was going to come out of his mouth next. There was always something bubbling under the surface. You knew he was angrier than he looked.

"We all tried to keep him off the sales floor. He was

good at telling us what to say, but he just wasn't good with customers, and he realized that himself."

"Did Paul and he get along?"

"Honestly, no. That isn't to say they might not have had a good relationship outside the business. But once you work for family, it's all intertwined. Not many fathers and sons work together well. It's not easy to be an intelligent son around an intelligent, domineering father."

I asked Alan if he had ever seen Paul act the same way as his father.

"No. In the ways his father was extreme, Paul was moderate. I've never seen Paul get as angry as his father. He was always rational and reasonable."

"Did the relationship improve as the years went on?"

"Over the years, I think it got worse. That doesn't mean they didn't love each other."

"Would Paul ever pick a fight with his father?"

"If anybody was going to pick a fight, it would have been Joe with Paul," he said.

Alan said he had a similar opportunity to go into a family business, but because he anticipated what he saw between father and son Luskin, he went to law school instead.

I empathized. Through my teens, I had dreaded having to make the same decision they made, but as it turned out, there was no family business for me at that time. I followed my bliss, as Joseph Campbell would say, as Barry Levinson had followed his into television and the movies.

Perhaps he didn't want to sell appliances either.

February 22

I wish I could work on just one story at a time. Someone I met recently gave me a source on another story, and talking to him on the phone for the first time, I chatted about the Luskin story. Since the source had been in Miami for a long time, I figured he'd remember the Luskin's stores.

"Yeah. His father did it," he said.

"What? It took me three and a half years to figure that out! How did you know that?"

He said his father was in the electronics business only a few blocks from Luskin's in Hollywood. He said those rumors had been around for years.

Within the hour, I got another call from a man who identified himself as Calvin Burns, who asked if I knew who he was.

"Of course. You're the Amtrak Police officer who arrested Cohen and Manley." My FOIA request from Amtrak had arrived the day before, although it didn't contain much I didn't already have.

Burns got my phone number from the FOIA request, and wanted to know why I wanted the information. It was one of his first cases as a drug interdiction officer, and still one of his biggest.

"We called them 'the Tough Guys,'" he said, referring to Cohen and Manley. "We said, you look like the guys in the movie, *The Tough Guys,*" a movie title that had escaped me. Then, when police opened their bags after obtaining a search warrant and saw the guns, they said, "Damn, they *were* the Tough Guys."

"They were a couple of amateur hit men, just some old-time criminals who would do anything for money. They probably had killed people," Burns said.

I asked about two disputed points: first, both Cohen and Manley had said they never gave police consent for a dog to sniff their bags.

"Oh, that's what they say? Okay," Burns said sardonically. In fact, he said, younger people now routinely tell Amtrak Police "Fuck you" when they ask if a dog can smell their bags. Then they just walk away.

But Amtrak's drug interdiction unit was new in 1987, and Cohen and Manley might not have been prepared to answer that way when they were approached.

The second point was whether he believed the 3½ ounces of cocaine Cohen and Manley were caught with had come from Florida. Cohen said he took it to Florida so his girlfriend wouldn't use it.

"Yeah, right," said Burns. "He bought it in Florida because it's so much cheaper there."

But remember, Gregg Bernstein had dropped the drug charges against both Cohen and Manley after the murder-for-hire story surfaced. He had insisted that the case that came to trial was not a drug case.

Burns said he was friends with Roy Cheeks, who was now the spokesman for the ATF office in Baltimore. He gave me his phone number, and suggested I call him.

February 23

The next day, at almost the same time, Roy Cheeks called me.

He introduced himself. "I got Manley to roll over," he said.

"I know that. But only from reading the ATF case file I got in FOIA." Now that I had the file—thanks to Manley's death certificate—Cheeks could come out of the woodwork.

I asked if ATF had sent everything in the file, and he said it had. "But what about the report of what Manley said to you? That's not there."

He laughed. "I don't write down notes," he said, that way, he doesn't have to produce any notes later. "I keep it all in my head."

I tried to piece together a chronology of his contact with Manley, although Cheeks said he really couldn't talk about the case without the permission of his superiors. He was there in Baltimore City Jail on August 20, 1987, the day Cohen and Manley were informed they had been indicted.

"I remember Manley shaking, and giving me a look like 'Can we talk?' I thought, *Let me try the hard one first* (Cohen)—*to see if he'd flip.* Cohen told me, 'Fuck you.'"

"And Manley didn't say the same thing?"

"He did. Only it didn't have the same forcefulness."

Cheeks asked whether I had met the characters. He was close to Marie—"Marie loved me," he said, and he felt bad for Joe Liberto.

He said Joe Liberto, as I knew, had been offered a

deal, "and he was getting ready to take it. He wanted either no time, or a cap at one year." But it fell through because the prosecutors couldn't guarantee that the judge would agree to exactly what they would recommend. Instead, Joe Liberto took his chances at trial and lost.

"He was going to tell us about Joe Luskin. I think he thought about it."

"So, tell me, what's the Joe Luskin story?" I probed.

"You got me," he said.

I explained my Joe Luskin theory. Cheeks said they knew Joe Luskin was at the meetings where the conspiracy was planned. He provided Marie's license tag number.

I didn't get the answer to where Cheeks learned that. But he did say later that Jim Liberto talked to him after the trial ended.

"He said his brother wasn't as involved as the rest of us—don't quote me on the words, it was something to that effect. But at that point, we didn't need to hear how many meetings they had had, or anything like that."

I wanted to get that one straight. "Are you saying Jimmy admitted to you that there was a murder-for-hire, just that his brother wasn't as involved in it as the others?"

"That's right," Cheeks said.

"Listen. Did Jimmy Liberto—or Joe Liberto—or anybody else specifically mention Paul Luskin, as opposed to Joe Luskin, in the conspiracy? Are there any direct statements you know of that would prove my theory wrong?"

"I don't remember," he said. "If I knew something, I would have told the U.S. Attorney's Office. There's no pressure on us to make up stories for convictions."

We talked about Susan. He recalled the scene at sentencing, when the marshals took Paul away as Susan jumped up to try to touch his hand. The guards yanked him away, "passing close in the night, but never touching.

"Oh my God," he remembered.

He thought Susan knew about the murder-for-hire, although when I asked if he had any direct information, he said he didn't. He was at Baltimore-Washington Airport the day Susan got off a plane and into a car with Paul after the FBI in Miami, using a picture of Susan that Marie had given them, had followed her to Fort Lauderdale airport.

Cheeks and other agents hailed a cab to follow them, but the funny story was they had no money on them. Paul's car drove all the way to Washington, and the cab fare was $104. When they got out, they showed the driver their badges, and promised to pay him later. They did. The cabbie told them, "Hey, I always wanted to be asked to 'Follow that car!' "

If Paul was innocent, he asked, what about his phone call to Marie on the day of the assault? I explained that the phone bill documented that Paul called at 4:41 P.M., even though Marie's Aunt Ruth said it was sometime earlier than three o'clock. The real time of the call matched many other calls when his children were home. Although, I said, the calls by the codefendants that morning were not as easily explained.

Cheeks asked if I had talked with the FBI, and I said I had tried to reach Pat Connolly when I wrote my magazine story, but he hadn't returned a number of phone calls. In more recent attempts, I hadn't located him. Cheeks suggested I call Jeff Hill, Connolly's partner.

FOURTEEN

March 1995

March 1
FBI SPECIAL AGENT JEFFREY HILL

It took a few days, but I got FBI Special Agent Jeff Hill
on the phone. He, too, needed permission to speak with
me, but if I could get it, it was okay with him.

I told him that I had talked to all the codefendants,
but not Manley. "Well, you won't be. Manley is dead."
He said before Manley died of a coronary, he had had a
heart attack in prison.

When I mentioned Joe Liberto, he told a story;
Liberto got food poisoning the night the FBI questioned
him at his home in Florida. "He accused us of doctoring
his food."

"You mean at the restaurant, before you met him?"

"Right," he said.

I told him Jim Liberto recently had admitted to me
that he was part of a drug ring. "Here I am, telling the
FBI."

"You're not telling me anything we didn't know."

That that was something the government didn't admit
at trial, I kept to myself.

"Have you talked to Steve Allen?" he asked. Yes, I
said. "Has he talked to you about the phone call he said
we missed that would have sunk Luskin? I don't know if
he's just a smug little son of a bitch, or it really exists."

"When did Allen say it?"

"He might have mentioned it to a prosecutor after the

342

trial. Not having it wasn't fatal, because we won the case."

March 2
FRANK GRATE, METALLURGIST

Three years before, I had spoken with Frank Grate, a forensic engineer and metallurgist, about my barrette-solder theory. But without charts from the FBI lab, he couldn't tell me much.

Now, since I had found those charts in Ben Darden's files, I went to visit him, hoping he could make some sense of them. Ironically, his office was just around the corner from the building that used to be Luskin's Hollywood warehouse store.

The FBI had used a scanning electron microscope to determine what elements were present in the two metal fragments removed from Marie's scalp. They labeled them Q15A and Q15B. (In the lab, "Q" refers to something unknown, or questioned, "K" refers to something known.) Both were small, but Q15B was minuscule.

Grate showed me that on the charts, Q15B had large peaks indicating the presence of lead and very small peaks showing calcium and copper. Q15A showed lead and calcium, but also antimony, rhodium, and phosphorus.

Q15A, being larger, could undergo further testing. Using another sensitive process called X-ray fluorescence, the FBI had measured it for three trace materials. They found: .02 percent copper; .8 percent antimony; and .015 percent arsenic. The other trace materials were even less. Subtracting, Grate announced that the remainder of the fragment was 98 to 99 percent lead.

"Is that consistent with a bullet?" I asked.

"Oh, definitely. Absolutely. Those are all numbers well within what you'd expect from a bullet."

(Later I asked the same question to a production manager of a bullet manufacturer in Miami, who agreed. A bullet needs to be soft, he said. If it was hard, it might crack as it passed through the hot barrel. The softness of a bullet also explained why it could fragment, or deform on impact.)

I asked about solder. Was that within the range of possibility?

Grate went to his bookshelf and found a book called *Solder and Soldering* that had a chart of various solder compositions, including impurities. He already knew solder could in fact have copper, antimony, and arsenic.

The chart listed seven common examples of commercial grade solder—the kind that would be used to hold a barrette together. The lowest concentration of lead was 40 percent, the highest was 70 percent. The second ingredient was tin—together in each example, tin and lead made up at least 98 percent of the composition. The FBI lab had not shown the presence of any tin in the fragments.

Another chart showed the strength of various mixtures of tin and solder. Pure lead was five times softer—and weaker—than the strongest combination, which was roughly 60 percent tin, 37 percent lead, with 3 percent antimony.

"This is not solder. I can assure you of that," he said.

"Is there anything else you can think of that would be 98 percent lead?"

"Not that I know of. Can I be one hundred percent sure it's a bullet? No. But in most probability, it's a bullet."

If it was a bullet, it was a murder-for-hire.

If it was a bullet, Cohen lied and Manley told the truth that Marie was shot.

"What about the calcium, rhodium, and phosphorus?" I asked.

None of that would be in a bullet, Grate said, but a bullet might have collided with a bone in Marie's scalp and picked up a detectible trace of calcium. Grate had studied that effect three years before as a defense expert in a case.

The rhodium was something else. Its presence surprised Grate, who at first wondered whether the handwritten "Rh" on the chart wasn't a scribble that meant "Pb," the symbol for lead.

He checked another source, and read that rhodium—a member of the platinum group of metals—is used in jewelry finishing because it resists corrosion so well. In fact, "white gold" jewelry is not silver-plated, as I had always thought, but rhodium-plated.

Phosphorus, the book said, was sometimes used in a rhodium bath to create a plating solution.

So the barrette theory was vindicated after all. It wasn't solder from the barrette in Marie's scalp, *but maybe some of the barrette itself that had scraped off and stayed with the bullet.* Both the bullet theory and the barrette theory might be right.

STEVE ALLEN

In the evening Steve Allen returned a phone call, from his carphone on his way home. I filled him in on some of the latest news, and then brought up that phone call that had been bothering me so much. I told him that both Alvin Entin and now Jeff Hill had mentioned it to me.

Alvin had said it was a call Paul had made from his carphone to the Marco Polo, at about the right time. Hill didn't know what it was, except that the call could have sunk Luskin.

"I didn't say that. I said there was a piece of evidence you guys missed. I can assure you it's not a phone call to the Marco Polo. I won't even confirm it's a phone call. It's not all that significant, and I'm not sure it implicates Paul or not."

I tried to get more, but he wouldn't give it up, and I knew he couldn't. "I won't say what it was without a waiver of privilege from Paul. It wouldn't be in Paul's best interests to talk about it now."

"What if I asked Paul about it?"

"Paul doesn't even know what it is. As an attorney, I make observations, and I don't always share with the client what they are."

"Tell me. Could it possibly lead to Joe Luskin?"

"It's possible," he said.

I hadn't talked to Steve since our meeting on the day after Thanksgiving. I realized I hadn't detailed the theory about Joe Luskin's involvement, to the possible exclusion of Paul.

He listened as I outlined it. "It's an interesting theory. It's a plausible explanation of the events," he said.

"Steve," I pleaded. "My last theory, that there wasn't a murder-for-hire, was a plausible theory, too. But it's not plausible anymore. You're really not giving me a strong affirmation. I'm seeing if I can disprove this so I don't have to discover two weeks after my book comes out that I went off half-cocked again and have to go 'Oops, Sorry.' "

He laughed. "That's all I can give you. Until the case is resolved a hundred percent, I'm not in a position."

When I got off the phone, I took inventory again. It probably was a phone call, but alright, not from Paul to the Marco Polo. It couldn't have been a call Paul made to Baltimore; it's inconceivable the FBI would have missed that. It must have been a call made somewhere in south Florida. It couldn't have been a local call because Hollywood to North Miami (which includes Turnberry) are free calls—except for cellular phones.

Allen did reiterate that Paul had always told him he was innocent, so whatever Steve knew wasn't a direct admission of guilt from Paul. *He's probably where I am,* I thought, *he only has an opinion whether Paul was involved or not.*

He did say that if Paul was involved, Susan didn't know it, and wouldn't have stayed married to him if she knew he had planned a murder.

And after talking to Roy Cheeks and Jeff Hill, it's obvious the government didn't have any certain evidence that Paul was involved—except Manley, whom I now considered a dubious source on the subject.

March 3
PAUL LUSKIN

Paul called, and I told him what Frank Grate had said. When I said this proved it was a bullet, and therefore, a murder-for-hire, he laughed, a little bit mockingly.

"It means either Joe Luskin was behind it, or you were," I said.

"But there are a lot of compelling reasons why it would be Joe and not you. First, Joe had twice as much motive monetarily than you. Second, the connection to Joe Liberto was clearly his, not yours. Third, he had an intense dislike for Marie, and your personality is different from your father's, as mine is different from my father's."

"That's true," he said.

"The question is, Were you in it as well? Regardless, you happen to be lucky she wasn't killed, because you'd be on Death Row right now, and your appeals would just about be ending. If I was on the case, finding this out, I'd be dramatically racing against the clock with this stuff."

"You're probably right."

"At least I know that the only way you're going to die in prison is if you swallow another chicken bone. Your problem is poultry, not the executioner."

"I just don't believe it," he said. "I think I would have picked up something, somewhere, like in Baltimore City Jail someone would have told me."

"You underestimate those people," I said. "They're hard guys. They must have looked at you like you're some privileged character from Miami, and not trusted you for a second." I thought of "Baby Huey," but resisted the temptation to say it.

"I don't know," he said. "If she was shot, I think it was in the course of a robbery. I don't think my father had anything to do with it."

"Cohen tried to kill her because she didn't give him the money he expected? I don't think so. I'm sure you'll think about it some," I said, as we had to end the talk.

"I'm sure I will," he said.

March 4
PAUL LUSKIN

"I thought about it all last night," Paul told me in the afternoon.

"Naaaah," he said.

He didn't want to believe it was a bullet. He raised some of the points I had already answered talking to

Carl Haemmerle, the firearms examiner: What about the noise? Powder burns? Why didn't the shot hit the mirror?

He even reminded me that it could have been lead from a blackjack. "It couldn't, Paul, because that meant the leather bag had split, and there would have been lead pellets all over the carpet."

He suggested we'd have to know the metal composition of all Marie's barrettes to prove that the fragment hadn't come from there.

"Paul, barrettes wouldn't be made of 99 percent lead. They'd be too soft. There isn't anything else obvious that's that composition. It was a bullet."

"It doesn't make sense," he said. "The drug stuff, Cohen and Manley trying to kill Jim Liberto, who was their connection to getting paid."

"It's entirely possible they were doing both drugs and murder when they came to Florida," I said. "As for trying to kill Jim Liberto, I don't know, they weren't really forward-thinking guys. Maybe they were going to rob him, and that would have counted for what they would have been paid."

He had to cut the conversation short. "Well, for all the things we've discussed over the years, I disagree." Again the nervous laughter.

"Okay. Fair enough." I laughed back.

SUSAN DAVIS

I explained the findings to Susan. She had already heard it from Paul the night before.

She wasn't convinced, or at least, didn't like what I had found. She offered some of the arguments Paul had made, but I replied you couldn't argue with the content of the metal.

"Well, maybe that's why Joe Luskin never went to visit him in prison," she said.

I grasped I was taking control of the story at last. I could hear Paul falling back on his heels, listening to what he did not want to hear. Susan had just stayed silent, cool, resistant. When I suggested before we hung up that she had something to think about, she responded no, she wasn't going to think about it at all.

At last, the power had changed from the story's characters to the storyteller. Our roles changed; now I had more to tell than to listen to. And disappointingly, they were not as good listeners as I had been. On the other hand, I was not that good an interview subject. I was still holding back a lot of what I knew. Well, so had everyone else.

Don't fall in love.

A while back, I recognized that I had fallen in love. That was step one. Now at last I could say I was in love no longer. If the story went against Paul Luskin, so be it.

"I narrate in order to become myself," I read that night in a story called *The Black Book,* by Orhan Pamuk, a Turkish writer. Both he and I gain our voices by telling the stories of others. Now I am at the center of a story about events that happened years ago to others.

March 6-9
LEAD ALLOYS

Shamed a little bit that I didn't have all the answers before concluding that the fragment was a bullet, I began a tour by telephone of America's lead smelters and casters, with the assistance of the *Thomas Directory of American Industries.*

I talked to Herb Doyle, general manager of Ney Smelting, in Brooklyn. He said part of his business was sales of casting metals for costume jewelry. I read him my metal fragment's composition from the FBI charts, and he said it did not sound like a piece of costume jewelry. He checked a spreadsheet of work orders going back thirty years and found that 96 percent lead was the highest concentration his company had been asked to compose for that application. The remainder was tin. Since I didn't have any tin at all, that eliminated the possibility it was a barrette, he thought.

But I thought back to what Dr. Charles Kokes, the medical examiner who testified for the prosecution, had told me in 1991: "The simplest explanations are almost always the correct ones. There was lead—bullets have lead—it was a gunshot wound. I'm not aware that any barrettes are made of lead. That's for health reasons—lead is very toxic."

Wrong. But that also meant the defense had missed a marvelous chance to destroy Kokes, defeat the bullet theory, and maybe win the case. Even if it was turning out that Marie was shot after all.

"People don't know their costume jewelry is made out of lead," Doyle said. "Ask them. They'll say it's made out of gold, or silver. But what's underneath that? They don't know."

Doyle called me back that afternoon. He had talked to some colleagues, who suggested that my metal fragment alloy was typical scrap from battery plates, recycled for their lead. That lead would be 99 percent pure—like mine—with antimony, a little arsenic, a little copper, but there wouldn't be any tin in it.

If the fragment matched battery plate lead, he said, that could take me in either direction, a bullet or a barrette. It's the cheapest lead you can buy—homemade bullets are made out of it; or possibly, overseas costume jewelers, casting very cheap stuff, might use it. He knew a caster in Taiwan, and promised to ask him by fax that night.

Bob Whitney, an applications engineer for Yuasa-Exide, a battery manufacturer in Reading, Pennsylvania, agreed that my alloy—even with all its impurities—"definitely" sounded like a lead acid battery. "The .8 percent antimony is right in the ballpark," he said.

By now I was wondering if I had spoken too soon.

Next I talked to Steve Kaplan, of Hallmark Metals, in Cranston, Rhode Island. Hallmark's specialty is mixing and selling the metals that others make barrettes from.

I read him the numbers. "It's very unlikely this was from costume jewelry," he said. His two most popular mixtures are 88 percent tin, 9 percent lead, 3 percent antimony; and 35 percent tin, 62 percent lead, 3 percent antimony.

Kaplan said the cheapest, lowest grade metal for

costume jewelry would be 97 percent lead, 3 percent antimony. He also said nobody uses battery plate lead for costume jewelry, although there was a company in Providence that briefly did about fifteen years before, when they were first starting out. But it didn't work well.

"From my experience, jewelry manufacturers couldn't get the alloy to fill the cavity in the mold," he said.

"More than likely, it wasn't part of the barrette. None of the alloys we make in the industry are 99 percent lead."

Not a barrette. Now I needed to confirm whether battery plate lead was used in bullets. I found Fred Stallings, plant manager for Zero Bullet, in Cullman, Alabama. He also agreed it was proper to assume my alloy was battery scrap. However, he said, not only homemade bullet makers used it, but all the major bullet manufacturers used it too.

He also argued against the barrette theory. "Nobody would wear a barrette that density of lead," he said. "It would be very soft, and it would blacken the skin."

We discussed some loose ends. He dismissed the idea that the fragment could have been lodged by a gun hitting a head (as Marie claimed had happened), but he was intrigued by the blackjack idea. That could have left any conceivable alloy lead fragment.

I argued that the blackjack cover had to break, lodging a fragment in Marie's head but scattering no pellets on the floor. Also, she never saw a blackjack.

If it was a bullet, Stallings wanted to know why it had fragmented. Since it didn't go far into the skull, did it hit something else?

I told him the barrette Marie was wearing had broken. That could explain it, he told me.

We settled on this: the fragment wasn't a barrette; it wasn't likely a blackjack; she wasn't hit with a gun; the alloy was well within the possibility it could have been a bullet, and if it was, the breakage of the barrette may answer why the bullet fragmented.

There were no other obvious options. We agreed this was most likely a gunshot.

* * *

I called a local police supply house in Miami, where a salesman described a blackjack as like a little club— maybe ten inches long and flat, covered with leather, filled with lead.

I asked if blackjacks commonly left lead fragments behind. No, he said. More likely it would leave a pencil-like smear than a fragment.

Herb Doyle called back with news from Taiwan. "People do use battery plate lead for costume jewelry. But nobody they know would put rhodium on it."

Battery plate lead would have a lot of pitting in it, he said. It wouldn't make sense to put an expensive plating on the very cheapest alloy.

We talked about blackjacks. He agreed that from an alloy point of view, the fragment could very well be from a blackjack, but he had checked and found that almost all blackjacks are manufactured with double-jackets so they don't leak all over the place. That reduced the practical chance that the fragment came from a black-jack, he thought.

He wasn't as successful finding bullets made of 99 percent lead and 1 percent antimony, with no tin added. He thought it sounded like a homemade bullet. But not five minutes after we hung up, he called back; someone had just handed him a faxed request for a quote asking for precisely that combination to make a small batch of bullets.

"I just got off the phone. Usually they ask for some tin in there, but not this order. So it could be used to manufacture bullets."

I had talked with a spokesman from the Lead Industries Association in New York earlier in the week, and he mailed me a pamphlet called *Properties of Lead and Lead Alloys*. It listed a hundred or more descriptions and chemical compositions of alloys, including one called "Bullet Alloy," unified number L52560:

It was 99.2 percent lead, .75 percent antimony. An almost perfect match for my specimen.

March 9

Out of curiosity, I reopened the book of telephone
calls the defense had assembled to show that the phone
traffic between the codefendants proved a drug conspiracy, not a murder-for-hire. I had taken a duplicate
copy from Darden's files. Perhaps I could figure out
Paul's phone call Alvin and Steve Allen were vaguely
referring to.

One of my few clues was that Alvin said it was on a
"critical date." Trusting it wasn't a call Paul made to the
Marco Polo, I found myself returning to the day of the
assault, March 9, 1987.

I had also copied the pages of Paul's car phone bill
between March 9 and March 12, and studied it. This was
the phone traffic on March 9:

11:25 a.m.: A coin phone at the Marco Polo called
   Palughi's Restaurant in Baltimore, 3 minutes;

11:30 a.m.: Palughi's Restaurant called Joe Liberto's
   home number, 1 minute;

11:31 a.m.: Palughi's Restaurant called 305-920-3405,
   the published store number for Luskin's Hollywood
   store, 2 minutes;

3:48 p.m.: Another Luskin's line, 305-920-3440, called
   the B. Lipsitz Company in Pittsburgh [where Paul was
   working as a consultant], 1 minute;

4:28 p.m.: Paul, in his carphone in Pittsburgh, calls
   Luskin's, 305-920-3407, 12.2 minutes;

4:41 p.m.: Paul, still in his carphone, calls Marie's
   number, 2.1 minutes. [Marie's Aunt Ruth Wapner
   testified she took the call, but didn't say Marie had
   been assaulted. Paul had told me in 1991 he routinely
   called his daughter Diana between 4 and 5 P.M., then
   called Shana between 8 and 9 P.M. He added that
   Marie had left him a message the Friday before to call
   her on Monday];

4:42 p.m.: Paul calls Luskin's, 305-920-3405 [the same
   line Palughi's had called earlier in the day], 1.1
   minute;

8:58 p.m.: Paul calls Susan, 10.1 minutes;

9:07 p.m.: Paul calls Marie's house, 3.0 minutes;

9:12 p.m.: Paul calls the toll-free number for U.S. Air;

9:18 p.m.: Paul calls his parents' home phone.

Then on March 10, there are three calls of note from Paul's car phone:

12:04 p.m.: Paul calls Luskin's, 305-920-3405, 2.5 minutes;

12:06 p.m.: Paul calls Marie, 6 minutes. [This call was noted by Detective Soccol, who was present taping an interview with Marie];

8:32 p.m.: Paul calls Susan, 18 minutes.

I had two sources besides Paul to explain to me the subtleties of the Luskin's store phones. One was Nikki Hart, the manager of the stores's executive offices, who testified to the grand jury and at trial; and Goldstein. I learned:

- 920-3405 was the Hollywood showroom floor phone number. Joe Liberto, the Hollywood store's general manager at that time, didn't have an office but liked to hover around the phone, which was near the store entrance.

- 920-3407 was one of the lines to the executive offices, which was separate from the showroom floor. That line reached Nikki Hart or any of the Luskins, but not Joe Liberto.

- 920-3440 was the Luskin family private line in the executive offices, and would not be answered by anyone else.

Now reexamine the list of calls:

At **11:30,** someone at Palughi's called Joe Liberto's home number, then the Luskin's store on the line Joe Liberto would pick up.

At **3:48,** the Luskin family line called Paul at B. Lipsitz.

At **4:28,** Paul called the administrative offices line—
most likely returning the earlier call. Perhaps he
called the private family line first, and after getting no
answer, called the line Nikki Hart or someone else in
the offices would pick up.

At **4:41,** Paul called Marie's house.

At **4:42,** Paul called the store number—the same one
Palughi's Restaurant called earlier.

Nikki Hart testified that Joe Liberto was rarely in the
executive offices. Goldstein told me the offices were
always occupied up to five o'clock and usually six, there
was always someone in those offices, which precluded
the possibility that Paul called there and got no answer,
then called the showroom floor number to leave a
message for someone in the offices.

Then why did Paul Luskin call the number Joe Liberto
might pick up on March 9, 1987, the moment after
calling Marie's house?

And why on March 10 did he call that same store
number again, then immediately call Marie?

Believe it or not, the government missed the true
significance of those two calls to 920-3405.

I reread Gregg Bernstein's closing argument:

"Well, we know that some time between ten and ten-
thirty in the morning, Marie Luskin is shot in the head
at her home and that home is only a short ride, about
twenty minutes, I believe the evidence was, to the Marco
Polo Hotel. And what do we see? At 11:25 in the
morning, well within enough time for Sonny Cohen to
drive back to the hotel, a telephone call is made from the
coin phone, a pay phone at the Marco Polo Hotel, to
Palughi's Restaurant. And who is at Palughi's Restaurant, ladies and gentlemen? We know who's at Palughi's
Restaurant. Jimmy Liberto. That call lasts about three
minutes. And what do you think Sonny Cohen is telling
him? He's telling him that the job is done, that she's
dead, as Mr. Manley testified, the bitch is dead.

"And what does Mr. Liberto do? Immediately after that he picks up the phone and calls his brother Joe Liberto to let him know that in fact it's happened. Joe Liberto apparently is not there because one minute later he calls again to the Luskin's store, to 3405.

"You heard what 3405 is, ladies and gentlemen. That's the main store number. It's not the office number. It's the number in the retail store directly next to the office, where Joe Liberto works. There can be no doubt that that's who he's calling. And they have a conversation. Whether he gets through to him or not I don't know.

"Let's look even further because we need to involve the other defendants as well because they're all involved in the conspiracy. At 4:28 in the afternoon, ladies and gentlemen, there's a telephone call from Paul Luskin's car phone to 920-3407. Now, what is 3407, ladies and gentlemen? You heard Nikki Hart. That is the number in the office, used for business calls. It is not 3440. Remember the number 3440? 3440, ladies and gentlemen, is the private family line. Don't let the defendant suggest to you for a minute that he's spending twelve minutes on the afternoon of March 9 while his wife got shot, just chatting with his parents.

"No, that call is to 3407, to the privacy of the office where he can talk to Joe Liberto, I submit to you, about what had happened.

"Is that beyond the realm of possibility? I don't think so, ladies and gentlemen, because then look what happens. That telephone call lasts twelve minutes, and twelve minutes later takes us right to 4:41 P.M. And what does he do? He makes a call to Marie Luskin's house. Is that just a coincidence, ladies and gentlemen? Is that just a coincidence, or is this Paul Luskin talking to Joe Liberto about what has happened and then checking up at the house to find out if in fact the deed has occurred?

"And you heard the testimony of Ruth Wapner, Marie Luskin's aunt, how she received a call that day, that afternoon while she was watching the house, from Paul Luskin and how she didn't tell Paul what had happened, but simply said, 'Marie is not here.'

"So now Paul Luskin says, What happened, I just

spent twelve minutes talking to Joe Liberto about how the fact that she's been killed, and now I get this phone call to Ruth Wapner which suggests to me that she's not.

"What do we see Paul Luskin do? One minute later he calls the store. Does he call 3440, does he call to talk to his father or his mother? So that when the defendant tries to suggest to you that this whole flurry of calls by Paul Luskin is to set up some visit between him and his children for his daughter's birthday, if that's true, ladies and gentlemen, then why doesn't he call on the private family line where you heard Nikki Hart say the family transacted the business?

"No, ladies and gentlemen, immediately after that call to Marie Luskin, he calls 920-3405, and that is the store and that is where Joe Liberto worked and that is where Joe Liberto could be reached, and I submit to you that there can be no doubt about what that telephone call is about, no doubt at all."

In Luskin's closing argument, Steve Allen caught Bernstein's flaw:

"For the government theory to work in this case, the government has got to have someone in the Luskin's executive offices involved in this crime almost because the government alleges there were calls—remember, 920-3405 is in the Luskin's showroom. Joe Liberto has access to that phone, as do other people. And by the way, you heard the showroom and executive offices are right next door and people go back and forth. But Joe Liberto is not allowed to use the phone in the office. Nikki Hart told you that.

"But the long and short of it is if the government's theory is that the 3407 was used in this conspiracy, then someone in the Luskin's executive offices has got to be involved, and there is not a shred of evidence of that."

Further, had the government simply forgotten about that twelve-minute call at 4:28—instead of applying it untenably to Joe Liberto—they could have focused on the call that really left question marks, the 4:42 call from Paul to 3405. Steve Allen offered no explanation for that (nor any testimony about it), nor Paul's call to 3405 the next morning. Of course, since Bernstein didn't raise the March 10 call, why should Allen have?

In the defense's own compilation book, there are forty calls between Paul and the Luskin's store lines. Thirty-seven go to or come from the executive office numbers or the Luskin family line. Three are from Paul to the showroom line, where Joe Liberto could be reached. One is March 9, one March 10, and there is one more June 25 at 7:38 P.M.

Is the phone call from Paul to 920-3405 on March 9 the call Steve Allen says the government missed that would have "sunk" Luskin?

I checked my notes from 1991, and found that I had asked Paul then about that call. He told me he was calling his sister Nance, who was working on the store floor, in the advertising office. He added that the call couldn't have been for Joe Liberto, because it was a Monday, and Joe Liberto didn't work Mondays. In fact, he had said the same thing in his 1991 sworn statement.

I asked Goldstein if he remembered whether Joe Liberto had worked Mondays. He called someone else who had worked with him at Luskin's, who reminded him that the store had managers' meetings every Monday and Friday morning, and everyone was required to be there.

"Joe Liberto would not have had Mondays off," Goldstein said.

Nikki Hart testified exactly the same thing in cross-examination by Joe Liberto's attorney Mike Libowitz.

"Were managers' meetings regularly scheduled at the Hollywood store?"

"Yes."

"Were those managers' meetings scheduled on Mondays and Fridays?"

"That's correct."

"And that would have been in 1986 and 1987?"

"That's right."

"Joe Liberto was required to be at the managers' meetings?"

"That's right."

"In Hollywood?"

"In Hollywood."

I told Goldstein that Paul said he had called 3405 to reach his sister Nance in the advertising office.

"That's not right," he said. "The advertising office was in the administrative offices."

Was it time for the theory to change once again? Was Paul Luskin involved in the murder-for-hire of his wife?

"There was no reason for Paul to call the store line," Goldstein said. "There was no one else he could be calling. Everyone else is a flunky salesman." And since Paul had been gone from the business for more than six months, he wouldn't have known any of them, he added.

"I always figured the Luskins were a little devious. Liberto was such a scumbag. We wondered if he had something on the Luskins, and if that's why they brought him back. That's what we all thought.

"Joe Liberto didn't do shit. He had no ability. He could sell, but he couldn't manage. Why would you have someone like that around? Except for extreme loyalty."

We speculated again on who would have been the instigator of a murder-for-hire—Paul or Joe Luskin. The absence of other calls from Paul to Joe Liberto would seem to prove the silent presence of Joe Luskin in between.

Joe Liberto's counsel Mike Libowitz pointed that out, too, in his closing argument. It was established that Susan told Paul that Marie would attend the Single Parent Support Group, but Paul was in Pittsburgh, and there was no record in the government's argument of any certain communication between Paul and Joe Liberto.

"For the Bennigan's theory to work, what's Paul going to do with this information? It's got to pass to Jimmy Liberto, to Sonny Cohen.

"The only possible explanation for that is more people in the conspiracy. Four is not enough. Maybe for this Bennigan's idea to work, we need more guilty people.

"How about Joe Luskin? How about Mildred Luskin? Well, they're talking to Paul. Maybe Paul tells them, maybe they tell Joe Liberto." But the government didn't suggest that at all, Libowitz said.

"But that's the only way, the only way this Bennigan's idea works. Joe, or Mildred, or both, must therefore be involved."

From there, Libowitz argued that the elder Luskins weren't involved, and, he said, Paul's information about Bennigan's never crossed the synapse to Joe Liberto, or farther.

I recalled the letter Joe Liberto wrote to Judge Motz in 1989 that "my life has been hell worrying about whether the threats made by Joe Luskin to me would come true."

"I don't think Paul had the balls for something like this," Goldstein said. "Joe Luskin—he'd pull your eyes out. Paul Luskin? He was a motherfucker, too, sometimes, but he'd be friends with you later. Joe Luskin, he was unrelenting."

March 10
MAIL

I got mail from Paul with the word "Personal" typed on the envelope. That was a first. Inside was a rather formal memo written in the style he usually used to correspond with his attorneys:

TO: ART HARRIS
FR: PAUL LUSKIN
DT: 6 MARCH 1995

Art:

I have discussed some of your materials with Bill (Genego) and we agree that only the materials concerning Brady/Jencks (discovery violations) are relevant at this point.

Additional theories of the case are unimportant at this point, for unless there is a hearing and new trial, your latest theory would be moot.

If you will, limit your paperwork to these issues so that Bill can get on with the finalization of the briefs and spend a minimum amount of time in other directions.

If there is a new trial, we will get to ask the right questions and research the fragment or fragments properly, ala O.J.

cc: Bill Genego
    Henry Gradstein (Paul's brother-in-law)

I think I have to come clean about my mom. She's a mystery and detective book fan from way back, and those Erle Stanley Gardner (Perry Mason) books she exposed me to when I was growing up probably inspired me more than I realized. I told her about the phone calls to the store and read her this letter, and she came to my same conclusion.

"I think you've solved it. He's telling you that you're getting too close."

I expected more resistance from her. She had been a Paul Luskin supporter from the moment I mentioned the story to her. Now, she said, there was still one important issue remaining: the relative guilt of Paul versus Joe Luskin.

"Nobody followed the money," she said. If they had, it would have led them to Joe Luskin. As it was, she thought, had Paul won the trial, the government would have reopened the investigation and found Joe Luskin. It put a damper on the defense attorneys.

Perhaps the story was that Joe told Paul in advance about the murder contract, but Paul was powerless to stop it. He had to do what his father said. Paul was definitely not the ringleader, she thought, and he got far too long a sentence.

March 11
A DIATRIBE

I got the reverse argument from another friend who had been through a terrible split-up and divorce recently. She asked me a compelling question, and followed it up with a diatribe:

"Who was supposed to find her, if she was supposed to be murdered?"

"Well, it was a Monday morning, and the kids were

usually at school. But the youngest child was home sick that day."

"So we know who was supposed to find her. Wonderful. You said he loved his kids, but that doesn't sound like loving them to me. That's totally devastating your child. I'd call it being a manipulative, uncaring, selfish person. I think it's pathetic. Even if he was going to sit back and let his family do it, and not stop it. Your parents are getting divorced, and the next thing your mother's dead? Every child needs to have both their parents."

Almost four years into this, for the first time since I realized the Fourth Circuit had rendered the facts of the case inaccurately, I consider the thought that Paul Luskin, a charming man, is not a good guy. Allowing myself the role of parole board for the moment, I ask: Has this man learned anything, admitted anything even to himself? Has his arrogance been humbled?

How can I still support him? What should I do now besides nothing, just let the legal process take its course?

When I gave him the ATF reports, I gave him his key out. But he doesn't want to use it, because the way out the prison door is also an admission of guilt.

Crazy. Bernstein's means were questionable, but he got the right result. At least part of it.

Paul, Susan, and I, three exiles from Baltimore to Casablanca, aka Miami. From the same high school. He got involved in a murder attempt, she married him, I got to narrate the story.

What is it about leaving home? You lose your anchor, but also your baggage. I can think of no larger act of self-liberation.

We become different people elsewhere. We are free of the limits and parochial expectations set upon us at home, and we can blossom to our fuller potential. Conversely, it's so much easier to drift from the straight and narrow and lose all one's groundings. When I got here in 1978, I needed to remain most of the same person who left home. It was a challenge to apply the values I had learned up until then.

I don't regret leaving.

Had all the Luskins stayed in Baltimore, this story would not have happened.

Early in my journalistic career, I cultivated detachment. Right now I wish I could cry tears for Paul Luskin. I'm close, but can't, nor can he seem to cry them for himself. I did not want the story to end this way. I hoped much too hard.

I think I can't cry because I realize now just how far I broke my cardinal rule of detachment, and I won't consciously let myself break it again.

March 12

My mom can't believe Paul Luskin would participate in such a villainous act as allowing his daughters to discover their murdered mother's body. "He'd have to be an uncaring person. He may have hated his wife, but he loved his children," she said.

As we talked, I realized there was one possible alternate explanation in Paul's slight favor. The phone call to the store showroom line was at 4:42. I have no evidence of any previous calls he made to that line or to Joe Liberto's home in the time period the government called the conspiracy.

It is plausible that Paul Luskin learned about the murder attempt only at 4:28 that day, when he returned a call to the executive offices number, assuming he then talked to his father. Following that presumption, Paul then called Joe Liberto, then Marie's number to find out for himself if it was true. After all, if he had advance knowledge of it, making those two phone calls and leaving a record of them was stupid—and otherwise inconsistent with the lack of other phone call evidence.

"It would mean the son has kept his mouth shut all these years, rather than implicate his father," she said. "He's taken a chunk out of his own life. Maybe that's the reason his father didn't visit him in prison."

Which answer?

* * *

March 27–31

There is a nine-hundred-pound gorilla in this story—
the Luskin divorce file. I'm not really exaggerating the
weight that much—there are definitely a few hundred
pounds of legal work in the ten boxes the Broward
County Courthouse clerk's office is obliged to keep. I
had spent some time with it in 1991, but back then, I
didn't understand just how much the criminal case was
predicated on the divorce case.

I decided to revisit the gorilla.

By March 1995, nine and a half years had passed since
the case had been filed, but when I wrote down case
number 85-29089 for a clerk at the window, he recognized it. "Oh, no, the Luskin case," he said. He also
knew it was the second largest civil case (by volume) in
the history of the county; only a case against Toyota is
bigger.

I found some remarkable things:

On November 25, 1986, Marie filed a motion to
compel Joe and Mildred Luskin and Luskin's, Inc. to
produce their financial records dating back to 1975. The
elder Luskins responded that because the company was
privately held, they had never compiled financial statements, and brought testimony to that effect. In fact, Jack
Luskin, who Marie had called as a witness to prove that
Luskin's of Florida was worth $9 million, agreed with
his brother that no financial statements existed. Despite
that, Marie asked Judge Nutaro on March 5, 1987, to
impose sanctions on the Luskins for failing to produce
them.

March 9, 1987, was the date of the assault.

On April 13, 1987, Luskin's had gone to federal
bankruptcy court to ask for protection. Since July 1986
they had closed seven of their thirteen stores and they
owed $1.8 million to their largest creditor, Sony. Howev-
er, Luskin's corporate attorney told the *Hollywood Sun-
Tattler* the next day that business would go on as usual
and he anticipated a "speedy reorganization" involving
consolidation of their existing stores into new "super-
stores."

On June 17, 1987, Judge Nutaro again ordered the Luskins to produce the records. When they still hadn't complied two weeks later, Barry Franklin renewed his motion for sanctions.

On June 29, 1987, Joe and Mildred filed a motion to the court:

"Recently, Marie Luskin, for no apparent reason other than ill will caused as a result of these proceedings, has refused to permit Joseph and Mildred Luskin to have any contact whatsoever with their grandchildren."

On June 30, Judge Nutaro heard Barry Franklin's motion to prevent Paul Luskin from legally defending himself against any future motion Franklin would file, or from asking for any further discovery, until he paid all his delinquent support, which had put him in contempt of court. On July 1, Nutaro signed that order.

On July 23, Barry Franklin served notice that Judge Nutaro would hear arguments for sanctions against Joe and Mildred Luskin on July 29 at 8:45 A.M.

James Manley testified that Cohen had told him on July 25 there would be a $25,000 bonus if they killed Marie by the evening of July 28. Manley said it was because the divorce trial was coming up.

Barry Franklin was asked at trial about Paul's parents' failure to produce those records.

"Now during this time period, were you also litigating the case against the parents as well?" Gregg Bernstein asked.

"Yes," said Franklin.

"And were there any discovery disputes going on at that time?"

"A big one."

"And what did that concern?"

"That concerned opportunity for representatives from either my office or the accountants that were retained by Marie Luskin to go into the books and records of Luskin's, Inc."

Paul tried to diminish the importance of that July 29 hearing when he gave his 1991 sworn statement. He agreed that its purpose was to reveal Luskin's, Inc.'s books, but added that "these books and records were in the hands of the trustees of the federal bankruptcy court."

In the government's closing argument, Gregg Bernstein had made a brief reference to those books.

"And isn't it interesting how beginning in November of 1986 and carrying through July of 1987—which is during the period in which we heard all of the events in this case—how during that time, countless motions are filed to get those books and records and they're never successful?

"What was in those records? What did these people have to hide, ladies and gentlemen, that made them go to the steps to not turn those records over, the steps that Paul Luskin would take to have his wife murdered to make sure that she was not ultimately successful?"

The words "these people" stand out. Can we truly believe that Paul Luskin, solely, took it upon himself to murder Marie for the larger benefit of the family business?

There were two letters dated July 10, 1987: Paul, *pro se*—acting as his own attorney—wrote to Judge Nutaro that he believed that "the Court is so personally biased and prejudiced against (me) that the Court cannot rule in good faith."

And also addressed to Judge Nutaro, there was an incredible, unsigned three-page letter:

I am writing without the knowledge or permission of any of the parties in this case. I am not signing my name because I do not want you to put me in jail.

It seems that you may be personally responsible for the economic and physical destruction of a very nice family. You may be operating on the fringes of the law, but you certainly have discarded any semblance of justice, fairness and understanding; instead you have shown yourself to be a merciless, prejudiced, scornful person. Since you took over this case, Paul Luskin has been having severe episodes of chest pain. He has also experienced dizziness, breaking out in cold sweats and slight blackouts. Mrs. Luskin has had a cerebral aneurysm diagnosed, along with essential hypertension. You are probably aware that this aneurysm could burst at any time, resulting in paralysis or even death. Mr. Luskin is also experiencing uncomfortable physical symptoms of stress. If anything happens to any of these people, you will be responsible. Your relentless attack of these people is totally unjust and a flagrant abuse of judicial discretion.

Many people also feel that you are seriously misjudging this case, to the extent that all who have heard of your decisions feel that your reputation for being an "off the wall" judge who loves to put people in jail and flaunt her authority is well deserved. I for one am petrified of you.

For example, Judge Reasbeck was thrown off this case for being prejudiced against Paul Luskin. At the time he awarded Marie Luskin $8000 per month, he stated on the record that he knew Paul could never afford that amount, but that the award was punitive. You have chosen to uphold this prejudiced ruling by continually denying modification and motions to vacate the order. At the time of the award, Paul's net income was almost $10,000 per month, so the award was an incredible 80% of net. As his salary decreased, since Luskin's was in economic trouble, he became unable to pay. He borrowed money to the extent of his ability to borrow. When he was fired from Luskin's, he got a job at SEH at $1000 per week. You refused to modify the order, thus forcing Paul to pay 200% of gross. You froze his assets and bank accounts, so he was unable to pay that way. You held him in contempt of court for non-payment, thus making it impossible for him to get a job and earn some money without the threat of incarceration over his head. You must have heard the cliché, "You can't squeeze blood out of a turnip." Yet this is what you *are doing. It is ludicrous to expect Mr. and Mrs. Luskin to pay temporary support to Marie. They did not marry her, and you can see that she isn't very nice to them. She denies them visitation, respect and common courtesy.*

I have been told that there is no such thing as debtor's prison in this country. But I have also been told that if Paul does not pay the court-ordered amount, he will be in contempt until he does. Since there is no way in the world that he could ever come up with the arrearages, he would have to spend the rest of his life in prison. This is so discouraging and depressing. I have been told that the way around you and your rulings is through the appellate court. But after seeing how our system of "justice" operates, why would I have any more faith in that court system than what I have already seen: that a judge can really hate a person and decide to "get" that person and punish him until his whole life is ruined, so that he has no future, so that he never sees his children again. So for Paul Luskin, this country is a dangerous place.

You have also ignored the fact that Marie Luskin's lifestyle has not changed one bit, in spite of the fact that she claims she has no money. She is living in a mansion with in excess of 9000 square feet of space. She has a live in maid, Sylvia, to whom she pays $1000 per month. She has a Tuesday and Thursday maid to whom she pays $400 per month. She has a pool service, a gardening staff, a personal interior decorator, a nutritionist. Yet she refused to pay tuition for the girls next year, at a cost of less that of the live in maid. You can see who is number one with Marie.

On the other hand, Paul Luskin is living in a small apartment. He does his own cooking and laundry and cleaning. He has no maid, nothing. He is driving a borrowed car. Marie is driving the marital Mercedes.

Marie has not looked for employment, preferring to sponge off the rest of the world. She has a college

*degree and taught English for many years. In fact,
when Shana was born, Marie refused to quit work
and Paul took care of Shana until the maid came. At
one point, Marie left the marital home, leaving Paul
and Shana alone for a few weeks. Then she returned
to them, quit work and became a queen. Now she
feels like she should spend her time having her hair
and nails done while everyone else bows and scrapes
to her, granting her every wish. You are perpetuating
this.*

*Although this letter is harsh, I don't believe that it
could make you any more prejudiced than you
already are. Everyone believes that you have pre-
judged this case, and that you will ignore Broward
county guidelines for child support, that you will
ignore equitable distribution of marital property,
and that you have a personal vendetta in this case.
At least I have had the opportunity to vent my spleen
and give you my own personal opinion of the way
you run your courtroom.*

*Usually, when a judge gets so personally involved
in a case that the judgments being made are as
ludicrous as yours, they remove themselves from the
case. Please step down before the destruction you are
causing becomes irreparable.*

There was another issue that the divorce file helped
resolve. Paul and Alvin Entin had given me conflicting
responses on when they first learned about the criminal
case.

At various times they said it was when Susan had been
served a subpoena to testify to the grand jury. I asked
Susan and she agreed. Although she couldn't remember
the numerical date, she recalled it was the day of Yom
Kippur. (She said she'd never forget being served; at
least a dozen federal agents descended on her house to
do it, scaring her half to death.) I checked; that was
October 3. That was also consistent with how Susan
testified at the divorce trial. She said she called Entin
after she was subpoenaed; Entin told her to call Steve
Allen.

But Paul gave a different answer in his 1991 sworn statement: "When Gregg Bernstein called Alvin Entin around the first week in October of 1987."

At the criminal trial, prosecutor Wick Sollers asked Susan the same question. Steve Allen then objected and Judge Motz sustained it, so she didn't have to answer. But while discussing it at a sidebar out of the earshot of the jury, the following colloquy provided an unexpected clue:

"When was she served with a subpoena, Steve?" Alvin Entin asked.

Allen answered: "She wasn't served with a subpoena until late September because that's how I first got into the case, and I got into the case about September 16. Gregg, my first call to you was about the first of October, and you called me to tell me that Susan Davis was going to go to the grand jury, so frankly, she wasn't even served until about the first of October."

Follow carefully: Steve Allen told me in 1994 he was originally hired by Alvin Entin to investigate the charges against Cohen and Manley, and talk to Bernstein. When I asked him how the Luskins knew the names Cohen and Manley, he said he didn't remember. But at trial, he was speaking only four months after the fact.

Steve Allen's September 16 is a very significant date; that's the day Manley signed his plea deal. Up to then, the government had not leaked the investigation to anyone besides Marie. And Marie would not have been likely to have told anyone else named Luskin.

But back at Baltimore City Jail, when Manley didn't come back that day, Cohen realized he had flipped. On September 17, Cohen rushed to call the FBI, telling them he hoped to make a cooperation deal to reduce his own potential sentence. However, he only mentioned his participation in a drug ring, not a murder-for-hire.

Cohen said in jail he was in daily contact with Jim Liberto. Did Jim Liberto contact the Luskins, directly or through his brother, to tell them there was a problem? Did the Luskins then tell Alvin Entin, who got Steve Allen into the case on September 16?

September 18 is another significant date: that's when the FBI interviewed Joe Liberto. Joe Liberto said in his

1994 pleading that he immediately told Joe Luskin what had happened.

Paul's assertion that he didn't learn about the murder-for-hire until Bernstein called Entin in the first week of October is diminished by Entin's apparent knowledge on September 16. Although Joe Luskin undoubtedly paid all or some of Entin's fee, Entin was Paul's attorney, not Joe Luskin's. Presumably, Entin would have discussed the issue directly with his client.

Once again I am reminded of Steve Allen's notes from the conversation he had with Steve Miles, dated October 28, 1987—less than two weeks after Paul was indicted, around the time that the family reportedly was scared Joe Luskin was going to be indicted as well:

> Joe can tie up whole case. Hired by Paul. Price tag $65,000 to be paid by Paul.
>
> Plot struck before he was fired. He pointed out the house.
>
> Joe saw the guns.
>
> Plot to kill.

According to Paul's diary notes, Joe Liberto was fired December 10, 1986. Two weeks before, Marie had filed the motion to compel Luskin's Inc. to produce their financial statements. But why would Paul "hire" Joe Liberto to arrange for Marie's killing, then just after fire him from the store—yet keep him on the murder-for-hire?

Remember, Joe Liberto and Steve Miles are old friends. Did it sound like Joe Liberto was telling Steve Miles it was Paul—instead of Joe Luskin? Given a choice, and given that Paul had already been indicted, and Joe Luskin hadn't, might Joe Liberto have wanted to help Joe Luskin, his mentor, instead of Paul Luskin, who he hated and who had fired him?

I had also copied from Darden's files Paul's chronology of everywhere he had been from December 1986 to his arrest in October 1987. Within that time, Paul flew all over the country, but he also made two summertime visits to Baltimore at which time he saw his parents, who had flown north. The first was July 7–8, which covered his dad's birthday.

But Paul also visited Baltimore the weekend of August 1–2, with his parents present again.

Cohen and Manley were arrested on Amtrak Thursday July 30. Remember, Cohen told me at Lewisburg that during his ten-day window he had an opportunity to raise bail, the Luskins and Jim Liberto were supposed to have shared the burden of posting $500,000 in property bond. Cohen then would have fled, and the case would have fallen apart.

At the divorce trial, Barry Franklin asked Mildred Luskin when she first found out about the murder-for-hire allegations. She answered:

"When my son called and told me that there was a problem. He said to me he had a problem in Baltimore and that he was being accused of something."

"When?" asked Franklin.

"When he called me from Baltimore. Up until I went to Baltimore I never knew exactly. I flew up right away."

It's obvious Mildred was talking about her trip on August 1–2.

At the criminal trial, Steve Allen introduced Joe and Mildred's plane tickets for that weekend as evidence. They flew Fort Lauderdale to Baltimore at 9:10 A.M., returning the next day at 4:05 P.M. I don't know when they bought the tickets.

Further, an old friend of Paul's, Barbara Sindler, testified for Paul at trial that she saw him at Obrycki's Restaurant in Baltimore the evening of August 1, and he was with his parents.

Also, Paul's car phone records show his last call in Pittsburgh on August 1 at 7:08 A.M., and his first call in the Baltimore-Washington cell at 10:03 A.M. His diary says he drove from Pittsburgh to Baltimore to pick up his parents at the airport, and he stayed overnight with them at a family friend's.

Paul's diary also says he was in Baltimore on August 15–19, but he wrote he spent time with Susan. He saw Susan again between September 11–13—this was the trip to Washington when the FBI put a tail on Susan from Fort Lauderdale. There is no indication on either of those trips that Paul's parents were present.

It's a horrible thing to implicate a man on his mother's inadvertent testimony.

I checked the phone records: on July 22 at 12:59 P.M., there is a two-minute call from the showroom line at Luskin's Hollywood store to Jim Liberto's home. Then on July 29 at 2:08 P.M., there is another call, for five minutes.

Then, on the afternoon of July 30—the day Cohen and Manley are arrested—there are three calls between Paul in Pittsburgh and his parents' private line at the store, beginning at 4:52 P.M. Mildred's testimony would have us expect they were calls from Paul to his parents. However—and this is very significant—the reverse is true; his parents' line calls him. Within the next hour and a half, they speak for forty minutes.

I was also reminded of what Joe Luskin told Detective Soccol when they first met. He was out of town the day Marie was assaulted. He was in Baltimore.

FIFTEEN

Oscar Wilde

From *De Profundis:*

For a year I wept every day at the same hour and for the same space of time. In prison tears are part of every day's experience. A day in prison on which one does not weep is a day on which one's heart is hard, not one day on which one's heart is happy.

I have got to make everything that has happened to me good for me. The plank bed, the loathsome food, the hard ropes, the harsh orders, the dreadful dress that makes sorrow grotesque to look at. The silence, the solitude, the shame, each and all of these things I have to transform into a spiritual experience. There is not a single degradation of the body which I must not try and make into a spiritualizing of the soul.

I have no desire to complain. One of the many lessons one learns in prison is, that things are what they are and will be what they will be. Suffering is one very long moment. We cannot divide it by seasons. We can only record its moods and chronicle their return. With us time itself does not progress. It revolves. It seems to circle around one center of pain. For us, there is only one season, the season of sorrow. The very sun and moon seem taken from us. Outside, the day may be blue and gold, but the light that creeps down through the thick glass of the small iron-barred window is grey. It is always twilight in one's heart. And in the sphere of time, motion is no more.

We who live in prison, and whose lives in there is not event but sorrow, have to measure time by throbs of pain, and the record of bitter moments. We have nothing else to think of. Suffering is the means by which we exist, because it is the only means by which we become conscious of existing; and the remembrance of suffering in the past is necessary to us as the evidence of our continued identity.

Love of some kind is the only possible explanation of the extraordinary amount of suffering that there is in the world. If the world has been built on sorrow, it has been built by the hands of love, because in no other way could the soul of man reach perfection. Far off, like a perfect pearl, one can see the City of God. It is so wonderful that it seems as if a child could reach it in a summer's day. And so a child could. But with me and such as me it is different. One can realise a thing in a single moment, but one loses it in the long hours that follow with leaden feet. We think in eternity, but we move slowly through time. And how slowly time goes with us who lie in prison I need not tell again.

For the last seven or eight months, in spite of a succession of great troubles reaching me from the outside world almost without intermission, I have been placed in direct contact with a new spirit working in this prison through man and things, that has helped me beyond words: so that while for the first year of my imprisonment I did nothing else, and can remember doing nothing else, but wring my hands in despair, and say, What an ending, what an appalling ending! Now I try to say to myself, and sometimes when I am not torturing myself do really say, What a beginning, what a wonderful beginning!

Epilogue

When Bill Genego filed his appeal in April, he didn't argue that Bernstein may have let Manley perjure himself; I figured because that would have led us to Joe Luskin. Without it, I knew Judge Motz wouldn't overturn the conviction, but I thought he would feel Paul had done enough time already. So Paul and Susan were crushed when on September 19 Motz denied the motion.

Paul Luskin is a strong man; stronger than he probably thought he was. He has survived nine years in prison and still won't say what really happened. For the last year I didn't know if I should keep helping him because I thought he was a liar, or too full of pride. But even with his father gone, I don't believe he can say to his children, Susan, or anyone else named Luskin that his dad tried to kill Marie. He's apparently willing to do his full term, thus blowing the rest of his life, to preserve this fiction.

I'm not even sure he can admit it to himself.

But I truly think he *is* innocent—except maybe for knowing after it happened. After spending a day with him in prison, he made me realize the phone call and travel evidence isn't conclusive. But no way, *no way,* would Paul have let the murder happen if he knew it in advance, and let his children find the body.

I think Paul's silence defines what being a Luskin is. Maybe it is true magnificence.

Who among us has ever encountered such a tragic American epic?